AVID

READER

PRESS

TAKE UP SPACE

The

UNPRECEDENTED

AOC

BY THE EDITORS OF

MAGAZINE

Introduction by
REBECCA TRAISTER

AVID READER PRESS

NEW YORK | LONDON | TORONTO | SYDNEY | NEW DELHI

Avid Reader Press
An Imprint of Simon & Schuster, Inc.
1230 Avenue of the Americas
New York, NY 10020

First Avid Reader Press hardcover
edition February 2022

AVID READER PRESS and
colophon are trademarks of Simon &
Schuster, Inc.

For information about special
discounts for bulk purchases,
please contact Simon & Schuster
Special Sales at 1-866-506-1949 or
business@simonandschuster.com.

The Simon & Schuster Speakers
Bureau can bring authors to your
live event. For more information
or to book an event, contact the
Simon & Schuster Speakers Bureau
at 1-866-248-3049 or visit our website
at www.simonspeakers.com.

Manufactured in the United States of
America

10 9 8 7 6 5 4 3 2 1

Library of Congress Cataloging-in-
Publication Data has been applied for.

ISBN 978-1-5011-6697-6
ISBN 978-1-5011-6698-3 (ebook)

About This Book

Though barely five years into her public life, Alexandria Ocasio-Cortez is an irresistible subject for a biography, which this is, but the book also takes a different form. It tells her personal story but is also a portrait of a nation changing fast enough to create the conditions for her rise. AOC's influence is revolutionary, both in terms of the agenda she is pushing, redefining and popularizing a kind of socialism for an America rarely hospitable to such ideas, and in the way she pushes it, inventing a new kind of political discourse—colloquial, brash, and direct, very much an outgrowth of her generation's life on social media. As Rebecca Traister explains in her introduction to the book, this is Ocasio-Cortez's real contribution to American politics. She has transformed the way it is practiced, maybe forever.

To tell that story, this book proceeds along two paths. At its heart is Lisa Miller's gripping account of AOC's life and her swift rise to power. This narrative is complete, but it is not exhaustive. Within her text, you will find numbers, much like footnotes, directing you to multiple types of stories by other authors: oral histories, essays interrogating her ideas, even a chapter rendered in graphic-novel style. You'll also find dissections of her political performances, including speeches, congressional testimony, and social media livestreams. This extended commentary starts on page 204, right after the biography.

We hope you will read the whole book, but it has been constructed so you don't have to. Read the biography, and then dig deeper into whatever else interests you. If we've done this right, whether you love her or loathe her (or are the rare person who falls in between), you will come to understand both Alexandria Ocasio-Cortez and the context in which the AOC phenomenon became possible.

CONTENTS

AND...

Alexandria
Ocasio-Cortez.

Cards Against Humanity

AOC went into the game in the summer of 2019. We had 200 cards on our shortlist: She was No. 1. Everyone said, "This is a killer card." We're looking for people who provoke strong emotional reactions. Early on, we put Steve Bannon in. But now you get that card and you think, "This game is old and lame." AOC is not ephemeral—ten years from now, she's still going to be a political person of prominence.

DAVID MUNK, CO-CREATOR OF CARDS
AGAINST HUMANITY

BEFORE AOC, AFTER AOC

Politics can be divided into two eras.

~~~~~~

By

REBECCA TRAISTER

At around 11 p.m., one week after a right-wing mob breached security at the United States Capitol on January 6, 2021, a ripple coursed through social media. Congresswoman Alexandria Ocasio-Cortez had taken to Instagram Live, her first major public statement since emerging from the bowels of the nation's Capitol complex, where she had hidden as armed combatants roamed the halls with their zip-ties, guns, and Confederate flags in hand.

The insurrection had been a gleeful, feral power grab, an angry strafing against Donald Trump's loss and the victory of Democrats over the nation's hard-right wing. Those armed insurgents had had their revanchist sights set on AOC herself, both metaphorically and physically, storming the Capitol fueled by rage at the leftist politics and broader representational shifts she has so swiftly come to embody. The nature of the onslaught also had put her in literal peril: Those who blitzed the Capitol did so with an energy that made clear they would have relished the opportunity to hurt or humiliate, dominate or punish, this woman, the young, hypercelebrated, beautiful—and in that circumstance, vulnerable—stand-in for everything they were there to repudiate.

Ocasio-Cortez had tweeted in the immediate aftermath of the attack that she was unhurt, but in the week following, her public voice—typically loud and steadily engaged—had gone unusually silent. Yet now here she was, closing in on midnight, very much herself, and very much online.

Within minutes of the start of her informal address, 110,000 people tuned in. As she spoke, Instagram hearts flew up the right side of the screen and comments flooded in front of her face: praise hands, thumbs-up emoji, "Preach!," "YES." Her speech was met with relief and adoration by some; derision, irritation, and fury by others. All of it was characteristic of how people interact with Ocasio-Cortez, whether warmly or aggressively: The communications were intimate, immediate, wholly unmediated.

Meanwhile, Ocasio-Cortez was just talking, speaking in what had, over the course of her time in politics, become her familiar conversational style, telling the still-incomplete story of what had happened to her. "It is not an exaggeration to say that many, many members of the House were nearly assassinated," she said, making news by explaining that one encounter had made her feel that her life was endangered.

She spoke for an hour and two minutes—part explainer on impeachment and the 25th Amendment, part history lesson about the first day the Capitol had been breached since 1814. There was poetic railing on the nihilism of the white-supremacist project, and the earnest vibe of a self-help session, rich in the language of trauma and self-care.

She offered the reassuring warmth of Oprah; the fire-and-brimstone of Jonathan Edwards; the inspiration of John F. Kennedy; the intimacy of an FDR fireside chat. It was exhausting and reassuring and scary and comforting and extremely weird. It was kind of wild, and actually there was no real, full precedent in American history for what it was or how it should be received.

Ocasio-Cortez's statement was the one that many Americans had been waiting through those hard days to hear—whether to cheer or to mock. But she wasn't the president, or the president-elect, or a former president, or the governor of the Massachusetts Bay Colony. She wasn't the Speaker of the House. She wasn't even a martyred political legend—not Hillary Clinton or Shirley Chisholm—whose losses inspire sassy T-shirts and tears. Alexandria Ocasio-Cortez hasn't yet lost anything, politically.

She is a 32-year-old congresswoman from the Bronx in just her second term in the House of Representatives. History suggests that, as a young politician who has no famous parent, is not a member of a political dynasty, and was never married to a rock star, only a handful of people should know her name at this point in her nascent career.

But after just three years in government, Ocasio-Cortez feels like a symbol of her own brand of insurgency, armed not with guns or Confederate flags but an insistence on an entirely new approach to taking and using power.

She, too, stormed that Capitol, as an elected member of Congress, bringing with her a new generation and its communicative habits and ideological perspectives. In her brief tenure, she has become her own kind of political monument: such a piece of the political firmament that partisan constellations have calibrated around her. Surely she has always been there and could not have just arrived in our collective consciousness in 2018.

I have covered women in politics for fifteen years and, like many others, had barely clocked Alexandria Ocasio-Cortez's existence until the days before she beat House Democratic Caucus chair Joe Crowley in the Democratic primary in New York's 14th Congressional District in June 2018. Yet it's genuinely hard for me, often, to remember a time on my beat, or what the dynamics around women in American politics were like, before AOC.

It can be maddeningly difficult to write about Alexandria Ocasio-Cortez without sounding extreme, like a fangirl or a hater. That's because her trajectory is itself extreme; to simply lay out the facts of her three-year entrance into and rise within American politics is to trace the path of a rocket. How do you accurately describe velocity and flare without sounding in awe of it? How do you speculate about where it's heading without acknowledging the seismic force of its takeoff?

I often have to remind myself—every time I tune in to one of her speeches, like one of her tweets, watch an Instagram video of her dog stealing bites of dinner, and then wait for whatever it is to send her critics into apoplexy and her fans into ecstasy—that however powerful she is, however solid her political base feels, the fact is that there is no model for what she's doing. Going from zero to Congress, primary victory to superstardom, political neophyte to fetishized celebrity, the Bronx to *Vogue,* bartender to House floor, Democratic Socialists of America member to souvenir votive candle. And all that unprecedented power—all that extremity—is also exactly what makes her position so precarious.

Because everything compelling and new about AOC makes her a target for scrutiny, over-identification, and, in many cases, disappointment. In Ocasio-Cortez, many of us are watching something beyond improbable. For such a vast range of people, she has proved that things that long seemed impossible might well be possible. Anyone and anything that has that power is going to become an object of near-religious fascination. But most human beings cannot withstand that level of intensity, projected at themselves.

• • •

AOC comes from a generation that believes we are not supposed to venerate individual politicians, rather rally behind their ideas. Individuals are imperfect and inevitably flawed; we cannot pin our hopes on them. The focus of political change, the young left believes, must be on structural reforms.

Ocasio-Cortez is among the most talented proponents of the conviction that the challenges faced by the United States, both in its past and in its future, are systemic in nature. That even electoral politics, so long calibrated around specific leaders, can in fact be fueled (like the activist history that oriented her politics) by movements and coalitions. Young politicians, moving into local, state, and federal offices around the country, conceptualize power very differently from their forebears: Instead of it coming from the top down, emanating from cloakrooms and other discreet enclaves for the elite, these insurgents argue that the power to make political change can and should come from the bottom up. It is closer to an idealized version of representative government than the United States has ever known and a view of political leadership that would make room for the inclusion of entire swaths of the United States that have long been held at the margins.

Nobody stands in more efficiently for this conundrum than Ocasio-Cortez herself. Because there is no way to reconcile the conviction that leadership is not driven by individuals with the fact that AOC has the kind of grip she does on our collective imagination in large part because she has the knockout charisma and communicative talents of a political supernova. She addresses organizing and coalition-building in practically every post, every speech. And yet people tune in to those speeches and retweet those posts because they are hers. Ocasio-Cortez possesses a combination of qualities that make her an effective interlocutor for the ideas and structural revisions her generation wants to make, but she exists at odds with one of those central tenets: Her power is partly in her person, and that means she is open to all the pitfalls that come with being the kind of leader we are supposed to be weaning ourselves from. Masses of people pouring their energies into ever-evolving ideas is one thing; masses of people pinning their hopes to a single person is a recipe for disenchantment and anger.

Already you can hear the complex judgments over transgressions both political and personal: leftists who held her up for toppling machine Democrat Joe Crowley but now find her unappealingly conciliatory in her willingness to work with Nancy Pelosi; centrist women who embrace her representational symbolism but find her progressivism alienating; guys who love her gamer–just-one-of-the-guys persona have been put off by her embrace of trauma-talk; Bernie Sanders acolytes who preferred her support of their hero to her own heroism. And also the right just hating her.

The impossibility of fulfilling every constituent's every wish is endemic to any aspiring politician, but Ocasio-Cortez's burdens are heavier in part because of her unusual identity. As a young woman of color, she bears symbolic representational weight. She is, crucially, our first female wunderkind politician. Being first, hacking a path through thickets of bias and improbability and amped-up expectation . . . that's a serious burden, with steep costs. It is perhaps too easy to forget, when Ocasio-Cortez leans on the language of trauma and self-care, the toll of ceaseless attacks and public villainization from one side, beside the heightened pressures applied by millions who long for her to be their impossible ideal on another.

Unfortunately for her, we simply have nothing to prepare us for the space she takes up.

In her 20s, and after only one seriously contested race, she has displayed a political precocity that made her an instantly formidable contender for national spotlight. In a way, we have practiced comprehending youth and power in male leaders, especially in white men: young Kennedys, Cuomos, Bidens, Clintons, Roosevelts. We know what it means to feel one way or the other about Paul Ryan or even about the young Barack Obama. We have ways of conveying and absorbing their ambition, talents, of comprehending and forgiving their stumbles. We care less about their outfits but also know how to talk about their hair, their partners, their jawbones, their physical appeal in ways that are not confusing; they're just about power.

The women who preceded Ocasio-Cortez into politics—including Chisholm and Clinton, Margaret Chase Smith and Pelosi, and House stalwarts from Barbara Lee to Patsy Mink to Gwen Moore to Barbara Mikulski—mostly did not come in so young; they could not have. They would not have been taken seriously enough; they first had to prove themselves professionally in law or public service or business; they had to defend their reputation as women (as we have traditionally valued them) either by raising their children before entering politics or by eschewing motherhood entirely.

This is not a country that has a deep history of having trusted women, especially young ones, with political authority; it has relatively little practice in how to treat them—or make sense of voters' extra strong feelings about them.

Recall that when Clinton first ran for president in 2007, just eleven years before AOC's primary challenge to Crowley, an entire Washington *Post* story chronicled how she was disguising her cleavage, so new was it to have a person with breasts in the bright political spotlight. Recall that Clinton herself became New York's first female senator just six years before that; that there have only been two Black women ever elected to the United States Senate; that no woman of color has ever been governor or senator in New York; that no Black woman has ever been a governor in any state, in any year, ever; that only 13 Latina women currently serve in Congress; that in 2021, just above 25 percent of Congress is female.

And now here we are. Democratic politics upended by a woman who gained her office in her 20s, a Latina from the Bronx and Westchester, with no background in policy-making; a bartender. She has a boyfriend; she uses social media to communicate with fans and fight with political foes, and also to cook ramen noodles in front of millions of people while chatting with them about structural inequality and mass incarceration. And every one of these things winds up meaning so much.

We are so much more used to treating young women, especially those who fit traditional models for beauty—as Ocasio-Cortez certainly does—as celebrities or fashion icons, not as policy-makers. Which is part of what informs the obsession with Ocasio-Cortez: There is no denying that her look, her approach to fashion, that Stila lipstick, is part of how she has become comprehensible to us, and that on some level she understands this, even though her actual job, as a congresswoman, doesn't have anything to do with how she looks or what she wears.

But those things do have to do with the job of women in the United States who want to be liked and admired broadly: the big eyes and red lips and flowing hair; the casual self-possession and undeniable glamour; her prettiness. They all make it easier for people to love Ocasio-Cortez. They make her fun to watch and listen to, easy to put on T-shirts and coffee mugs. Like so much in this country, this is unfair and miserable, but it is also true.

AOC's beauty not only works as a draw and a point of fixation; it also drives and exacerbates the hatred of her critics. That's because she is not ornamental. And her choices to do things they do not want her to do (to be too progressive, to be not progressive enough) combine with her undeniable aesthetic appeal to remind them that they do not have control over her. This beautiful woman is autonomous, capable of self-direction; that stands in for a reminder that she is not theirs to possess.

Here is the nub of one tricky but crucial dynamic underlying the physical threat to AOC during the Capitol raid and beyond: If Americans are not yet comfortable with women in representational numbers in politics, they are certainly not used to young and beautiful women wielding legislative power over them. Some men on the left, who, via AOC, experienced the frisson of good politics voiced by a woman they also found alluring, onto whom they could project their own desires—both ideological and sexual—react to her self-determination as a particularly vivid and personalized affront. Her deviations from their strategic or political script may be imaginatively entwined with a sexualized rejection. For some men on the right, troubled by a woman they can't help but be aesthetically drawn to, but whose politics they abhor and whose power they cannot seem to quash, there are related, and dangerous, impulses in play. This is, after all, a country in which many men are increasingly, violently angry at—and want to punish—the women who have the power to reject them.

The beauty opens up milder forms of antipathy as well. It's what her colleague from Georgia, Republican representative Marjorie Taylor Greene, was playing on when she tried to insult Ocasio-Cortez for having "single handily [*sic*] put an end to all 'dumb blonde' jokes." This insult was a way to call her stupid but also to point out that she is not a blonde. American beauty standards built around whiteness, youth, and traditional apprehensions of femininity are a comfortable way to put women in an aesthetic but not an intellectual mold, fueling resentment of and underestimation of them. If her aesthetic appeal is an issue, so too will be whatever decisions Ocasio-Cortez makes around family and her personal life in coming years.

After January 6, her colleague Katie Porter, in whose office AOC found refuge, would tell the media how Ocasio-Cortez said, in the midst of her frenzied terror, afraid she might be about to die, that she hoped one day to have children. While it was likely meant to humanize the congresswoman, remind people of her humanity, her desire to love and mother and make a family, its revelation also felt almost like an intimate violation. That's in part because that decision lies at the nexus of the confusion in the United States about how to treat women in the public eye.

Magazines and television cover pregnant women obsessively by focusing on baby bumps and maternitywear, but America's treatment of women of childbearing age—from the way the government polices reproductive freedom and limits access to reproductive health care, to the way the media fetishizes pregnancy and dismisses mothers of young children—is key to the history of attempts to maintain racial, class, and gender hierarchies. Whether or not AOC has a child, there will be so many other poison pills ahead of her, neatly tucked into existence as a woman in America who ages out of cool, whose body becomes less interesting to the masses, whose skin eventually wrinkles and sags, who inevitably loses the beat of technology and pop culture, who becomes meaningfully older than the kids who make the next wave of politics. When she entered the House, she was the bright contrast to the shoulder-padded '80s and '90s warriors who preceded her, but someday—should she stay in politics—she too will wear the metaphorical shoulder pads. Like every woman lucky enough to grow old, Ocasio-Cortez will be asked to navigate the rocky shoals of middle age, in which the fans will be less plentiful, less adoring, quicker to turn on and demonize her.

• • •

Sometimes when I think about Alexandria Ocasio-Cortez, and what the next few years could bring—in terms of her life, in terms of the path she takes—I imagine that she might just pull a Bartleby: might decide that she would simply prefer not to. In truth, it was what I had been thinking in the days between January 6 and her first social-media address: that maybe she would just quit.

Because who needs this? Who needs the risk, the fetishization, the enmity of so many of the most powerful people in the country, the scrutiny of her every professional and personal choice, of relationships and body and clothes and ideology, every day, from one's mid-20s to . . . forever? Why would anyone choose to be the guinea pig, the trailblazer, if one could do something else, something just as meaningful but far easier, out of the glare, absent the grinding threats?

But I wonder if perhaps my own occasional hunches that Ocasio-Cortez could just drop out of politics aren't tied to my own lack of imagination, which in turn is tied to the lack of established script, the pathlessness ahead of her. Maybe it's my own exhaustion, considering the many choices ahead of her, that makes it all feel unnavigable, and perhaps unbearable in its risks.

Because those risks are not all about how she'll be received with bias; they're not all about our failings—in the media, as a white capitalist patriarchy, as a violent misogynist gun culture, as an electorate intolerant of nuance or human weakness. She might fail, too. In that she might, someday, just lose.

But even if she does lose, she has created a new paradigm, with its own new rules and parameters. She may be working on an unsolvable puzzle—the personal, the professional, all of it—but her efforts will make it easier for those who come after her to crack. The knottiness of it is also what makes her historic.

The kinds of choices she makes will wind up providing for others the thing that she did not have: a model. Just one more, yes, but a big bright memorable map for young progressives, young women, for women of color with ambitions to change the way power is wielded in the United States.

And every additional road map makes it easier for others who come after to find their way. Ocasio-Cortez understands this. In a second Instagram Live in early February, weeks after her first, in which she described things she was thinking as she hid during the Capitol raid, terrified that she was going to die, she said that she considered that if her path were to be abruptly halted, "then people will be able to take it from here."

Of course, it is an indictment of the nation—its violently unjust history and present—that anyone might reasonably be forced to contemplate becoming some sort of sacrificial lamb to political progress while hiding in an office bathroom. But the fact that a 31-year-old second-term congresswoman could have (correct) confidence that she had already played a role in bridging past and future is a testament to how much American politics has shifted around, and has been shifted by, Alexandria Ocasio-Cortez in just a couple of years.

This brief span—a blink of America's eye—has entailed explosive change; hers has been one of the most incredibly propellent political stages of any politician in American history. And whatever happens next—to her, because of her, in reaction to her—this young person for whom there is no solid precedent has alchemically altered the nation and its possibilities.

To point confidently at AOC as someone likely to shape our future does not mean that she will, necessarily, be governing us through that future. Her path, like the Democratic Party's itself, is far from fixed: It's fraught, perilous, electric, and ultimately unknowable. There is so much combustible energy poured into this one figure. Her learning curve has been as steep and fast as her ascent. But if the nation is to grow—to learn better how to elect new kinds of leaders who want a new kind of politics—its own learning curve must keep pace.

A LIFE IN
FOUR CHAPTERS

———

By

LISA MILLER

CHAPTER 1

Just Relentless

CHILDHOOD / 1989–2007

A t Yorktown High, there were two types of kids who competed in science fairs. There were the kids who memorized their presentations in advance, using the long bus rides from Yorktown to other parts of Westchester and beyond to cram, codifying hundreds of hours of experiments into junior-varsity TED talks. Memorization was the safest course for the shy or anxious kids who feared an unforeseen question from an intimidating judge. And then there were the kids who preferred to wing it, to have the science part nailed, sure, but to deploy all that absorbed knowledge as a chance to communicate—to *connect*. These kids, who instead listened to music during the bus rides, saw each individual encounter with each new judge as a fresh opportunity to engage a stranger in the thrilling drama of science. This, everyone agreed, was a more perilous tack. It was improv. It was salesmanship. It was *politics*, and in the history of the advanced science program at Yorktown High, no one was better at it than Alexandria Ocasio-Cortez.

Back then, she was known as Sandy Ocasio, a *Harry Potter* fanatic whose Puerto Rican parents were ambitious for their children and had moved north from their home in the Bronx to one of the most affordable corners of the gin-and-tonic suburbs for the public schools. The message Ocasio-Cortez received growing up was that she shouldn't dress "ghetto"; upwardly mobile people wore blazers and "don't show up in hoop earrings and a nameplate and, I don't know, *baby hair*," as she has said. At Yorktown High, she was well liked, but in her majority-white suburban school, where the lacrosse jocks ruled and the popular girls were blonde, she lacked social capital. Brown-skinned, opinionated, but guarded, she found her people among the science geeks, a band of so-called outsiders. These were the Asian and South Asian kids. The children of immigrants. The girl with the stutter.

In her junior year, Ocasio-Cortez became consumed with an idea for a science experiment. She wanted to show that antioxidants, the compounds found in such healthy foods as blueberries, pecans, and artichokes, extended lifespan in *C. elegans,* the roundworm. Her mentor, a longevity researcher at Mount Sinai named Charles Mobbs, was skeptical and thought it was likely a dead end. But, at 17, Ocasio-Cortez displayed a precocious insistence that would later become a trademark. She was sure that her idea could work—*would* work—and she made her case with so much of what Mobbs calls "frankly, charisma" that he approved her approach. In the end, she was right. She showed that certain antioxidants do extend the lifespan of *C. elegans,* in some cases to 45 days from 12.

As each science fair approached, Michael Blueglass, the science teacher, would drill the kids on their presentations, forcing them to consider every potential setback or pitfall. Judges, he warned, could be imperious, condescending, distracted, bored. The best recourse, always, was to tell a great story, and to tell it well—which is to say, to not get caught in the weeds of data or methods but to imbue the narrative with the excitement of discovery, to reach for the big themes and stick to them. Ocasio-Cortez was a natural at all of it, savantlike at synthesizing masses of technical information and retelling it in a captivating way, conveying authority with an off-the-cuff intimacy that made listeners feel they were hearing something fresh. The single, tiny flaw in her presentations was that she didn't always know how to dial her energy down, or temper it for optimal effect.

In 2007, her senior year, Ocasio-Cortez took second place in the microbiology category at the Intel science competition, the biggest, most prestigious precollege science fair in the world, which has served as an incubator for future recipients of the Nobel Prize. The winning photo shows her at the apex of high-school geekdom, looking businesslike in a blazer and a collared shirt, no earrings, her hair pulled back, wearing a lanyard with the badge of a competitor and, pinned to her lapel, the hefty prizewinning medal.

The prize was a big deal, but a different event better predicted Ocasio-Cortez's future success. Each year, Blueglass asked the kids bound for the Intel fair to present before the local Board of Education, and in 2007, everyone was gathered in the cafeteria of a local middle school. Just before Ocasio-Cortez's turn came, an assistant superintendent excused himself and left the room. When he returned moments later, she was in full swing, talking about her roundworms as if they were the main characters in a new sci-fi drama and forecasting cures for cancer and Alzheimer's disease. Believing he was seeing a ringer from a pharmaceutical company or a university, he leaned over to his boss. "*Who*," he whispered, "is *that*?"

• • •

"Women like me aren't supposed to run for office." Alexandria Ocasio-Cortez said this in her first campaign ad, the one that went viral, which showed her putting on makeup in the bathroom mirror. She didn't resemble any politician anyone had ever seen. She was young—28—when she made her run for Congress, where the average age of her would-be colleagues was almost 58. She was Latina and female in a profession dominated by white men. She was fashionable—interested in music, photography, literary fiction; she played video games—compared to the career politicians who were often ridiculed for being out of touch. But her difference went below the surface. She didn't just preach about wealth inequality—she lived it, another downwardly mobile millennial who had been nursing class resentments for years. As a bartender weighed down with family responsibilities and debts to pay, she had no family connections, no social clout, no access to elite routes to power. Barack Obama and Bill Clinton—they had been nobodies from nowhere, too, but they were men and they had attended Harvard, Yale, Columbia, Georgetown, and Oxford between the two of them, given multiple chances to impress the kinds of people who could guide them to the political stratosphere. The facts of Ocasio-Cortez's life made her not just an unusual candidate for federal office but an impossible one. She was exactly the kind of American whose hopes for any social mobility had been crushed by a rigged system perpetuated by officials elected to represent the people's interests.

This was her first feat: converting her vulnerabilities into political power. She had a good, relatable story to tell and a natural gift for storytelling, but it was her audaciousness in the absence of any discernible path forward that made her amazing. She claimed power simply by assuming it could be hers and then asserting that assumption in public. This was part of the thrill, initially, of being an early spectator to the phenomenon that would become AOC: her kamikaze yell of *Why not me?*

She amassed more power by continuing to align herself with the powerless and then pushing her agenda for long-overdue justice through social media, gaining millions of followers who identified with her along the way. Her use of these platforms, while unprecedented, should not be surprising. She is a millennial, after all, native to reality television and influencer culture, and she was cognizant of the way smartphones had already been utilized to magnify a political movement's tactics and mission. (Neither the Arab Spring that began in 2010 nor the 2016 presidential campaign of Bernie Sanders—nor the phenomenon of Donald Trump—would have been possible without Twitter.) But she was better at harnessing technology, and more naturally so, than any politician before her, attaining fluency in all the different languages of Facebook, Twitter, Instagram, and Twitch— she is a digital polyglot—and then speaking to their denizens about her struggles, which were theirs, too. Having won her election in New York's 14th Congressional District, she upended the usual relationship between the government and the governed. Instead of constituents, she had fans and friends, communities overlapping with communities. She lived out loud on her phone. She gave tutorials about the true inner workings of government for free to the masses.

And in this way, she gave the political process back to an alienated generation that, because of her, began to regard American democracy for the first time as something that belonged to them. As enacted by Ocasio-Cortez, politics could be, like the internet itself, iterative, horizontal, intimate, spontaneous, collective. Her very person in the congressional chamber proved that representational government didn't have to be fusty, cynical, and self-interested. It could be young, mad, and moral. "Movement" politics is not a new concept, but with Ocasio-Cortez at the helm of the progressive left, the movement grew bigger and broader than ever before, more diverse and more powerful. With the ability to shame and punish, to praise and fundraise, to make careers and break them, the left under Ocasio-Cortez has changed both its composition and its tactics, and the lines between grassroots activism and elected politics have blurred for good. "Radical ideas are starting to become mainstream at a faster clip than at almost any other point," she has said. "It's really incredible how quickly we can elevate our consciousness in such a short period of time."

Before she was 32 years old, Ocasio-Cortez was arguably one of the two or three most influential politicians in the land. Once inside the halls of power, she held her lines, able to summon the fury of her partisans with a few taps of her fingers on a screen. Her Republican opponents mocked and threatened her. Moderate Democrats ostracized her. Her mother worried about her. It was in this crucible that Ocasio-Cortez transformed herself into nothing less than the embodiment—the face and the voice—of the newly ascendant progressive left. Elizabeth Warren and Bernie Sanders may have preceded her, but it was Ocasio-Cortez who came to represent, both in the public mind and the political sphere, the morally righteous left flank in the existential war against the status quo. So strong was the magnetic pull she commanded that by 2021, even the president could not inch toward the moderate center without first considering the consequences. Before the first anniversary of his inauguration, Joe Biden, who campaigned as a civility-loving centrist, was signaling his principled alignment with a younger, browner generation whose egalitarian, anti-capitalist priorities had previously been dubbed "radical."

In three short years, Ocasio-Cortez went from mixing margaritas to mastering the finest of all the political arts: to continue to present an authentic and believable self without sacrificing an ounce of her power. No politician in memory has so adroitly integrated her natural talents and deployed this holistic understanding of American political theater so strategically.

It's a lot to carry. AOC's friends say that, actually, she is an introvert, a person who prefers to go home after a long day and watch *RuPaul's Drag Race* or play *League of Legends*, so this level of naked exposure, this constant pressure from colleagues and the press, the nonstop threats, the responsibility to her causes and her constituents—any human would crack under all this weight. This is a risk that Ocasio-Cortez seems cognizant of, and so she has apprehended a spiritual wisdom that people much older and more experienced can spend whole careers failing to grasp: that the most powerful thing a person can do is be willing to walk away from her power. She tries to start each morning sipping a big glass of water garnished with a lemon slice. "I have to practice nonattachment to ego and to esteem," she has said. "I can't be attached to keeping my seat as a member of Congress if I'm going to do my job." This Zen, the caring and not caring in an atmosphere where amassing and guarding power is the name of the game, is just another provocative thing about her. Her ordinary day is a teetering balancing act. She has to maintain her position among the power brokers in order to agitate against them while continuing to persuade her following of her authentic disinterest in power in order to earn their trust. One false move and she's done for.

Ocasio-Cortez is, on top of everything else, a master illusionist, building a genuine connection with people—she's so *real* and so raw—even as everyone in her audience comprehends that, on some level, it's artifice. This is politics, of course, but in her case, the performance infuriates people, especially those invested in the way politics have traditionally been transacted—and so the shredders, the haters come after her, seeking every which way to diminish her potency or discredit her story. The controversies started even before she was elected. In an editorial leading up to her primary race, former senator Joe Lieberman said she was not the future of her party. "Joe Lieberman, whatever," she responded after she won, in the same breath neutralizing his assessment and establishing a new front in political combat. During a six-week period in 2019, Fox News mentioned her name, on average, 76 times a day. She has been called dumb, naive, silly, uninformed, despicable, and belligerent. Even the most insignificant things about her become controversies: her haircuts. Her fashion shoots. Her astrological sign. When you look up her birthday on Google, you find a bitter debate about whether she was, in fact, born at 11:50 a.m., as a staffer has said, or whether she fudged the time so that astrology Twitter would hold her in higher regard. As she matured, Ocasio-Cortez drew ever-more-explosive flak, so that when, in September 2021, she attended the Met Gala in a white mermaid dress with the slogan "Tax the Rich" scrawled in red on her back, the whole world, at least on Twitter, felt obligated to take sides. Was she sucking up to power or giving it the finger? Abandoning her causes or furthering them? The answer didn't matter as much as the vitriol, which was completely disproportionate to the event. Sometimes it seems the problem is that she's a *girl*.

It's useful, then, to remember the high-school science nerd. Because when AOC was just Sandy, running around the halls of Yorktown High and twisting arms so that everyone in the science class would chip in to buy Mr. Blueglass an Xbox, she was exactly the same person she is today: a combatant who regards "no" as a dare, whose intelligence radiates from her, who is relentless and unafraid of the white men in charge, who has an appetite for boring and backbreaking work. The kid who spent the summer counting roundworms too small to see grew up into the woman who told the right story in the right way and found voters no one ever had before.

•••

Alexandria Ocasio-Cortez was, in fact, born at 11:50 a.m. on October 13, 1989 (a Libra, with Sagittarius rising), the first child of Sergio Ocasio and Blanca Cortez. Sergio met Blanca while he was visiting relatives in Puerto Rico. Blanca, who didn't speak English, moved to be with Sergio in the Bronx. Gentle, hardworking, and religious, Blanca is a petite woman with a wide smile. Physically, her daughter resembles her, but in most other ways, Ocasio-Cortez is more like her father, the parent who chose her name. Sergio, a second-generation resident of the Bronx, who died at age 48 from lung cancer, was larger than life, warm, and driven. "He grew up poor, he took a lot of pride in being of the people and not above anyone," Ocasio-Cortez said. He didn't like pretense, "and he told off-color jokes all the time." But he was curious about the world; his close friends teased him about being "a closet intellectual": "When no one was looking, he'd be reading the *Bhagavad Gita.*" Sergio left "his little books" all over the house. Alexandria picked them up, and as soon as she was able, she read them too.

"I was a total daddy's girl," Ocasio-Cortez said. "Anything that he did, I wanted to do." The connection between Ocasio-Cortez and her father was deep. Even when Ocasio-Cortez was still an infant in a bibbed onesie, she and her father seemed to inhabit their own world, and in photographs, the pleasure they derived from each other is obvious. They had a "soul tie," as she put it, bigger than every other love; it made other relationships feel thin. (Gabriel, Ocasio-Cortez's brother, who was born three years later, experienced a more complicated dynamic with Sergio. "I was a difficult son, he was a difficult Father," he once wrote.)

In her father's presence, Ocasio-Cortez has said she felt nothing less than "truth." She felt "home." She tells the story of being about 5 years old when her father announced he was going on a road trip with his buddies. "I wanted to go so badly," she said, "and I begged and I begged and I begged, and he relented." Somehow Sergio persuaded his friends to join him in indulging his daughter. "It was, like, four grown men and a 5-year-old girl." Traveling south from New York, the group stopped in D.C. "It was a really beautiful day, and he leaned down next to me, and he pointed at the Washington Monument, and he pointed at the reflecting pool, and he pointed at everything, and he said, 'This all belongs to us. This is our government, it belongs to us, so all of this stuff is yours.'" Recollecting that day many years later, Ocasio-Cortez began to cry.

Sergio supported the family with his small business, an architecture firm based in the Parkchester corner of the Bronx. Built during World War II with an investment from MetLife, Parkchester started out as a whites-only development of redbrick eight-story apartment buildings with green spaces in between meant to keep working- and middle-class Irish, Italian, and Jewish families from bolting to the suburbs. In 1968, the city forced Parkchester to integrate, and soon after, a Harry Helmsley–run company started flipping the more than 12,000 rental units into cut-rate condos. During the era when the Ocasios lived there, one-bedrooms were selling for between $35,000 and $39,500 and the apartments had fallen into disrepair. Soon, the residents of the Parkchester development were largely Latino and Black, with a growing Indian, Bangladeshi, and Pakistani population and a small core group of elderly white people who had never left. It became a neglected, crime-saturated spot: Residents complained of graffiti, vandalism, and frequent robberies. In 1999—about five years after the Ocasio family moved away—police shot at the African street vendor Amadou Diallo 41 times outside his home, killing him, about a mile from the Parkchester subway stop.

Even so, it was an improvement for Sergio, who had spent his childhood in the far more violent South Bronx during the 1970s, a time when "the Bronx was burning," Ocasio-Cortez said, repeating an old line. "Landlords began to turn into arsonists because the insurance payouts were more valuable than the families that lived inside those buildings." Sergio's own scrappy childhood was likely similar to those of other second- and third-generation kids, influenced by a strong Puerto Rican identity against a backdrop of gang war. Sergio grew up with five people in a one-bedroom apartment, and in high school traveled by subway each morning to join the upwardly mobile ranks at Brooklyn Tech. Sergio "barely had a father," Gabriel said, "barely an outline of a father, and he was operating off of that." So owning a one-bedroom apartment in Parkchester, even with the crib in the closet and the mattress on the floor, was a step up and also a way out. Sergio made his living fixing up the apartments in the complex.

The red lips, the gold hoops, the happy references to *mofongo* and *lechon*—all this is an explicit homage to her Nuyorican heritage, which Ocasio-Cortez soaked up among the cousins, uncles, and aunts in the Bronx and in Puerto Rico. Ocasio-Cortez speaks imperfect Spanish, searching for words and muddling her syntax, a familiar predicament for bilingual children who speak English all day. She gleefully reps the Bronx in public (never mind that more than half the population of her district is in Queens), welcoming comparisons to Cardi B, going on *Desus & Mero* to pay tribute to the bodega

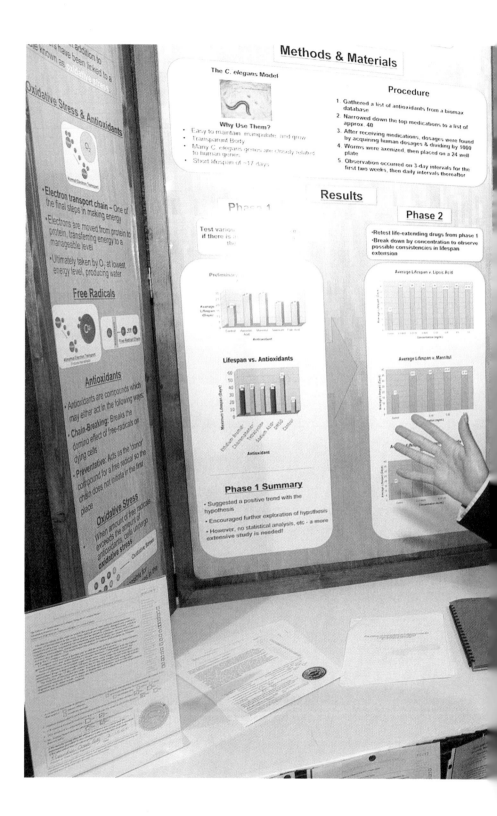

iscussion/Analysis

s average increase:
ic acid's average increase:
O's average increase:

cases, lifespan was increased by
100%
in the evidence given, **antioxidants**
xtend lifespan
O, Lipoic acid proven most
ctive

Conclusion

thesis upheld
ative stress plays key role in
legans aging
xidants reverse or hinder the
ts of oxidative stress, causing an
sion in lifespan

Future Research /
Applications

rse assay will be conducted –
ounds that cause oxidative stress
e checked to shorten lifespan

ine antioxidants to see
res will affect lifespa
be utilized for begi
nerative diseases
neration, etc.

eview of L

al, R.S., and R. W
xidative stress, ca
striction, and agi
.5271 (July 1996
d the system by w
s is created.

nda, Yoko, and Sh
xidative Stress a
ormation in th
s ele

*In 2007, her
senior year of
high school,
Ocasio-Cortez
won a prize for
her science
project on
roundworms—
which she
completed despite
skepticism from
her mentor.*

egg-and-cheese sandwich, and razzing Manhattan- and Brooklynites for considering her home borough, as tourists would, as nothing more than the location of Yankee Stadium and a certain big zoo. With all due respect to President Trump, she said on her first appearance on *The Late Show With Stephen Colbert* in 2018, he was born in Queens: "I don't think he knows how to deal with a girl from the Bronx."

When she was about 5 years old, her parents moved the family away from the Bronx, having purchased a small ranch house on a corner lot in Yorktown Heights. Parkchester had failed to live up to its promise. What Sergio and Blanca wanted, like generations of ambitious and concerned parents before them, were good public schools for their kids.

The move to Yorktown has become part of the Ocasio-Cortez legend, a dislocation she returns to again and again, for it gives her an opportunity to speak in a personal way about structural injustice and insist that poor people should not be held responsible for their poverty. "I was born in a place where your Zip Code determines your destiny," she said early, in the ad that went viral during her primary campaign in 2018. As a surrogate for Bernie Sanders for President in 2020, she expounded on the point, saying, "My mom and my dad looked at the quality of education in the Bronx. And they looked at 50 percent dropout rates. They looked at the inequity of education, the inequity of education funding, the fact that teachers weren't paid, the fact that kids weren't given their tools to succeed, and that, frankly, it not only had to do with their income but it had to do with their melanin too. And so . . . my family made a really hard decision. And my whole family chipped in to buy a small house about 40 minutes north."

She emphasizes the details of her difference when she talks about her childhood in Yorktown. While her mother cleaned white people's houses, she read books on the stairs, sometimes helping out when a toilet needed scrubbing. In her college essay, she wrote about how she and her mother cleaned out a neighbor's refrigerator as his wife was dying because it was the way they knew how to help him best. "We served the wealthy in Westchester County so that I could go to school with wealthy kids," she has said, her tone matter-of-fact. Where she felt most at home, she says, was in the Bronx.

It's not that in Yorktown she didn't fit in. She did. She had friends and converted a shed in the backyard into a clubhouse for them, hanging curtains and pictures on the wall. She did well enough in school, although "I wasn't an amazing student, because I liked learning on my own terms," she said. She regularly went to church and Girl Scouts. Teachers recollect her as extremely independent, a self-starter—the kind of kid you could leave alone to do a job or assignment and come back to find it done without any help.

Like many working-class kids, Ocasio-Cortez grew up absorbing the fine stratifications of class. Yorktown, in the 1990s, was ground zero for the soccer mom and the minivan. At her house, the family ate a lot of rice and beans, and Sergio built a loft bed for Alexandria so that, in her small bedroom, a desk for homework would fit underneath. During the summers, when both parents were working, they would sometimes send Gabriel and Alexandria to stay with Blanca's family in Puerto Rico. Sergio had been raised in the Roman Catholic Church—Ocasio-Cortez was initiated in those sacraments—but Blanca was Pentecostal and on the island had attended small, rural churches where people believed in miracles and faith healing; any service might include someone being overtaken by the Holy Spirit, speaking in tongues or falling to the ground. On her summer visits, Ocasio-Cortez would accompany her aunts and uncles to these services. "I'd drive up to the mountains—deep, deep, deep up," she said.

"The roads aren't even paved, and we'd be in this car, this van, careening on muddy roads that were dark, to get to the top of a mountain, to a small, tucked-away church. And there I witnessed the Pentecostal tradition, which has a lot of similarities with the Black Baptist tradition. With the role of music, and people catching the Spirit." She would ride horses with her cousins in her flip-flops.[1] (MORE ON AOC'S COMPLEX RELATIONSHIP WITH PUERTO RICO, SEE PAGE 204.)

On weekends and during school holidays, the family drove down the Taconic to the Bronx, where Ocasio-Cortez hung out with her Stateside cousins, most of them boys, many of whom she regarded as brothers. Some of these extended family members grew up to be cops. But one of her favorite cousins, the "largest and funniest," was imprisoned during the "fever pitch of 1990s mass incarceration," along with countless other kids she called "baggy-pant boys" who, she has said, fit the description of so-called "super-predators and thugs." On his upper arm, her cousin had a tattoo of Jesus on the cross. As a child, sitting on his lap during family celebrations, Ocasio-Cortez would beg to look again at the inked image: the crown of thorns and a banner above it that read "Only God Can Judge Me." It fascinated her. The leftist, socialist-leaning notions that propelled Ocasio-Cortez to Congress—that social engagement is the salve to class alienation, that the collective is more powerful than the individual, that only activist movements can upend racism and inequality—these were entirely absent from her childhood home as political concepts.

From a very young age, Ocasio-Cortez understood that to attain the level of comfort and ease she saw in the suburbs would require extra-hard work; her parents impressed upon her that she was responsible for her own success. Sergio, especially, fervently believed that people made their own luck and that through perseverance and imagination ascent was possible. He himself worked around the clock and rarely showed up to school events. "I don't know that I ever met her father," says Lisa Stamatelos, her Girl Scout troop leader.

"My dad instilled in us that we would have to always be ten steps ahead," Gabriel said. "I have never felt cared about by the system. I never saw a cop that I trusted. There was nobody on the government payroll that gave me any type of joy." If a political label had to be applied to the environment in which Ocasio-Cortez was raised, it might be "libertarian"—a DIY mind-set that prioritized grit and self-reliance and contained a deep suspicion of elites and institutions. "I grew up in a house that was actually proudly independent," Ocasio-Cortez said. "I grew up in a house that said you need to be watching all of these people. Because none of these people could be trusted. To consistently deliver. Maximally. For you."

Evidently, this perspective was shared in the mostly white, working-class neighborhood where the Ocasio-Cortez family lived. In the 2016 presidential election, the precinct of Yorktown Heights voted overwhelmingly for Trump. As a candidate and as a member of Congress, Ocasio-Cortez would wrestle with this. Could she build a working-class movement, based on shared experience and grievance, that would transcend race, generation, geography, and culture? Given all they had in common, could her Yorktown neighbors ever— hypothetically—be persuaded to vote for someone like her? Or are Americans so loyal to their inner circles and clubs that such political mixing is impossible?

Latino voters have been called "the sleeping giant": They would be an intimidating bloc if they rose up. But, mostly, they haven't. More than 30 million Latinos in the U.S. are eligible to vote, yet only about 60 percent are registered. The explanations are wide-ranging, from fear (of reprisal because of the immigration status of family members) to lack of access or interest because of language, cultural, and economic barriers. Politicians have historically not done enough to directly address these concerns. Many older Latinos tend to also be conservative on issues such as abortion and gay marriage while favoring progressive social policies on education, health care, and the environment. They do not fit neatly in either party, and their diversity—a Cuban dentist has different priorities from a Mexican dishwasher—means they can't be appealed to in a uniform way. Latino men, especially, taught through religion and culture to regard their roles as head of the house and family provider as sacrosanct, tend to favor calls for lower taxes and personal responsibility. In 2020, 36 percent of Latino men voted for Trump.

As a child, Ocasio-Cortez lived these realities: Her maternal grandmother, Clotilde, lived with them, and every year extended family would join Sergio and Blanca to celebrate their wedding anniversary with a traditional pig roast in the backyard. But the family was also strict and religious, with gender roles firmly entrenched. Gabriel said he never came out to his family as gay because he feared rejection. It was "a Roman Catholic family," he explained, "and tradition has kept our family alive; abiding by the tradition was survival." So real was this fear of exclusion that Gabriel did not dare declare his sexual preference even after his father was dead. Because of his sister, "many people assume that there were many progressive values in the way we were raised, but the reality is that we were righteous when it came to our beliefs and morality about class."

Being Puerto Rican, the family both was and wasn't an immigrant clan. They are American citizens, of course. But they were *like* immigrants in that their identity, their heritage, their language, and their culture were rooted in a Spanish-speaking Caribbean island. Blanca was a foreigner here. Ocasio-Cortez related to the immigrant experience, and she shouldered the responsibility of her parents' sacrifices and dreams for her with a sense of duty and respect. She met their expectations. She checked every box. She belonged to the Girl Scouts way into her teens—far beyond the point when most kids bail. She went to church. She bought every new *Harry Potter* book. She joined clubs and sought out leadership positions whenever she could. In addition to science fairs, she did indoor track, Model U.N., and Key Club. She went to high-school parties, but she was never that girl—no drama, no boyfriends that anyone can remember, "certainly not somebody who you'd see doing a keg stand or funneling beers," says one of her classmates. Even as an adult, she was reprimanded by her mother when during a Facebook live blog she said "fuck" out loud.

"I grew up between two worlds in many different ways," she has said. "Between the Bronx and Westchester, between the United States and Puerto Rico, between rich and poor." It wasn't something she complained about or rebelled against as a kid. She internalized all the discrepancies, learning to be extremely adaptable, *versatile,* sensitive to what different people expected of her and responsive to the different rules and norms that governed her separate worlds.

Later on, as a grown-up, she described how this training in code-switching worked on her psyche. Women, and especially women of color, grow adept at anticipating what others expect and then delivering on that while keeping other parts of themselves separate and private. "When you're a woman of color, there are just so many things about you that are"—here, in an interview at SXSW, she searched for the right word—"*nonconforming.*" She wriggled uncomfortably in her seat as if her clothes were too tight, then she reached her arms out wide, as if for a hug. "I happen to have been born with straight hair, but my nieces have, like, 'fros," she said. "And we're taught to, like, put our hair back and be small and articulate in a certain way and essentially try to do an impression of power. Which, really, are subconscious signals to try to act like white men. It's down to how you are forced or encouraged to speak, the idea that some ways of speaking are less legitimate, the idea that some ways of dressing are less legitimate. We don't say 'legitimate.' We say 'unprofessional.' So if you say 'ain't,' or you say 'my mama,' it's 'unprofessional.'" Here she uses air quotes to underscore her point: a professional woman who has ascended so high still seems to feel as if she's always pretending.

It explains so much. The girl who grew up in a small ranch house, sharing a bathroom with four other people, spent her days at a prosperous high school for the white children of the prosperous—the campus, with its football field and illuminated scoreboard, resembles the set of *Glee*—raking in science prizes. She remained close with her Puerto Rican cousins, and during high-school summers attended a program aimed at cultivating leaders among Hispanic youth. This same person became the congresswoman from a majority-minority district who lives with her white boyfriend and travels regularly to the Capitol, where she gives speeches to a group of majority white men in an edifice built by enslaved people, first used by the House of Representatives in 1857 and dominated since that time by white men. Even before her first day of work in D.C., Ocasio-Cortez had built for herself a comfort zone. The Squad, whose four founders bonded together as incoming freshwomen in 2018, operates as an affinity group, a club where self-identified outsiders may give one another protection, affirmation, and support.

In one very special aspect, Ocasio-Cortez's upbringing liberated her. Sergio may have been in certain ways a conventional Latino father and husband, but his adoration and his unwavering belief in his daughter gave her confidence and a deep, possibly exaggerated faith in her own ability to shatter the constraints of class, race, and gender. On Facebook, before she announced she was running for Congress, Ocasio-Cortez paid homage to her father, who encouraged her to think for herself. "When I was 9 years old," she wrote, "I ran to my dad when a man on TV argued that women should primarily bear children and support the home. He listened, then turned to me and asked, 'Well, why shouldn't they?' It kicked me off-balance, because I expected him to fight for me; tell me that the TV man was wrong. But instead, he made me articulate an argument and figure out how to stand up for myself and all people. He helped me find my voice, and then he amplified it."

"He really made me believe that I had true power in this world," she said another time. That started, as a young person, with her ability to dominate any room. In college, she viewed every late-night revelation or half-baked insight as an opportunity, something to be unpacked, examined, and attacked. Being with her could be exhausting. *"It's a joke, just take the joke,"* a friend recalls thinking. One of her mentors remembers her, in her early 20s, conducting a seminar in a classroom full of people older than she was. And when he, the mentor, tried to interrupt her, she asked him to be quiet. *"You little pill,"* he remembers complaining to himself.

"We are just relentless, and we learned that from our parents," Ocasio-Cortez once said to an audience of first-generation college students. It would seem that permission she received as a child to hear her own inner voice as her most reliable guide allowed her to begin to trust her own sense of what really mattered. "No amount of money or makeup can compensate for loving yourself," she has said. "Make sure that you do that. That is the one foundation of everything. And if you need a little boost, or if you're feeling particularly challenged that day, look in the mirror and say, 'I'm the bomb.'"

CHAPTER 2

Deeply Conflicted

THE COLLEGE YEARS / 2007–2016

I n the fall of 2007, Ocasio-Cortez enrolled in Boston University. She registered as a premedical student with a plan to become an OB-GYN: "I wanted to be a healer," she said. But in the spring of her freshman year, she interviewed for an internship in the Boston office of Senator Ted Kennedy, at around the same time that he was diagnosed with a brain tumor. Emily Winterson, who ran Kennedy's immigration office at the time, found Ocasio-Cortez rather unlike the other eager young interns in the office—women, mostly—who saw the internship as a career-making chance and spent lunch hours sitting around the conference-room table eating takeout sandwiches with members of Kennedy's permanent staff, saying yes to everything and hoping to impress. Ocasio-Cortez wasn't like that. She rarely stayed for lunch. She didn't ingratiate herself. She didn't seem to care whether she was well liked or not. Kennedy and John McCain had been working on an immigration-reform bill together for years, and though it never came up for a vote in the Senate, it has been the foundation for all immigration bills since. Ocasio-Cortez was obsessed with how legislation was made, the nuts and the bolts of it, and she buttonholed Winterson whenever she could, asking endless questions. Winterson remembers her as focused and respectful, and that she wrote "fantastic" letters to constituents. "Her eyes are very intense, and they're very beautiful," she recalls. "Her intelligence would just pop out at you." Despite her interest in the process, however, Ocasio-Cortez held herself back. "She isn't an easy person to get to know," Winterson says. "And I didn't feel, when she left, that I knew her."

It's possible that Ocasio-Cortez, still a teenager, may not have felt comfortable with the pomp and pageantry associated with the office of the Lion of the Senate. Going into her interview, she felt jitters—unusual for her. "I mean, I was *prepared,* but walking in I felt like an alien," she said. She noticed, during her initial meeting in the senator's library, "this old pair of glasses, kind of like *perched,* presented on this thing. And I turned to the guy who was interviewing me, and he pointed at that and he said, 'Those are Benjamin Franklin's glasses.' And I was like, '*Whoooooa.* This is history. *This is it.*'"

Ocasio-Cortez has since spoken at length about the temptation all ambitious people face to do the next thing and the next, to reach for positions and prizes, when it's far more important—crucial—to listen to and trust one's inner voice. "For me," she wrote in a poem in college, "not knowing is half the fun / It's the uncertain moment before a first kiss / It's trying to remember if your seat belt clicked." Ocasio-Cortez compares her own sense of life direction to a metal detector, a *beep-beep* sounding in her head when she's fulfilling her

purpose, a warning silence when she is not. She later told a friend
the job "was not a good fit."

Addressing a group of first-generation college students the spring
after she was sworn in to Congress, she talked about this, the magnetic pull of amassing elite credentials that distracts a person—
especially one who aspires to politics—from the heart of what matters.
"You can't think that the high—that the prestigious things—are the
things that qualify you to your community. They're important,
though. They're not things to throw away. Strive. Thrive, professionally. Figure out these spaces. Learn how to write. Learn how to read.
Learn how to educate yourself. Succeed in those spaces." But elite
credentials are no substitute for lived experience, she said. "If you
get that seat, and you don't have the context of the people you're
fighting for, you're not that much better than anybody else in the
system."

• • •

Just as she was starting her second year at BU, Ocasio-Cortez got a
call from her mother. Sergio was extremely ill. So Ocasio-Cortez went
home and visited her father in the hospital. They spent hours watching *Star Trek* and talking, and as the conversation went on, the tone
shifted, and Ocasio-Cortez began to get the feeling—and she knew
he had it, too—that they were saying good-bye. As she was leaving
the hospital room that day, he called her back from the doorway.
"Hey," he said. "Make me proud."

After her father died, Ocasio-Cortez was lost. She has called it "an
unmooring."

She was 18 years old, facing a situation that no amount of dog-
gedness could fix. She couldn't talk, charm, work, or argue her way
out of the crater her father's death made of her life. All of her other

important relationships—with her mother, grandmother, brother— seemed to wither. "I felt alone in the universe," she has said.

A week after her father's death, Ocasio-Cortez was back at school. A month later, she turned 19. She phone-banked for Barack Obama, voted, and breathed a huge but qualified sigh of relief when he won. "The air the morning after he was elected smelled different," she has said. "Like, that's how it really felt." She buried her sadness in to-do lists. She refocused on her grades, intent on raising her GPA (and ultimately graduating cum laude), and joined more clubs—decisions she would later come to regret. She was "dealing with it by not deal- ing with it," she would say later. "It took me a long, long time to really process what happened and the loss of my dad at a young age . . . because I kept not processing it. Just because you're able to go to school and do well and maintain a job and what have you—it doesn't mean that the thing hasn't hurt you." But eventually some self- protective impulse kicked in; she knew she needed a break. So she signed up for a study-abroad program in Niger and, in the fall se- mester of her junior year, escaped the geographical locus of her grief.

In Niger, she discovered a way of life that was the antithesis of how she'd been raised: There, work was just how people occupied themselves during the day. The real living began in the evening, when people would gather, make tea over an open fire, and listen to music and talk. "That was the point," Ocasio-Cortez has said. "That inter- action was the sun around which life revolved, our fellowship and connection to one another." This was the first glimmer of a new thought—that Americans had it backward. The grind was a scam. "I remember feeling at that time that Americans were so poor," she has said. "That level of enjoyment just does not exist in American life."

And in a birthing room in Niger, where Ocasio-Cortez was pur- suing her interest in medicine by helping a group of midwives, she experienced one of those mind shifts that can occur while one is immersed in entirely unfamiliar cultures and customs. It was an all-female space—the mothers, the midwives—the male doctors only summoned in the event of trouble, and Ocasio-Cortez was struck by how easily the women wore their power, so sure of their role as "the glue." One day, the laboring patient was exactly her age, 19 years old, and Ocasio-Cortez understood that whatever material differences between them were the consequence of circumstance, or luck, and that what bound them was existentially bigger and more important. The baby the woman delivered, a boy, was stillborn. Ocasio-Cortez held the mother's hand, and as she watched the medical team try and fail to revive the infant, she had the thought—an idealistic thought—that if she was lucky enough to have been born to loving parents in a wealthy country, then she should do everything in her power to help others thrive. "I believe that people, all people, belong to one another," she would say in a speech during her senior year.

Upon returning to Boston, she switched her major. Doctors could only treat one patient at a time. "I wanted to focus on healing sick systems," she said later. She decided to pursue economics and international relations, which better satisfied her inner communicator. You had to digest a lot of data, but "the real quest is discovering the story."

•••

It's hard to remember just how mannered the public conversation around race and justice was during the presidency of Barack Obama. From the start, Obama's critics on the left (and even some of his allies) warned that the election of a Black president would do nothing to address the racism pulsing just beneath the surface of the country, and that Obama's anemic response to the Great Recession and his deference to Wall Street would accelerate income inequality at an unprecedented rate, creating a massive and discontented underclass. As early as 2009, leftist activists worried that the president was too politically opportunistic and not sufficiently self-critical to make racial and economic justice a real priority, and without an organized activist movement to his left, he would feel too little pressure to do so. Obama's Blackness gave the white liberal Establishment cover to speak of racial harmony as a benign matter of togetherness and reconciliation, and any ferocious language or sentiment was instantly quashed.

This was the cultural and political environment in which Ocasio-Cortez had her consciousness raised. In 2008, the Howard Thurman Center for Common Ground at Boston University was a 4,000-square-foot space in the basement of the student union, a lounge where students would study, play board games, and talk over coffee and takeout from Panda Express. It was home base for a self-selected troupe bound together by their interest, broadly speaking, in social justice. Ocasio-Cortez reigned there like a queen.

Howard Thurman, the Boston University chaplain after whom the center is named, was a Black Christian theologian whose 1949 book, *Jesus and the Disinherited*, deeply influenced the Reverend Dr. Martin Luther King Jr. Thurman dreamed of an equitable multiracial society, attained through difficult conversation among openminded people, so that grievances, curiosities, frustrations, and rage might be aired and, through honest grappling, new alliances forged. When Ocasio-Cortez attended BU in 2007, 7 percent of the student body was Hispanic American. Two percent was Black. The Thurman Center had almost no profile at all.

But it was a charged space, a political incubator, and it attracted kids interested in the issues of the day who liked to challenge and be challenged, who relished verbal combat and confessional exchange. "If you wanted to have difficult, uncomfortable conversations, it was the place for you," says Eric Baker, who works at a think tank and became friends with Ocasio-Cortez at the Thurman Center. "And the best part was you weren't judged or written off or told, 'You're not right for us because you're not the wokest person who ever lived.' No. It was 'Let's have this conversation and tell us your concerns, your curiosities, and we'll work through this together.'" The political slant of the center leaned left, but it also attracted conservatives, libertarians, and unaffiliated rhetorical bomb-throwers.

The centerpiece of every week was a Friday-afternoon event called "Coffee and Conversation" in which the dean of students, a lawyer named Kenneth Elmore (one of few BU faculty members of color at the time), would stand in the middle of a semicircle of chairs and introduce a topic. "I think I'm going to vote for John McCain," he would say, drawing fire. Sometimes as many as a hundred students would attend, and a controlled and mediated gladiator fight would ensue, with people picking sides, making bombastic and reflective comments, antagonizing and supporting one another. Ocasio-Cortez picked her moments. "She was very precise," says Baker. "She would let everyone else go and then she would raise her hand, and people would pipe down, the ruckus would temper. And then she would give her answer in this eloquent, succinct, very deliberate style. People would be like, 'Oh, this is amazing.'"

• • •

The group debated the topics of the day: the war in Afghanistan, the tea party's activist-like tactics for pulling the Republicans to the right, the effect of oil spills on marine life, whether Barack Obama was living up to his campaign promises. They talked about race in

America and whether young people's voices were being heard. They argued over Kanye West. In addition to their coursework, they read King, and Thurman, and Nikki Giovanni, and when the sessions were over, the kids stayed for hours, talking more and listening to music—everything from Adele and Mariah Carey, to Jay-Z and Disco-Tex and the Sex-o-Lettes—sometimes till three or four in the morning before walking en masse back to the dorms.

Ocasio-Cortez had an official leadership role. She was an ambassador, charged with circulating, welcoming newcomers, reaching out to the excluded, and defusing conflict. She was also a magnet. "Every guy went through their phase where they had a crush on her," Baker says, "and she'll probably stab me in the heart for saying that."

Riley Roberts, a tall, red-haired finance-and-sociology major from Arizona, was a participant at the Thurman Center, too, often sitting off to the side. A technology nerd with an interest in how "heretical" thinking, as he called it, could challenge the status quo, he was one of her main sparring partners. "Riley was, for lack of a better term, the shit-starter," says Baker. "Riley's just as smart as anyone you've ever met, probably smarter, but he would actively say things just to stir the pot." Roberts would become especially provoked when the conversation began to have the collegiate, navel-gazing feel of collective concord. "Riley was just like, 'This is dumb. Why are we all going around in a circle saying the same thing?' He enjoyed intellectual combat," Baker observes, "and I think she enjoyed his pushback." The two got together sometime senior year, but they didn't make a show of it. Ocasio-Cortez had always kept her romantic life private; some of their friends didn't know about their relationship.[2] *(MORE ON "THE BOYFRIEND," SEE PAGE 210.)*

In the summer of 2009, fans of the French pop band Phoenix made a video to accompany the single "Lisztomania." It was a mash-up of dance clips from Brat Pack movies: Ally Sheedy, Andrew McCarthy, Molly Ringwald doing mid-'80s punk-pop dance moves. The video went viral, and the following year the kids at the Thurman Center decided to make their own version.[3] *(MORE ON* DANCE VIDEOS, *SEE PAGE 214.)* At sunrise one morning, more than a dozen students gathered on a BU rooftop to twirl and heel-toe and goof around. Ocasio-Cortez was cast as the Ally Sheedy character, and she's sexy as she leans back against a pillar and freestyles some salsa moves. At one point, she drops to her knees, and her hair flops over her bowed head as her fists pound the air. Baker was directing, yelling from off-screen: " 'Die more! Play more dead!' It was just a blast," he remembered. Ocasio-Cortez was totally game: " 'Hell, yeah. Let's go be silly on a roof,' " he remembers her saying. Even then, Ocasio-Cortez was an extremely serious and conscientious person who knew how to bust out once in a while. Nine years later, in the members-only room adjoining the Oversight Committee's meeting room, Ocasio-Cortez hit the floor beside her California colleague Jimmy Gomez and did a series of push-ups while her peers cheered her on.

But it was her senior-year Martin Luther King Jr. Day speech from just months before graduation in 2011 that best showcases what Ocasio-Cortez would become. She mounts the podium with all the poise in the world. She's untrained, for sure: She has not grown into her confidence yet. Having immersed herself in the speeches of King, she emulates the cadences of the great preacher, offering a swooping, stylized series of verses and refrains that feel like a costume she's wearing, something too big for her but so delicious that she can't take it off. But here, in nascent form, are thoughts, and even phrases, she would sharpen over the years. "This time is a cusp," she says, of a period of massive innovation, ingenuity, and growth. And then she downshifts to her point: It is a moral failing that we overlook the people who suffer on account of mere circumstance, that education has become a commodity for rich people while Bronx children "cannot count by coincidence of their Zip Code." This Zip Code language would be embedded in her ads and her stump speech seven years later.

• • •

Life out of college was a shock. A liberal-arts education is meant to cultivate an individual's potential—what Ocasio-Cortez has called inner "genius"—with curricula and clubs and like-minded friends and bolstering professors united in support of that effort. Exiting that bubble of approval is difficult in every case. But for Ocasio-Cortez, this transition was made even harder by the facts of her life. She had entered BU during an era of booming college attendance— Black and Latino enrollment nationwide, while still minuscule, had spiked between 2000 and 2010—and Ocasio-Cortez, like so many other people of color in her generation, had been seduced by the promise that higher education would open doors. Sergio had died without savings, without a will, and behind on two years of medical bills. Financially, the family fell off a cliff. Blanca, still cleaning houses, took on additional work as a bus driver and as a secretary to try to make the mortgage payments. Gabriel, a teenager, learned to leash the family dog on the porch to keep the bank inspector away.

None of the rules or promises that had guided Ocasio-Cortez to this point seemed to apply to her new reality. Sergio had told her she was special, destined for greatness, capable through intelligence and grit of attaining her dreams, and her education had reinforced that notion. But now she saw that it didn't matter how smart she was, what she knew, how ambitious or imaginative her ideas were. It didn't matter that she'd won science prizes; been chosen to give speeches; immersed herself in economics, music, and literature; and graduated

June 26, 2018: Ocasio-Cortez with her partner, Riley Roberts, in Sunnyside, Queens, on the day of her primary election.

cum laude. She was a petite young Puerto Rican woman with bills to pay. She moved into an apartment in the Parkchester development that had belonged to her father, with $25,000 in student loans and no health insurance. Up in Yorktown Heights, her family relied on food stamps.

Throughout high school and college, she had attended the National Hispanic Institute, a youth leadership program, and now she was given a paid fellowship there, helping the administrators develop high-school curricula, traveling the country to set up and lead summer programs, and receiving a grant to try to launch a series of children's books with Latino characters. Books had always been both a pleasure and an escape for Ocasio-Cortez: She loved the works of Junot Díaz and Pablo Neruda. *Consider the Lobster,* by David Foster Wallace, delighted her. She wanted to share that pleasure with young kids in the barrio, who, she thought, might more easily take to reading if they saw themselves reflected in the books. But she wasn't able to get the series off the ground. At around the same time, she rented space at a small-business incubator in the Bronx. People who knew her then remember her working on a tool to help educators track kids' emotional and mental health. She took meetings and reached out through her networks, but that project was going nowhere as well, and she became extremely discouraged.

"Alex, I think, had a Mary Poppins understanding that you follow a particular pathway and bingo! You're successful," says Ernesto Nieto, a co-founder of the NHI. And so, when she foundered, she felt she was to blame. Facing the disparity between how she saw herself and how the world saw her "was not very pleasant. That's the journey for a lot of Latinos. The same doors are not there for us as for somebody else."

On long car rides to NHI events, Ocasio-Cortez and Nieto swapped stories of losing loved ones at a young age, of living between the city and the suburbs, of shouldering the responsibility of caring for family. Nieto tried to frame Ocasio-Cortez's struggles as systemic, not owing to any shortcoming on her part. Only recent college graduates with family support could afford to gild their résumés with high-prestige, low-paying internships, or take the financial risk of starting a business. In the car, unburdening themselves to each other, Ocasio-Cortez and her mentor would cry.

Exhausted, Ocasio-Cortez turned to waitressing, which was at least reliable. "Working with young people, as immensely fulfilling as it is, did not pay the bills," she said. There was something liberating, finally, about abandoning the imagined, idealized path to a fantasy career in favor of meeting the pressing need. On a good night, she could earn hundreds of dollars—cash—which she would stash in a purse against future expenses. She worried about what her father would think of her life, whether he would be disappointed in her, but she also felt unshackled by admitting that this was what she needed to do for now. Whenever she tried to map her life in terms of achievements or goals, "I was deeply unhappy," she has said. "And when I started focusing more on *how* I want to be, I was much happier, even when I was a waitress."

At Coffee Shop—as well as its sister location next door, the taqueria Flats Fix—Ocasio-Cortez found herself, once again, at the center of a scrappy group of millennial outsiders. Founded in 1990, Coffee Shop was a model joint in its heyday. Owned by models, staffed by models, patronized by models, it had the after-hours feel of a high-tone speakeasy. "The revolving door of people that came through there was insane," remembers Jesse Korman, a photographer who often took work meetings at the restaurant and was dating one of the bartenders. "Artists and high-end celebrities and crazy tech entrepreneurs and music-industry people and normal people."

Speakers mounted behind the bar played Brazilian music and indie rock. By the time Ocasio-Cortez worked there, its flash had faded, but it retained the flavor of a hot spot.

The staff understood beauty was a prerequisite for employment there. Waiters and bartenders were often hired by the model-owner Carolyn Benitez, who appeared to conduct job interviews like casting calls. "She'd say, 'Come on and sit in the booth,' and she looks you up and down," remembers Maria Swisher, who worked with Ocasio-Cortez behind the bar. "She asked me how to make these two trashy cocktails that you really don't need to know how to make in order to be a bartender. A Slippery Nipple, or something. And I was like, 'I don't know, I can make you an old-fashioned.'" Bartenders were expected to look hot at work. "I think it even said in our manual we were supposed to look fashionable," Swisher remembers, "and it was always very unclear what that was supposed to mean." Ocasio-Cortez, sometimes rocking a red lip, her hair up in a messy bun, "probably dressed the most conservatively."

The front-of-house crew at the restaurant was an assortment of creative, idiosyncratic anti-authority types familiar to anyone who has ever been young in New York. Swisher was doing political theater; another bartender was a performance artist launching a fashion line; a third was a sailing instructor and tarot-card reader. "It was this free-spirited thing—*Hey, we're in New York City figuring things out*," Korman, the photographer and patron, recalls. The Coffee Shop girls, as he called them, were always high-energy, operating at a ten and yelling at one another across the room.

Swisher and Ocasio-Cortez became friends. Swisher had just moved back to the States from London, and she and Ocasio-Cortez bonded over the fact that they were both caring for their mothers, both uninsured, and constantly worried about money. "The United

States is kind of a rough place to be if you're not affluent and you're young—it's very easy to fall through the cracks," says Swisher.

Restaurant work has always been a temporary solution for people who are between things or hard up. Ocasio-Cortez has since spoken of the very exploitative nature of this work, the undocumented old men washing dishes in the kitchen, the front-of-house staff working mainly for tips without protections or benefits or scheduled breaks. She translates this experience into an equity fable of how, for some, bad luck can lead straight to financial calamity, forcing a person to hold down a demanding, demeaning job to keep from drowning, while business and government perpetuate the notion that misfortune is somehow the sufferer's fault. But this was personal for her. At the restaurant, "so many of the people that I worked with had parents that passed away or they were born in circumstances that led to these outcomes," she said. "Whereas in society we're taught you're there because that is what you deserve. You didn't work hard enough. You didn't educate yourself enough. You had messed up in some way."

But while she was stalled professionally, Ocasio-Cortez was also just living her life, working constantly, hanging out with the restaurant people and friends from BU, taking the 6 train home to the Bronx long past midnight. After work, the Coffee Shop crew often went to a bar nearby, a small, dark New York City place where everyone knew the bartender. Ocasio-Cortez was never a partyer, but like so many New Yorkers, she loved the adrenalized adventure of exploring undiscovered corners of the city. There was a kava bar on 10th Street that she and Swisher would visit; her friend Eric Baker remembers once meeting her at a hookah lounge after work. "I don't know if she had any fun, but I had a lot of fun watching her try hookah," he recalled. Ocasio-Cortez was clearly at a crossroads in life, "just turning over how she was going to move forward," Baker said. Though Ocasio-Cortez and Riley Roberts had split up near the end of college after dating for much of their senior year, they were back together, working it out and doing a long-distance thing—he was in Arizona helping start-ups with digital marketing and planning to move to New York—and when he was around, he would join the group after hours, talking about websites and music and tech.

In 2016, Ocasio-Cortez messaged an acquaintance from her Thurman Center days named Claire Wasserman, who was running empowerment seminars for women. She wanted to attend one called "Get Unstuck," about how to make professional pivots. "She was really unhappy working at the bar," Wasserman remembers. "I was shocked that she was struggling."

While Ocasio-Cortez was trying to get unstuck, the world was changing and not in the naively hopeful ways that she'd projected in the earnest speeches of her college days. In 2011, the year she graduated, hundreds of young people set up an encampment in Zuccotti Park in lower Manhattan. Calling themselves "Occupy Wall Street," they were protesting, among other things, growing wealth inequality and the outsize influence of money in politics. They introduced the phrase "one percent" to the vernacular, a tag that better illustrated a grim social reality than any economist's chart or graph. (They also advocated for canceling student debt and raising the minimum wage.) By 2014, when Ocasio-Cortez was waitressing and bartending downtown, college graduates carried, on average, $28,400 in student debt and unemployment among people ages 16 to 24 was higher than 15 percent. (Unemployment in the general population, meanwhile, was just over 5 percent.) That same year, 400,000 people took to the streets of New York City to protest government and business inaction on climate change, and Michael Brown was shot by police in Ferguson,

Missouri, leading to months of furious uprisings and the growing importance and visibility of Black Lives Matter. In 2015, a year before the election of Donald Trump, the phrase *downwardly mobile millennial* began appearing in the mainstream press. The tectonic plates of American politics were shifting, but very few inhabiting the established realms of media or government—not the New York *Times* or Hillary Clinton or Barack Obama—could see it yet.

At the restaurant, everyone debated politics constantly with a sense of urgency. "I always wanted to talk tons about environmental justice," Swisher remembers. "We talked a lot about health care. It was really personal for both of us." The bar at Coffee Shop was enormous and curved, with lots of little corners to escape to, and from their position behind it, Swisher and Ocasio-Cortez would hold forth during their Saturday brunch shift—dissecting the events of the week with each other and with the regulars who came to talk politics. They discussed Bernie Sanders, how he really seemed to have working people's backs, and what it meant to be "socialist." (Swisher, having recently relocated from London, had some perspective on that.)

During the 2016 election cycle, Ocasio-Cortez started canvassing for Bernie Sanders's presidential campaign, becoming a foot soldier in his young leftist insurgency. Slinging coffee in the morning and margaritas at night, "I didn't feel like I deserved a good life," she has said, and the Bernie campaign allowed her to "question those assumptions." Volunteers were organizing for Bernie on college campuses and Reddit; an offshoot of Occupy, called the People for Bernie Sanders, had a million followers on Facebook.[4] *(MORE ON AOC AND BERNIE SANDERS'S SYMBIOSIS, SEE PAGE 216.)* Ocasio-Cortez had joined the campaign through a small community organization called Bronx Progressives. But even her enthusiasm for Sanders was tempered by skepticism, frustration, and dissatisfaction. As she put it, if "Congress is jacked up and our Senate is jacked up, you could elect the best person in the world to the presidency, but if your two major bodies are compromised, you're not going to get anything done."

With their customers Ocasio-Cortez and Swisher also discussed their disillusionment with the New York *Times,* which seemed to have swallowed the party line—and the inevitability of Hillary Clinton as the nominee—without question and without seriously considering the concerns of people like them. It was "destabilizing," Swisher says, to see the "Paper of Record" in this light, as an Establishment mouthpiece, and it forced them to reassess the media in general. "How do you decide now what media you take in and what is trusted? And is there really media that is neutral?" Swisher says.

When Clinton won the nomination, clashes intensified at the bar. One regular argued for a third-party vote, saying that Clinton's anointment proved that Democrats and Republicans had become indistinguishable from each other—corrupt, owned by big business, and interested only in their own power—but Ocasio-Cortez refused to go that far. It wasn't helpful, she argued, to talk that way, to let cynicism and mistrust obscure meaningful differences between candidates. Hillary Clinton and Donald Trump were worlds apart, and it was immoral and obstructionist not to act decisively. "I remember there being a conversation where we kind of decided that to vote third party would be a thing we could only do from a place of privilege," Swisher said. "If you are the 80-year-old dishwasher working in our kitchen, it makes a hell of a lot more of a difference whether you have Hillary Clinton or Donald Trump as president than it does for either of us."

A writer for the *Guardian* was often at the bar, as was a guy from a small town in Missouri. There were homeless people, and neighborhood people, and a memorable venture-capitalist libertarian. "We kind of used to playfully tag-team him a little bit and give him shit about libertarianism," Swisher said. He was always talking about people pulling themselves up by their bootstraps, without understanding "that the fact he grew up in a Connecticut mansion makes his bootstrap different from everybody else's. We gave him the business about that a lot. It was fun," Swisher says.

The fun stopped on November 8, 2016, with the election of Donald Trump. Whatever activism Ocasio-Cortez and her crew had previously undertaken, whatever complaints, or demonstrations, or high-minded rebellions—these had always been done within the broader context of faith in the legitimacy of leadership. Barack Obama and the other grown-ups in charge deserved to be in charge, even if they sometimes misstepped or misspoke. But now the system had betrayed them, and a generation was ready to rise up. "We are not," Ocasio-Cortez later said, "going back to brunch."

CHAPTER 3

Wild Ride

THE CAMPAIGN / 2016–2018

Like his older sister, Gabriel Ocasio-Cortez had been a Bernie Sanders supporter, and one day in the dystopian, Trumpian fall of 2016, he had an idea. He had heard about something called Brand New Congress on a leftist YouTube show. Founded by former staffers of the Sanders presidential campaign, Brand New Congress was a political recruiting outfit seeking to persuade working-class people to run for national office without corporate or lobbying money; since Sanders's withdrawal from the race the previous spring, the group had been issuing calls on leftist media for people to nominate their friends, neighbors, and community leaders as prospective candidates in the 2018 midterms. Gabriel was driving, but it started to rain, so he pulled over to wait out the storm. "I hate driving in the rain," he said. "I'll take the snow. I'll take a blizzard, anything." Sitting there, killing time, Gabriel had the thought—born of equal parts loyalty, admiration, and intimacy with his sister's ambition—that would send Alexandria into orbit. "In our family, we have so much pride in making one another proud," he said. "Not just making one person proud. It's about making your grandmother proud, your sister proud, your mom proud, your dad proud, your cousins proud." He knew Alexandria would be great for this. He picked up the phone.

Life's auspicious moments are often only evident in retrospect. Ocasio-Cortez was likely in the midst of something else when she heard from Gabriel. Was she interested in running for Congress? "I mean, it's one of those things where it was, like, 'Eff it. Sure. Whatever,'" she has said.

From his car, Gabriel filled out the web form and hit send.

Meanwhile, Ocasio-Cortez and Swisher had started planning a trip to the Standing Rock Reservation in North Dakota. Swisher had a long-standing commitment to environmental justice, and "I just had this really strong feeling that I needed to go," she says. When she shared her impulse with Ocasio-Cortez, "she was like, 'I've been thinking the exact same thing, and we should just do it.'" Protests there had been ongoing since spring, and the two friends saw the pilgrimage as a purifying event, a way to reorient themselves toward what mattered and away from the shallow, the cynical, the self-satisfied—all the habits of mind that had blinded progressives to the real dangers of Trump.

For Ocasio-Cortez, the election result was just the culmination of everything that had gone wrong in America since Reagan and even long before that. The president-elect, though grotesque, was a *symptom*, she would often say later. "I know that guy," she once said, though she had never met him. "I know him really, really well . . . I have bartended for Donald Trump. I've had guys catcall me who are

Donald Trump in New York City." Even his profession—"shady real-estate developers"—was a familiar, old-school New York archetype, "not like an aberration," she added. A trip to Standing Rock would give her a moment to step off the treadmill and contemplate with seriousness the problems she cared about most: environmental degradation, racism, and control of the poor and the marginalized by politicians and businesses. A road trip would, in other words, give her a chance to think about a political future. From the moment they agreed to travel to Standing Rock, a run for office was "the elephant in the room," Swisher recalls.

The protests at Standing Rock had started in April as a local movement, with a small group of Lakota Sioux camping out in teepees and tents on the wide, grassy plain by the Cannonball River near their reservation in an effort to draw national attention to the $3.8 billion, 1,172-mile pipeline project planned by the Dallas-based oil conglomerate Energy Transfer Partners (DAPL, it was called). The bulldozers and drills were aimed both at ancient Native American burial grounds and at the river itself, a sacred site, which incensed the Lakota Sioux, who were already nursing a generations-old injury over a broken land treaty. For them, the pipeline was another instance of America trampling on Indigenous property and traditions without regard or respect for the people who held them, and it recalled a whole history of desecrations.

Since then, the protest had grown into a symbolic nexus of a generation's concerns, a new vehicle for the anger the activist millennial left had been expressing since Occupy over the inequities and disparities created by capitalism's excesses. By summer it had swelled to more than 3,000 travelers from all parts of the country, including the third-party presidential candidate Jill Stein and, later, the actor Mark Ruffalo. Confrontations with corporate security forces sometimes grew violent. Protesters were fired upon with rubber bullets and set upon by dogs, and published their battle scars on Twitter. But especially during the fair-weather months, Ocasio-Cortez said later, some people mistook the protest for a party, bathing topless in the sacred river and wearing feathers and other ornaments, the kind "that Forever 21 sells in their accessories rack." These were nothing but tourists, she indicated dismissively, "thinking that if they just walked the grounds and held hands with Native Americans and, like, you know, communed and—I don't know—like sat at a campfire and burned sage in a fire, like they would somehow be contributing or enlightened or giving in some way."

For Ocasio-Cortez, the trip was of the utmost seriousness, an acknowledgment that the volcanic grief and disillusionment that had defined her existence and that of her peers for so many years could no longer be endured. Something had to be done. "The America that we're living in today is so dystopian, with people sleeping in their cars so they can work a second job without health care. And we're told to *settle down*," she said. "At some point, these chronic realities do reach a breaking point, and I think for our generation it's reached that."

• • •

Swisher and Ocasio-Cortez decided to livestream their road trip at the last minute as an experiment, and the recorded segments from the road retain the feeling of a rough draft: young people with a new tool and an idea at play. Ocasio-Cortez's cell phone was mounted on the Subaru's dashboard, and she always handled it herself. "Hey, Santiago," she would say to her friends logging in to the stream. "Hey, Alex." She would wait for everyone to "hop on," and in closing, she would give her smile and wave, saying, "Thank you, thank you, I love you guys." In late 2016, influencer culture was blowing up, with

Snapchat crushing Vine and Facebook still outpacing Instagram, and a constant stream of unboxing videos, gaming competitions, political monologues, and makeup tutorials flooded YouTube. Ocasio-Cortez had a knack for the form. She and Swisher hit the highway on December 19, and at their first rest stop, Ocasio-Cortez maintained mesmerizing eye contact as she launched into a dissertation on the relative merits of Cheetos and Hot Cheetos, while at the same time negging Swisher's friend Josh Pereira, who was along for the ride and seemed maybe just a little full of himself. There were only a couple dozen viewers, but Ocasio-Cortez played to them. "Okay, fine," she said. "He's a regular Cheeto guy. I naturally picked up the *superior* Cheeto, which is the Flamin' Hot Cheeto." It was deft, the way she reduced the bearded white dude in the back seat to some lame bro. "FYI, *we just met.*"

There, in miniature, is the political attack she'd come to be known for. Changing to a slightly more serious topic, she continued, "I'm not trying to be difficult, I'm not trying to be down"—always a signal that she's about to lob some flak—but Hillary Clinton "didn't make a single visit to the United Auto Workers before the general election and then they're, like, upset that union workers didn't organize for her." And then she offered a version of the thesis that would define the next 18 months of her life. Democrats, she continued, "have also been very spoiled by Barack Obama because he [ran] one of the strongest organizing campaigns that we've ever seen, and that's what it takes. I think it takes that ground game." To her tiny late-night online audience, Ocasio-Cortez chatted and debated her way through the Midwest and the Plains, with Swisher and Pereira as her willing foils. She was better at going without sleep than her companions and more insistent on pushing through. They arrived at the camp on December 21, the winter solstice, after dark.

As the trio tumbled out of their car, they were bowled over by the brilliance of the stars. Strangers greeted them with hugs and offers of hot food and drink. A flute was being played in the distance, and the sacred fire—the camp's center, a prayer site, no photos allowed— burned bright. They were shown to their tent and given subzero sleeping bags and a camp stove. At Standing Rock, there was no commerce, no rent, no paychecks, no bills to pay. Cell service was sketchy, so there was no self-important busyness, no junk-food distractions.[5] *(MORE ON* THE STANDING ROCK ROAD TRIP, *SEE PAGE 222.)*

Ocasio-Cortez and her friends stayed for just a few days. Each morning, in the blackness before dawn, the whole camp was awakened by a couple of men on a loudspeaker telling jokes, singing, and saying prayers. "Remember why you're *heeere*," they would say. Every activity, from offering tobacco to the river to chopping wood to prepping dinner, felt like a rite. On their first day in camp, Ocasio-Cortez and Swisher spent hours at a gas station filling propane tanks. They had raised more than $1,000 in donations through a GoFundMe, and now they spent some of that money on fuel for the camp's main generator. They went walking with tribal elders. They observed the decision-making process in the women's council. Winter was not a period of active confrontation or conflict at Standing Rock. It was a time of spiritual fortification.

Ocasio-Cortez would later describe the experience as "transformative." She saw how her anger, frustration, and isolation could be channeled, productively, into principled opposition, how historical grievance could be converted into strength, and how worldliness— cynicism and spiritual fatigue—weakened resolve. "One of the things that was so powerful," she said, "is that they don't confront the situation with the same force their opponents give to them. They respond to being attacked by dogs with prayer. They respond to tear gas with prayer. They basically respond to attack with organization. They don't respond to attack with attack."

On this trip, Ocasio-Cortez had the revelation that political activism could be like a sacred mission. The organizers at Standing Rock liked to underscore the point, always speaking of social protest as a vocation. "What is your gift? What is your talent? What is your spirit telling you to do?" asked one of the tribal chiefs. For a young woman who aimed high, and was raised in the social-justice tradition of the Roman Catholic Church and steeped in the works of Thurman and King, this made sense.

"There is something to be said for seeing and smelling and tasting and breathing" another person's reality, Ocasio-Cortez has said. "Indigenous people who just wanted the same rights to their own land that anybody else had—it really internalized the intersection of racial and economic and criminal justice into one, and I felt like we had to do something."

Uplifted and rejuvenated, Ocasio-Cortez and her friends got back in the Subaru on Christmas Eve. Before they hit the road, they performed a car-karaoke version of Bon Jovi's "Livin' on a Prayer." Ocasio-Cortez rocked the air guitar. The plan was to drop her off in Bismarck, where she would catch a flight to Arizona to visit Roberts, while Swisher and Pereira continued east. But as they were departing Standing Rock and regaining cell service, Swisher recalls, Ocasio-Cortez's phone rang. It was a staffer from Brand New Congress with a serious question: How interested, really, was she in running for Congress?

• • •

They say you have to ask a woman seven times to run for office. Even the most ambitious women usually don't dream of the U.S. House of Representatives. Questions of likability, charisma, beauty, experience, smarts, aggression, and leadership get hopelessly tangled up with femaleness. The public eye, doubling as the male gaze, can destroy even the most capable woman through subtle and unsubtle misogynistic attacks, and in the early months of 2017, when Ocasio-Cortez began to wrestle with the idea of a run, there was no better living example of this than Hillary Clinton. Even with her elite education, multimillion-dollar war chest, institutional support, decades of experience, and recognizable name, the competent woman had lost the electoral vote to the incompetent man—who had roused his supporters at gigantic rallies with cries of "Lock her up!"

For Ocasio-Cortez, the notion of running for Congress was beyond far-fetched. It was insane. She was a bartender with little savings and few powerful social connections. Many of those involved with Brand New Congress formed a new group called Justice Democrats. Their mission was to launch hundreds of candidates in the 2018 cycle to replace every corporate-backed Democratic politician in Congress. Its larger goal was to repeal and replace, as it put it, the entire House of Representatives. Bernie's platform would be its policy template, and it would provide media training, back-end fundraising, and messaging support. One of the co-founders was a former Silicon Valley entrepreneur named Saikat Chakrabarti, who had in his previous life helped to invent an easy-to-use shopping-cart app called Stripe and thus was an expert at the technological back end of digital fundraising. It was he who essentially devised and led the small-dollar-donor revolution that made Bernie both the master and the mascot of the insurgent activist left.[6] *(MORE ON AOC'S RELATIONSHIP WITH CHAKRABARTI, SEE PAGE 230.)* Boiled down, Justice Democrats' big idea was to replicate the unprecedented success of the Bernie Sanders candidacy—but at scale.

They had received about 10,000 nominations for candidates, and as Ocasio-Cortez contemplated her future, its founders scrutinized her. "We were looking for examples in their background that they weren't going to sell out, that they were selfless and committed to other people," remembers Corbin Trent, another Justice Democrats co-founder. When you persuade someone to run for national office from nowhere, "you're getting people to take this leap of faith. You've got to be a little crazy, a dreamer or something. What we had to cull out were the crazy fucking narcissists and the people who just wanted power," says Trent. To that end, Justice Democrats eliminated people who nominated themselves, as well as those who said yes on the very first call.

Ocasio-Cortez didn't say yes right away. She needed to think about it.

• • •

Justice Democrats unanimously agreed on Ocasio-Cortez. She was so obviously smart—a quick study, a great talker. She cared about justice in an authentic way. "She's not good at being full of shit," Trent observes. Also—and this was not incidental—"she's just really pretty," says Trent. "That's like 30, 50 percent of being on TV."

Most tantalizing, she lived in NY-14, an hourglass-shaped, waterlogged district that sprawls over the Bronx and Queens, encompassing both Rikers Island and La Guardia airport. For 20 years, the district had been represented by Joseph Crowley, one of the most powerful Democrats in Congress—a close ally of Nancy Pelosi's and in the mix to become the next Speaker of the House. In the eyes of Justice Democrats, the toppling of Crowley by a Bernie-branded insurgent would be nothing less than a dream.

But Ocasio-Cortez was green, and Justice Democrats worried about that. Starting at the beginning of 2017, she and the Justice Democrats were in constant touch, doing calls and video interviews, and

Ocasio-Cortez lobbed more livestreams into the ether. Notably, she and Swisher made a livestream as they toured the Jefferson Memorial on January 22—the day after the first Women's March and two days after the inauguration of Donald Trump. They wandered the immense rotunda sharing one pair of earphones, looking euphoric. Ocasio-Cortez proclaimed her desire to find common ground with the people in MAGA hats, and she raved about the profundity of Jefferson's impact on America's founding documents. Jefferson "is one of my favorite presidents," she said. But Lincoln is my "all-time bae, for sure."

Waleed Shahid, one of the Justice Democrats, remembers a meal with Ocasio-Cortez at a Thai restaurant near Union Square after she had decided to run. When she remarked that "I think there are a lot of Trump voters who are anti-Establishment who might vote for me," it occurred to Shahid with a little alarm that she might not understand that only registered Democrats could vote in the Democratic primary in New York. He laughs about it in retrospect.

Ocasio-Cortez wasn't intimidated by what she didn't know. That was the thing about her, the confidence that she could learn anything, integrate it into her DNA, and then communicate it to all around her. "What struck me was the amount of bravery" she had, Swisher recalls, "in the sense of not being a perfectionist and just knowing that none of us need to be perfect in order to do what we are called to do. There were a lot of instances where Sandy seemed like she was a little bit out of her depth and wasn't sure that she was going to say the right thing or that people were going to like it and decided that she needed to do so anyway."

What seemed to scare Ocasio-Cortez was not *Can I do it?* but *How can I afford it?* She was already living on tips, saddled with debt, trying to help out her mother. Roberts had moved from Arizona into her apartment in the Bronx. He was trying to get a career going, and "she was kind of holding shit down," Swisher remembers. Ocasio-Cortez and Roberts had to talk about how she couldn't work as many shifts at the restaurant if she was going to run for office. "It was going to be a big transition," Swisher says. But then Ocasio-Cortez got Crowley between her teeth.

Crowley, a liberal stalwart, was the picture of the self-satisfied pol. Pink-faced and middle 50s, he was called "the King of Queens," making him a storybook foe for a small brown woman who knew what it meant to—as she once put it—work a double restaurant shift and be found "crying in the walk-in fridge . . . because someone yelled at them for bringing seltzer when they wanted sparkling." NY-14 is a majority-minority working-class district of almost 700,000 people. Nearly half of its residents are foreign-born. Half identify as Hispanic, and about 20 percent as Asian, but there are pockets of Yemeni immigrants in the Bronx and French-speaking Africans in Queens. The median per capita income is $30,000 a year, and the median age is 38. They are, overwhelmingly, the people who serve New York City: drivers, sanitation workers, home health aides, doormen, preschool teachers, grocery-store clerks, delivery people—and, of course, restaurant workers. Most rent their apartments and travel approximately 45 minutes to work each day.

That is the big picture, and within it, important disparities exist. Some of the city's poorest New Yorkers live in three big public-housing projects in NY-14. The fast-gentrifying neighborhoods of Astoria, Jackson Heights, and parts of Long Island City are in NY-14, too. There, millennials priced out of the real-estate market in Manhattan and Brooklyn can afford to raise families, creating enclaves of well-educated hipsters with left politics, known in city vernacular as "Queens mommies" and among Bernie Sanders supporters, favorably, as "class traitors."

Crowley, the son of an Irish American family of cops and teachers, had presided over all this diversity since he became a member of Congress in 1999, when his predecessor retired and handed him his seat. Since that time, he had never actually had to run in a competitive race. NY-14 was so deeply blue, within a blue city within a blue state, that his reelection every other November was always a given, and, with his lock on the district, the notion of mounting a primary challenge against him was widely regarded as foolhardy. Each election cycle, Crowley amassed millions of dollars from real-estate developers, private-equity firms, pharmaceutical companies, and private insurers and then seemed to sit back and wait for his win.

But Ocasio-Cortez and Justice Democrats saw him as vulnerable. They could paint him as out of sync: white in a brown district, older in a young one, beholden to corporate interests while representing the working class, and a comfortable representative of the way things were instead of how they ought to be. Crowley was born and raised in Queens, but having attained his congressional sinecure, he had moved with his family to the suburbs of Washington, D.C., and he sent his kids to school there, a choice Ocasio-Cortez saw as traitorous. The man who had all the name recognition in NY-14 didn't drink his city's water or breathe its air. Furthermore, Crowley positioned himself as a progressive, but as Ocasio-Cortez contemplated her run, she saw that she could point to a litany of betrayals. He voted to invade Iraq ("Disastrous!" Ocasio-Cortez said later). He voted for the Promesa Act, which gave financial control of the Island of Puerto Rico to an outside panel ("Sucking the island . . . dry").

It was Crowley's presumption of power that most provoked Ocasio-Cortez. He was absent in his district and, on the median, showed up to vote less than his colleagues. And yet he seemed to be rewarded for this show of laziness with the powerful position of chairman of the House Democratic Caucus. Life had taught Ocasio-Cortez that no matter how hard she hustled, she couldn't presume to attain anything. "When I think about my opponent trying to take Nancy Pelosi's seat, it's like, *Why?*" she said later, tilting her head back and smiling broadly at her own joke. "What has he done? It goes back down to the idea of equating fundraising with leadership. And they're not the same thing."

Looked at in a certain way, Crowley came across as nefarious, and this awakened in Ocasio-Cortez a crusading impulse. "King of Queens" wasn't just Crowley's brand: It was an allusion to the fact that in the Queens political machine, he was boss. In addition to being the elected representative from NY-14, he was the chairman of the Democratic Party in Queens, which meant, as Ocasio-Cortez correctly pointed out, that he was "responsible for his own endorsement by the party," a double role that she called "an astounding conflict of interest." Every challenge to an election in Queens would be ruled on by a judge selected by Crowley himself. Ocasio-Cortez took Crowley's dominance as a dare.

As she contemplated entering the race, Ocasio-Cortez viewed herself as a "poor, stray cat," scrappy and under-resourced, a self-perception that ultimately stimulated her ambition. "The most passionate I ever saw her was when she was going off about his record," recalls Waleed Shahid, "about how many people were afraid of him and she was the only person who could do it. People told her she was crazy. She made it into her shield. *I'm the only one who's going to run against this guy. Might as well do it one hundred percent.*"

By March 2017, four months after the vetting process began, Ocasio-Cortez had made her decision, though it wasn't yet public. That month, she attended a women's-empowerment event in a storefront near Grand Central station run by Claire Wasserman, the same college friend who organized "Get Unstuck." "Reinventions" was an invitation for women, mostly in their late 20s to mid-30s, to stand up and tell a story about how they changed their professional direction in a courageous or meaningful way. It was after work, and the room was packed with about 100 people. One woman spoke about coming out as queer and leftist after a GOP childhood. Ocasio-Cortez was seated near the back. When she stood up, there was no banter, no self-deprecating small talk—her voice was loud and clear. "People like me don't run for office," Wasserman remembers her saying. "People who look like me don't run for office, but I have always wanted to run for office, and I am going to do it." Wasserman cried. "And people *cheered.*"

The leaves weren't yet on the trees when, on the first weekend of April 2017, she joined Justice Democrats for a political boot camp down in Frankfort, Kentucky. She was 27 years old and still working in the bar. The weekend was designed to help the dozen or so inexperienced candidates get up to speed in advance of the 2018 midterm cycle, and it started with a recorded talk from Marshall Ganz, the Harvard public-policy lecturer and former organizer for United Farm Workers who helped Barack Obama build his grassroots campaign. He impressed upon them the importance of telling an authentic, believable personal story, which he called the "story of self." There was media training, kind of like speed dating, where the prospective candidates had to answer questions from mock Fox and MSNBC interviewers. ("They kind of put us through the ringer," Ocasio-Cortez said.) And there were warnings from civil-rights leaders. "You have to be fearless because they're going to come after you. They are. This is no joke, y'all," said Darryl Gray, a pastor who had marched alongside Ralph Abernathy in the 1960s and later in Ferguson.

In Kentucky, Ocasio-Cortez developed a close friendship with a woman named Cori Bush, a nurse from St. Louis who was also aiming to topple an Establishment Democrat in a primary race. (Bush would lose in 2018 and then win in 2020.) That weekend, she was convinced that this congressional bid was more than just an insane individual risk. It was a collective endeavor, a movement that reflected her generation's frustration. "We can only accomplish great things together," she said to the group assembled around the conference table. Over time, this notion would be honed to something more cutting. "We meet a machine with a movement," she would say again and again.

That same month, she made her official announcement with an Instagram post. It was a quiet salvo. No pundits opined, and no reporters showed up at her door. The post showed a photo of Ocasio-Cortez standing on a green lawn holding her "first campaign baby," who was mushing a dandelion into her face. Like a game aunt, Ocasio-Cortez is both grimacing and smiling. "In case you haven't heard, I've been nominated to run for office! U.S. Congress to be specific," she wrote. The post promised "a wild ride to come."

• • •

Ocasio-Cortez has always managed her own message and image; she has always been the best narrator of her own story. This was true at the science competitions when she was a kid, and it was true in her 20s when she was a restless New Yorker posting on Instagram the Thomas Piketty book she got for Christmas. It was true when she complied with a restaurant culture that expected her to look hot while at the same time refusing to trade on her sexiness. "She always looked amazing, and everyone thought she was beautiful," recalled Swisher, "but she's always had a good instinct on how to blend into a situation without bending to the demands of it. She never seemed out of place or too rigid or uptight, but she was not trying to fit into

June 24, 2018: Just two days before defeating Crowley, Ocasio-Cortez traveled to Tornillo, Texas, to demonstrate against the Trump administration's detention of children.

a mold." At the restaurant, people continued to call her Sandy, but on the campaign trail, she introduced herself as "Alex."

The most Ocasio-Cortez has ever copped to her own astonishing beauty is to refer to herself as belonging to a cohort of "young, brown women who are intelligent and whose faces are symmetrical"—"symmetrical" in this case a self-deprecating euphemism for "beautiful." Ocasio-Cortez would have been well aware of her impact on others. Her rhetoric could be confrontational and her politics countercultural, but her appearance conformed to society's conventions. With her wide-apart eyes, arched brows, and tawny complexion, she could have modeled for a skin-care line—and, in fact, later capitalized on these assets by shooting a makeup tutorial for *Vogue*.[7] (MORE ON AOC AND THE POLITICS OF BEAUTY, *SEE PAGE 235.*) Even before she entered politics, her looks gave her power. Absent the other markers of status or class, her beauty was a privilege that provided entrée to rooms and spaces that would have been barred to women older, rounder, or darker-skinned.

But the way she wore her beauty was original to her. Like many women raised by strict parents, she presented herself modestly. One old Coffee Shop photo shows her among a trio of servers, all wearing tomato-red cocktail dresses: Her colleagues rock cleavage and form-fitting styles, while Ocasio-Cortez wears a tentlike frock with a high, narrow neckline and what looks like a sports bra underneath. There was a hipster, thrift-store look to her that seemed to signal the belief that fashion and beauty should be democratized, accessible to and enjoyed by anyone who found them enjoyable, no matter their height, weight, skin tone, or ability to pay. But like the messy, twisted bun that would become a signature of her primary run, her casual presentation belied another reality. Her admirers dwell on how *natural* she is, but no natural talent—in baseball or chess or politics—attains the kind of power, popularity, and fame Ocasio-Cortez has without a constant, strategic self-assessment. It's tempting to imagine Ocasio-Cortez as having arrived in the political sphere fully formed, a prophet for the millennial left. But this view underestimates her. For every aspect of her political self has been carefully calculated and curated. By her.[8] *(MORE ON AOC'S AUTHENTICITY, SEE PAGE 237.)*

Kim Balderas first spotted Ocasio-Cortez lingering at the outskirts of a community event in Queens in the spring of 2017. And the first thing Balderas, who was 18 at the time and an active member of Black Lives Matter Greater New York, noticed was how she was dressed: polished, as if this summertime gathering were a high-stakes job interview. "She just stood out in the crowd. We were all in sneakers and chill clothing, and homegirl's in heels and a dress. We're like, 'Who the hell is this?' "

There has long been friction and a deep mistrust in local communities between electoral politics and grassroots organizations, mainly because the latter have, over time, grown weary of and cynical about the parasitic dynamics of representative democracy. The politicians need the community activists to turn out voters; when they come courting, they all make promises they won't keep. And once they win, politicians seem to be in the game to stay in the game, to satisfy their own egos and amass their own power. Using words like "compromise," they leave the issues—like the systemic racism and economic inequality that have a stranglehold on their constituents—and the people who got them into office, behind. Upon encountering Ocasio-Cortez, Balderas was firmly on the side of the grassroots. "I really stayed away from electoral politics," she said. "I felt for myself it was a waste of time."

But she kept running into Ocasio-Cortez at local events, and she grew impressed. "She wasn't talking about 'Let's all come together.'

She was talking about 'We should do something about these situations.'" One of the mantras of movement politics is that candidates don't matter; policies do. And Ocasio-Cortez "was speaking like an organizer. Like somebody who knew how to relate to class struggle. That's the biggest thing that made me say, 'Oh, she's not coming to play. She's coming to fight.'"

When, later that summer, Ocasio-Cortez sought the endorsement of Black Lives Matter Greater New York, Balderas understood that the stakes were high. People would take note and other endorsements might follow, and so, at the decisive meeting, she grilled Ocasio-Cortez. She wanted to make sure that she would stay strong on the issues that mattered to the organization, especially putting a stop to racist police practices and, as Trump-administration assaults escalated, the illegitimate targeting of immigrants by ICE. "I remember saying to her, 'The last thing I want is to have another white-passing Latina in office taking up space, saying one thing and showing up on TV as another.' I remember saying that to her, and she was taken aback." In response, Ocasio-Cortez said, "I don't run from conflict. I go after it," and Balderas understood that with Ocasio-Cortez in Congress, "we could get people to talk about these issues on a mass scale that didn't exist in our neighborhood before." Black Lives Matter Greater New York voted to endorse Ocasio-Cortez.

In Queens, the grassroots and electoral politics meet in the living room of veteran organizers Jo-Ann and Donnie Whitehead. They don't endorse so much as anoint, and they, too, were extremely impressed with Ocasio-Cortez. They invited her to their house in the fall of 2017; she arrived early and just hung out, talking to people one-on-one. And then someone accidentally spilled a glass of water on the rug, and Ocasio-Cortez—instinctively, raised by a mother who cleaned houses and after years of working in food service—"was the first one to take up a napkin and wipe it up," Donnie Whitehead re-members. "If you'd never seen her before, you'd think she just came to help set up or whatever. Me, I don't really listen to every word a candidate says; it's whether or not the attitude is in service to work-ing with people."

The Whiteheads offered to help and advise her as she petitioned to get on the ballot to challenge Crowley. "We indirectly had been fighting the Queens machine for, my gosh, I can't even fathom the years," Jo-Ann said. "They're great at kicking people out of the race, off the ballot for stupid reasons. *You have an extra comma in your address.*" They had six months to gather the requisite 1,250 signa-tures, but the Whiteheads advised Ocasio-Cortez to collect many times that number to insure against inevitable fraud claims by the Crowley camp. Ocasio-Cortez seemed to have no sense of how hard the job would be, and the Whiteheads didn't know whether she was naive or brave—or both. "Everyone has fears. But she seems to have a sense of 'You have to tackle your fears and do what you think is important and right.' It was just a good vibe."

Ocasio-Cortez had never been an organizer before, not really. She had volunteered, and she knew the language and tropes of civil rights. But her own incipient campaign was her first real immersion in day-to-day movement politics. The volunteers who hiked around Queens and the Bronx through the fall and winter of 2017 and 2018, shiver-ing as they helped to collect her petition signatures, were mostly teenagers and 20-somethings from BLM Greater New York and activists connected to the Whitehead's network. In the process, Don-nie Whitehead got pneumonia. They were "busting out at train stops, handing out flyers. We were just talking about politics and then we mentioned AOC," Balderas remembers. "It was such a powerful time, not only in organizing but in building community. We were all so excited. It was really beautiful. It was so committed. You felt like it was the right people, the right scene."

Since the prep trip to Kentucky, Ocasio-Cortez's social media had begun to reflect her progress as a candidate—more frequent posts of her public appearances and policy positions, but her marketing was not uniform. Volunteers were still wearing purple T-shirts that said "Brand New Congress," and Ocasio-Cortez was using an array of headshots that, while flattering, did not cohere. One night that October, Ocasio-Cortez texted Jesse Korman, her photographer friend from working at the bar. Did he have time for a quick photo shoot? She wanted something "more professional," Korman recalls.

A couple nights later, Ocasio-Cortez showed up at Korman's apartment after her shift and immediately started in about Crowley. "It was 10:30 p.m., and we're whispering because I have roommates who are asleep," Korman says. "I was like, 'Wow, Sandy, that sounds crazy. So you really feel like you have a chance to beat this guy?' She's like, 'I'm going to give it everything I've got.'" When they started taking photos, Ocasio-Cortez revealed herself to be comfortable in front of the camera. "She was quite collaborative and would say, 'Oh, let me lift my chin a little higher so I can get this better angle here; let me put my hair here.'" The shoot took a businesslike 45 minutes, and the images taken would soon be everywhere, on posters and palm cards and T-shirts, the lettering in Spanish and English evoking the iconic 1960 poster of the Cuban Marxist and guerrilla leader Che Guevara. Those portraits contain all the elements of the future AOC: Hair back, face unadorned, she looks beautiful but neither girlish nor young.

She was also finding her footing on Twitter. She began to float ideas there, to try out phrases and positions to see what hit. A bland tweet about ICE as a "criminal justice issue" morphed within months

72

to #AbolishICE, which garnered tenfold more "likes" than the original and became part of her permanent arsenal. "Social media is a place to find a more honest pulse of what people are talking about and what they believe," she said later in a conversation with the writer Ta-Nehisi Coates. "I use social media to listen as much as I use it to speak . . . I see what's building momentum, and then all it needs is an amplifier, which is why I think it's working—because I know I'm not the only one who believes these things."

In December 2017, Ocasio-Cortez sent a tweet that would help to define her future political identity. The issue at hand was a wonky one. The Trump administration had moved to repeal Obama-era rules around net neutrality, and one important segment of Ocasio-Cortez's prospective constituency—the techies and lefty gentrifiers who composed Bernie's base and had been settling in Queens for the past decade—were up in arms. A protest erupted online, and Senator Ted Cruz sent a condescending tweet aimed at neutering the outrage, in which he addressed the egalitarian-minded techies as "Snowflakes," an attempt to conjoin the issue of net neutrality with "trigger warnings," "safe spaces," and other foci of right-wing derision.

Ocasio-Cortez saw her opening. Cruz wasn't speaking directly to her, not yet—he had likely never heard her name—but he was a powerful man attempting to humiliate her friends to elevate himself. "Snowflake?" she tweeted, shaming Cruz for his manners. And then she made a move for which she has since become notorious. She used Cruz's record against him, pointing out that he had accepted campaign donations from Comcast, which could profit from the net-neutrality rollback. "Comcast paid you $36k to write this tweet. Campaign contributions are public record." It was, perhaps, her first slam dunk, receiving nearly 65,000 likes.[9] (*MORE ON* AOC'S GREATEST TWITTER DUNKS, *SEE PAGE 242.*)

•••

There was a big problem. As a candidate, Ocasio-Cortez was gathering strength and refining her message. But her campaign was floundering. It was January 2018, just a year after she'd first been recruited. With the primary six months away, she was still working at the bar, stashing grocery bags full of campaign literature beneath it during her shift and then going out door-knocking or to house parties afterward. Her mostly volunteer organization was more focused on message than money. Since her official announcement nine months before, it had raised just $60,000.

"She was not doing well," Shahid remembers. "I was trying to get her to take that seriously. I felt like she didn't understand how severe an issue this was. I asked her, 'Can we make a spreadsheet where you write down literally everyone in your life who could give you $50 or more?' And she did, but then it was like, 'Hey, you haven't called any of these people.' She was really punting on it." Asking her friends for money "made her uncomfortable," Shahid reflected, especially when the people in her life—in her family, at the bar—were already just scraping by.

Shortly after the New Year, Justice Democrats had come to a reckoning. They were adrift, having raised only $1 million since they launched, and had long ago abandoned their vision of supporting 400 candidates. Now they made the agonizing decision to go all in on Ocasio-Cortez, pulling back resources from every other candidate. The conversations within the group were excruciating and the calculus was brutal: Ocasio-Cortez was hands down its best candidate, and even if she didn't win—the likeliest outcome, most conceded—a solid turnout for her would send the loudest message to the protectors and preservers of the status quo. Other candidates were furious. Having been sold a dream of collective revolution—*a movement*—they were now told they had to fend for themselves. "I had to have really, really tough conversations with dozens of incredible people," remembers Alexandra Rojas, another Justice Democrats co-founder. Ocasio-Cortez wasn't part of the internal decision-making, but she took it in stride. Rojas sensed that her attitude was something like: *I need all the help I can get. Awesome. Let's do this.*

Before long, Justice Democrats took over the daily operations of the Ocasio-Cortez for Congress campaign. Chakrabarti and Trent moved to New York, Chakrabarti to run the strategic operation and Trent to handle communications, while Shahid began to seek endorsements from the institutional left. Some of the people who had been there at the beginning felt pushed aside. "There was not very much transparency about who was calling the shots," Kim Balderas recalls. "A lot of times Justice Democrats would come to events and be like, 'Oh, we actually want to do this and that.' I was like, *What the fuck? We've been spending a whole two weeks on this, and just like that—no conversation, no questions, no nothing?*" The suspicions of the grassroots were aroused: Would this be just another politician after all? "They would call those electoral people 'fake organizing,'" Balderas says.

Justice Democrats, as well as Ocasio-Cortez herself, saw the reorganization as a necessity. "I think Alex thinks she's strategic. She's thinking about the greater good, and I think Alex knows there are casualties," reflects Tia Keenan, who co-founded an activist group in Queens called Neighbors Against White Supremacy and was an early volunteer on the Ocasio-Cortez campaign. Crowley's stranglehold on Queens was real, and it would take a real operation to challenge it. Shahid had become discouraged. He would take Ocasio-Cortez to meet the members of Democratic clubs in Queens and other well-known activist organizations. She would give her stump speech, work the room, and people might even applaud. Then they'd say, "We appreciate your spirit, kid, and vote to endorse Crowley," Shahid remembers. Even in sympathetic rooms, Ocasio-Cortez was forced to play defense, having to address and respectfully respond to everyone's doubts about her. She once attended a small gathering in someone's living room, and "it was a bunch of white leftists basically being skeptical of this woman," Keenan recalls. "Really challenging her: 'How do we know you're going to win? We've invested in the way things are. Why would we abandon that investment?'"

But somehow, none of the doubters derailed Ocasio-Cortez. Winning the election was her only focus. "You don't become a powerful person by accident," Keenan reflects. "At a certain point, she had to realize, *Hey, this is possible. This can happen.* And then: *This just has to happen; it's mine to lose.*" She faced down all the obstacles as if she were playing a video game: "Step over these stones, slay a dragon, eat a mushroom."

Whatever Ocasio-Cortez might have really thought or felt about the skeptical political folks who underestimated her or the frustrated activists who mistrusted her or Justice Democrats, which piled all its hopes upon her back, she did not reveal. "Stop trying to navigate systems of power and start building your own power," she once advised two teenage Latina Girl Scouts during a Q&A at SXSW. At the end of January 2018, she posted a video to her Instagram Story that would mark another stage in the development of her public-facing self. Her face was inches from the camera. "We're not running to make a statement. We're not running to pressure the incumbent to the left," she said. She was learning to unleash her rage to push her purpose, this time not by emulating the cadences of King but by being entirely herself, anger issuing from her in a way that was raw and fierce but always on the safe side of controlled. The video has the feeling of a vent, but of course it's a performance, too. "We're running to win. We're running to organize. We're running to redefine the political landscape in New York City, and we're going to do it."

• • •

As a child, Ocasio-Cortez didn't grow up with any consciousness around political labels: The word *socialism* meant nothing at all. At BU, during the Obama era, there was no Democratic Socialists of America chapter on campus. But Ocasio-Cortez loved the politics of Bernie Sanders and agreed with his economic analysis: that "hyper-capitalism" was obliterating "human dignity" and that all the pressing problems of the moment, including racial injustice, could be viewed through the lens of class struggle.

But she would not have called this socialism, necessarily. "I don't read a book and decide what I am," she said. "I'm like, *These are my goals: Health care. Housing. Education.* If my belief that housing is a human right . . . if that makes me a socialist, then all right, I guess I'm a socialist . . . Some people may really disagree with me on the left, you know, you have to be, like, really pure and all this stuff, but for me, it's more tactile. What am I trying to accomplish? This is what I'm trying to accomplish. You can call that whatever you want to call that, but these are the things that I want." [10] (MORE ON THE HISTORY OF THE LEFT, *SEE PAGE 252*.)

When Ocasio-Cortez calls herself a Democratic Socialist, the tag threatens and infuriates her opponents. On the right, "socialist" is a dog whistle evoking communism and revolution: bread lines, onerous taxation, the removal of rights, government control, censure—some of history's most calamitous experiments. ("Marxist or this or that," as she has said.) Fox News obsessively tracks her allusions to socialism, and when Trump deployed the word *socialism* to implicate elites in wanting to appropriate voters' hard-earned money and property, he positioned himself as the freedom-loving alternative.

In the winter of 2018, as the ballot petitioning and the door-to-door canvassing swung into gear, her campaign started to seek the endorsement of New York City DSA. The organization, founded in 1982, had bumped along until 2016, when Bernie Sanders, a longtime independent then running for president as a Democrat, expressed his affiliation, and membership surged. In 2016, entrance polls at the Iowa caucuses showed voters under 30 preferred Sanders over Hillary Clinton by a factor of six to one, and naturally the overlap between Bernie's base and DSA's members was huge. DSA endorsed Bernie Sanders in the presidential primary that year, and when he withdrew from the race, it did not transfer support to Clinton. Any candidate seeking to align herself with Bernie's constituency and platform would be wise to get the approval of DSA, especially because—and this was important—the Queens chapter had a robust membership and email lists. In the guerrilla fight against Crowley, its members could be converted into a small but organized and disciplined army of Ocasio-Cortez volunteers. Of DSA members, Bilal Tahir, who ran Ocasio-Cortez's primary ground game, says, "They are hard-core militant folk."

But expediency does not preclude sincerity. Ocasio-Cortez officially joined DSA in January 2018, at around the same time she was seeking its endorsement. It felt to her like a natural progression. She had read the fundamental socialist texts as an adult, and then it was "just, Oh. I was already here! I didn't know this was a political way of being. I just thought it was a moral way of being."

The endorsement process must have been grueling, for it required Ocasio-Cortez to play up to a group of mostly white men committed to the intellectual purity of the socialist ideal. In the end, though, it worked. The Queens chapter of DSA was the first to get on board. "We were like, *She's a star. She's going to win. An exciting young Latina running against this old white guy in a majority-minority district—she's gonna wipe the floor with this guy*," remembers Aaron Taube, the co-chair of the chapter's electoral committee. The raw enthusiasm was dampened by the chapter representing the Bronx, whose members were less convinced. "(A) I didn't think she had any chance of winning," remembers Brian Elliott, then the co-chair of the electoral working group of Bronx/Upper Manhattan DSA. "And (B) I really just viewed her as this person who had some charisma and had politics I agreed with who was running a shot-in-the-dark congressional campaign." Privately, the Bronx chapter of DSA debated the "opportunity cost" of challenging Crowley, and worried about Ocasio-Cortez's inexperience and lack of institutional support. Besides, Elliott added, she wasn't off-the-charts incredible. "I think she's sincere. That's it," he says. "It's not like when she walks in a room, everybody draws their attention to her because she's just *that* magnetic."

At a meeting at the office of *The Nation* magazine in March, the endorsement committee of DSA New York City vetted Ocasio-Cortez. She was evasive about her stance regarding BDS, the Palestinian-led group promoting boycotts and other economic sanctions of what it calls the "apartheid state" of Israel (support for which is suicide for politicians in New York City, where the largest Jewish population outside Israel lives), but reassured the group that she would always be comfortable identifying herself as a socialist and her campaign as a socialist effort. "We wanted to make sure this is somebody who's not going to back away from our values and the values we want to push. The fact that she was able to confidently state yes to that made enough people comfortable moving forward," Elliott says. Ultimately, DSA endorsed her.

In the early spring months of 2018, the Ocasio-Cortez campaign deployed its volunteer troops across Queens and the Bronx to knock on doors and stand on street corners and at subway stops to build name recognition for Ocasio-Cortez and collect signatures to get her on the ballot, aided by DSA's own tight field crew. "They're like, 'We are going to make these numbers.' They did add some oomph to our organization," says Tahir. There were also BLM folks, restaurant people, and out-of-work actors. There were people who spoke Bengali and Spanish, and there were chalk artists who illustrated the candidate's name on well-trafficked sidewalks. In the end, the campaign collected 5,400 signatures, 4,150 more than it needed. Ocasio-Cortez earned her place on the ballot on April 12. The primary was set for the end of June.

• • •

Ocasio-Cortez sits in her living room in the Bronx, sipping from a takeout cup of coffee. It's the spring of 2018, and her apartment is a regular student-type mess: a worn couch covered with a weird knitted throw, a can of paintbrushes standing on a low shelf. Riley Roberts is there (he delivered the coffee), looking on with pride and humor in a purple T-shirt.

A documentary-film crew is collecting footage, and Ocasio-Cortez—caught in an apparently casual moment at home—uses the camera as an opportunity to deliver a short tutorial in the elements of effective campaign literature. In particular, she wants to show how inferior Crowley's expensive mailings are to her own. "Everybody in the district got this Victoria's Secret catalogue of my opponent," she says, opening up Crowley's glossy leaflet to a headshot of the politician. She displays the spread like it's show-and-tell. Then she grabs her own mailer, a simple purple postcard printed on both sides. She holds it up. "I'm not trying to gas myself up or brag or anything, but this is the difference between an organizer and a strategist. What am I trying to get people to do? Two things. I want them to know my name"—here she points at her name on the card in gigantic type—"and I want them to know that they need to vote." The primary's date is also huge.

She flips her card over. Again, her name. Again, the primary's date. Her platform is broken down into seven simple bullet points, starting with health care for all and ending with the abolition of ICE. Crowley has none of this. What he has is a vague declaration of intent. "'Taking. On. Donald. Trump. In Washington,'" Ocasio-Cortez reads aloud. Now she's openly mocking him. "'Delivering for Queens and the Bronx.'" She cups her hand to her mouth and speaks sotto voce. "'Deliver' is insider talk. 'Deliver' means 'pork.'"

She unfolds the two pages, accordion style, to their full poster-size width, revealing a glossy collage of Crowley hugging people floating on a baby-blue sea. "Okay, we got this big beautiful spread here. Where's the primary date?" She looks at the camera with big-sister impatience. Roberts, off-camera, snorts. "There is nothing about the path forward here. 'Trump' three times. 'Commitments' zero times." She holds her thumb and index finger up in a big round *O,* as if to say, *I'm done here; there's no help for this guy.*

Ocasio-Cortez loved the nitty-gritty of campaigning. She was interested in all of it and genius-level good at most of it. She walked the streets of the Bronx and Queens with a bullhorn, speaking Spanish whenever she could, buttonholing strangers, crouching down to speak to children at eye level. Most of the usual Democratic suspects—labor unions, Democratic clubs, progressive activist and community groups—still weren't giving her the time of day, but whenever anyone scraped together an invitation, she showed up, including one time to a Muslim fundraiser in Long Island, far out of her district. "People did some praying, and they gave money," remembers Michael Carter, an early member of her staff. Borrowing from Bernie's playbook, the Ocasio-Cortez campaign set the suggested donation at $27. Early mornings found her leafleting by the big Parkchester subway station near her home, an express stop on the elevated line, where the city's essential workers streamed up the stairs by the thousands each morning and back down at night.[11] (MORE ON THE DAY-TO-DAY CAMPAIGN, SEE PAGE 260.)

Ocasio-Cortez engaged people on the street in a natural way—attributing her people skills to her long years serving behind the bar. In the restaurant industry, "we spend so much time talking to people of different political opinions, and you don't get to run away," she has said. "At the end of the day, you still kind of like the guy. He's totally advocating for a position that you loathe, but you also know he doesn't dislike you personally." Online and on the floor of Congress, Ocasio-Cortez is known to be fierce, but in person she is, as she herself has said, "a little disarming." People like her.

Likability is a treacherous requirement for a politician—especially for a woman. Too likable, and she isn't taken seriously. Too serious, and she isn't likable. The ingredients are nonspecific, some combination of folksiness, sincerity, magnetism, and sex appeal shaken up into a telegenic cocktail. But Ocasio-Cortez had it nailed. Warlike in public but charming, even deferential, in person, she always kept her own voluminous personal drive hidden. She understood that female ambition is best expressed runically: A woman who wants to climb to great heights or accomplish big things hardly ever attains these goals by saying so.

Deep into the spring, Crowley was still behaving as though his opponent didn't exist, and Ocasio-Cortez was galvanized by this in the same way that she was by his entitlement. What did "representative

*Ocasio-Cortez's campaign poster
for the Democratic primary in
2018, inspired by a Che Guevara
poster from the 1960s.*

government" even mean if the habits and traditions of the electoral system had evolved to preserve incumbent power above everything else? "The definition of electoral insanity is electing these same guys over and over again and expecting our country to be any different," she has said.

Numbers became the singular focus of the Ocasio-Cortez campaign. They needed 15,000 votes to win, and to make that math work, they needed to flip Crowley voters. But they also needed to stimulate disengaged and unregistered ones. The conventional wisdom when running a primary campaign is to solicit votes from people who have voted in primaries before, Ocasio-Cortez has explained. "Only talk to those people who are showing up on special elections, off-year elections—these dates that kind of go by—only talk to those people." But in this case, those people already favored Crowley. "I knew that that wasn't going to work for me. And I knew that that wasn't going to work for our community because what you're saying is: Only campaign and only organize like one percent of the people in your district. And I knew that in order for us to have a better community, I needed to educate and expand the electorate. That is harder."

This is where Justice Democrats was an enormous help. Its email list had grown to more than 160,000 names, and it was sending out all its fundraising and other solicitations on Ocasio-Cortez's behalf. She wrote a statement of purpose on Facebook, which Chakrabarti converted into a Facebook ad, and then sent directly to the people on the email list. Those people became the targets for door knocks and invitations. They could be converted into volunteers. Justice Democrats also deployed a texting tool similar to the one Chakrabarti pioneered for the Sanders campaign, so that likely voters were flooded with texts—*Hi, I'm Joe, I'm your neighbor and I'm voting for Ocasio-Cortez*—an old trick now but in 2018 more of a novelty. "When someone said, 'I'm going to vote for you,' we checked on them, like, three times. 'Are you voting? Did you vote?'" Ocasio-Cortez said.

For most of the spring, campaign headquarters was the Parkchester apartment. Roberts "was really important in her process," says Michael Carter, the former staffer. "He was often there in the apartment with me and her when we were doing fundraising or strategizing." Roberts knew a lot about database management and search-engine optimizations. "He was behind the scenes pushing Alexandria out through Facebook, mostly, but by digital means overall. He did some work, too, with Google analytics, working on search terms, getting her name more searched, putting in some of the digital infrastructure that enabled her to get a high-enough profile that 15,000 people would vote for her."

Still, almost no one in the mainstream press was covering her. Justice Democrats spent $10,000 on a poll with about two months to go, and Ocasio-Cortez was 30 points down.

And then, on May 30, the Ocasio-Cortez camp pushed through all its social-media platforms its only video ad, produced on a budget of $6,500, and people heard Ocasio-Cortez say the words she would become famous for. "Women like me aren't supposed to run for office," she said in a voice-over, while footage of her applying mascara in her yellow bathroom played onscreen. With its whooshing trains and images of children and worn-out workers, the ad was gritty and pretty, extremely resonant for anyone who has ever commuted by subway to a job in New York. "Who has New York been changing for?" Ocasio-Cortez said. "Every day gets harder for working families like mine to get by. The rent gets higher. Health care covers less. And our income stays the same."

It was an appealing vérité picture of working-class struggle, urban style—and then, at about one minute in, there's the image that sent

June 26, 2018: Ocasio-Cortez, at her Election Night party in a Bronx pool hall, seconds after she was declared the upset winner over Joe Crowley.

the ad into viral orbit, garnering it 300,000 views within 24 hours, a humongous, insane hit. Ocasio-Cortez is standing on an outdoor subway platform, when she performs the ballet that a million commuting women have done a million times: She changes out of her flats into her heels while standing without losing her balance. It's a familiar working-woman trick, like taking a bra off while clothed, but "you never see people on TV doing that," says Naomi Burton, who made the ad together with her boyfriend, Nick Hayes, through their company, Means of Production. Hayes had been changing his camera battery when Burton noticed Ocasio-Cortez taking off her shoes: "I was like, 'Yo. Get this,'" Burton recalled. "As soon as we saw it played back in the footage, we knew. As a way to say, *You are me, I am you*, that was a huge moment." The week before the ad dropped, Ocasio-Cortez had raised less than $20,000, according to FEC filings. The week after its release, she raised twice that. Then three times. In the two weeks preceding the primary election, she raised nearly $200,000. In the final month, the Ocasio-Cortez campaign raised more than it had in the 13 months since her announcement combined.

The momentum began to change; everyone working on the campaign felt it. Michael Carter was out canvassing one day, and he found a pile of Crowley flyers on the ground—a signal, he thought, of the Crowley team's own disinterest. "I think one of his canvassers had just ditched and pretended they handed it out, and that really underscored the difference—why people were on our campaign versus theirs." Taube remembers watching Ocasio-Cortez speak at the opening of her Queens headquarters sometime in the middle of May. If she was good in February, she was great now. "We were like, 'Oh, she's really fucking good,'" he remembers. "It was like, 'Oh, wow, she could maybe do this.' It was just her presence. I can't even remember what she said. But I remember being struck by the way that she commanded the space with a bunch of people around her. It was a super-hot day, really muggy. There were a ton of people out, and she's just killing it, and people are coming off the train, and looking at what's going on, and you felt like something was happening."

Ayanna Pressley noticed it, too. Up in Boston, Pressley was running a primary challenge against the ten-term Democratic incumbent Michael Capuano, and early in June, she traveled to Manhattan for a fundraising house party. On the way down, she asked a mutual friend whether Ocasio-Cortez might be encouraged to drop by. She did. That night, the two unknowns shared their similar biographies. They had both gone to BU, both been responsible for taking care of their mothers. Standing on a multicolored rug beside a big-screen TV, Ocasio-Cortez said a few words—"On November 6, 2018, our nation will change"—and then Pressley followed up. "I can't wait till we win—we're going to start our own caucus," she said. Ocasio-Cortez tweeted, "Our BFF applications are already in."

Later, Pressley recalled her first impression of Ocasio-Cortez. "She's diminutive in size but large in presence. She's luminous. I felt literally the air shift and I looked to my left and it was her entering into the event space."

And then Ocasio-Cortez mopped the floor with Joe Crowley.

She was very nervous before their televised debate on NY1 on June 15. Sitting in her apartment on the worn couch, with the documentary crew filming, she prepares herself like a professional athlete. She takes deep breaths and lifts her arms from her sides, like wings, then over her head. She fans the air about her, as if she might fly. "I need to take up space. I need to take up space," she whispers to herself as if reciting a mantra. "I am here."

Roberts, off-camera, laughs a little. "What's that?" he asks.

Ocasio-Cortez smiles. Her red lipstick is on. On her right wrist, she wears Sergio's favorite watch, like a good-luck charm. "I don't know." She laughs at herself. "This is me taking up space."

It's as if she's burrowing into her own core, mining for her super-natural confidence. "I can do this," she says.

"I know you can," Roberts says.

"I am experienced enough to do this. I am knowledgeable enough to do this. I am prepared enough to do this. I am mature enough to do this. I am brave enough to do this." It's a prayer, a prose-poem. But then the thought of Crowley obviously passes through her mind, and she breaks her state, gets heated, starts jabbing the air with a highlighter. "And this whole thing, this whole time, he's going to tell me I can't do this. He's going to tell me I'm small, that I'm little, that I'm young, that I'm inexperienced." Then she exhales loudly, stretches her arms out in front as if she were taking a racing dive, and with flexed wrists pushes all her negative thoughts away.

Crowley performed exactly as she predicted. He condescended to her. He implied that she had better leave the hard work to the man in charge. He suggested that overthrowing Trump was too important to take a risk on an inexperienced and impudent girl. He fumbled a reference to Reddit. Ocasio-Cortez looked at him with lasers shooting out of her eyes, then she ripped him apart. For taking corporate money. For being in the tank for the real-estate lobby. For raising his kids in the suburbs when schools in Queens and Bronx were failing. For being weak on ICE, a charge he disputed. "If this organization is as fascist as you've called it fascist—and you have said it's fascist—then why don't you adopt the stance to eliminate it?" She bangs the palm of her hand on the desk. "This is a moral problem and your response has been to apply more paperwork to the situation . . . and that puts our communities in danger." Crowley sat there blinking, befuddled, looking like a person from the past encountering a creature from a future he'd never imagined and couldn't understand.

Less than a week later, Crowley failed to show up for a town-hall debate in Ocasio-Cortez's neighborhood in the Bronx, citing a scheduling conflict, and he sent a Latina surrogate in his place. Ocasio-Cortez turned it into her show. "We are making excuses for absentee leadership," she said. "This is not a debate . . . I am the only one running for Congress in this room." With about a week to go before the primary election, the New York *Times* finally turned its attention to the contest, chiding Crowley for his absence. Voters were right to wonder, "What are we, chopped liver?" the editorial board wrote. Crowley's "seat is not his entitlement," the Paper of Record concluded. "He'd better hope that voters don't react to his snubs by sending someone else to do the job."

The photograph is iconic by now of Ocasio-Cortez, in a crowded pool hall in the Bronx, responding to election results displayed on the wall-mounted TV showing her 15 points up. Her hand covers her mouth, her eyes are wide in disbelief, the mic of a NY1 reporter juts into the frame, poised for a reaction quote. It was June 26, 2018. She had received 17,000 votes—2,000 more than her goal and 4,000 more than her opponent. Three days later, she tweeted a photo of her sneakers, filthy with grime and worn through the soles. "Respect the Hustle," it said.

BILL
WEIDEMEYER

November 30, 2018: Ocasio-Cortez draws a lottery number for her new office on Capitol Hill.

CHAPTER 4

Breathing Fire

CONGRESS / 2018-PRESENT

On Wednesday, June 27, the Beltway and media Establishment—not to mention all of NY-14—woke to find the political planetary order had shifted. Ocasio-Cortez described the moment this way. "If a spaceship landed in your backyard, it's like, 'What the fuck is that? Is it going to hurt me?'"

The news desk of the New York *Times* had been rebuffing the Ocasio-Cortez campaign for months. Presuming a Crowley win, the paper had sent a staff reporter to his victory party and a freelancer to hers. The *Times* published its very first news story on the underdog candidate vanquishing a sitting congressman without the participation of the underdog herself. "Pretty much all of political journalism are doing an Ocasio-Cortez crash course tonight, myself included," tweeted MSNBC's Joy Reid. CNN published one of its first stories under the self-defeating headline "Who Is Alexandria Ocasio-Cortez?"

Ocasio-Cortez made her national media debut the next morning on *Morning Joe*, wearing the same navy-blue dress that she had worn in her campaign poster. She had been up late the night before at her victory party, a surreal experience. Initially, the crowd at Park Billiards Cafe & Sports Bar was just staffers, volunteers, friends, and the small handful of leftist and local media who had covered her campaign: *Chapo Trap House, The Young Turks,* the reporter from NY1 who had been ready with the mic in her face. "I cannot put this into words. I cannot believe these numbers right now," Ocasio-Cortez told her after gasping at the results up on the big screen. In the final tally, she crushed Crowley with 57 percent of the vote. As news of the upset surged out through social media, the energy in the room totally changed. The actress Cynthia Nixon, in the midst of a primary challenge against then-Governor Andrew Cuomo, arrived at the bar. National press sprinted uptown. Hillary Clinton was calling. The week before, Ocasio-Cortez had been a former bartender with an extremely uncertain future. Her campaign had spent just over $550,000 while Crowley's had spent $4.5 million. Now she was standing up on a chair thanking her staff and making promises: "We are going to rock the world in the next two years," she said. And when she added, "I can't do it alone," someone shouted back, "You're not alone!" and everyone clapped. Roberts took pictures. Later, campaign people formed a little human barricade to protect her from the growing crush, and Ocasio-Cortez sat down with a laptop and earbuds to pick her way through the avalanche of media requests.

Initially, for the first few microseconds of her inaugural appearance on MSNBC, she looked unsettled. A novice to live national TV, she took a moment to figure out where to aim her gaze. But she quickly recovered, and once she did, she gave a version of her stump speech, something she'd done thousands of times on the streets and in the living rooms of the Bronx and Queens. "We have to stick to the message," she said. "What are we proposing to the American people? . . . What is the vision that is going to earn and deserve the support of working-class Americans? And we need to be explicit in that vision and legislation. Not just 'better.'" The panel of white men and Mika smiled at her, gobsmacked.

The dress was a tactical choice. It was simple and flattering. It didn't wrinkle or bunch up. It didn't show too much skin. It signaled that she was the kind of working woman who liked to look good but had no patience for fuss. "If it looks like I'm tired, I am," she would later say in speeches. "If this is the fifth time you've seen me in this dress, deal with it."

• • •

Morning Joe was Wednesday. On Friday, Ocasio-Cortez went on *The View,* in a different dress, and was asked whether she would be running for president of the United States. Ocasio-Cortez hadn't even been elected yet. She had won an off-season primary race, and because NY-14 was so deeply blue, no one thought her Republican opponent stood a chance in November's general election. But technically speaking, the woman on whose back the newly adoring and astonished left was piling its future presidential hopes was still a candidate for Congress without a fallback plan. Ocasio-Cortez deferred the question as she would continue to do, alluding to presidential aspirations as a child, then backing away, saying, "I'm gonna work as hard as I can and leave it up to the universe." Her mother, Blanca, in the audience, smiled tearfully. Later that day, Ocasio-Cortez appeared on *The Late Show With Stephen Colbert,* walking onstage with her now-famous bilateral spirit-fingers wave. Colbert, full of beneficent awe, came clean and spoke for most of the country when he said, "I want to confess: I did not know your name on Monday."

Nancy Pelosi was less impressed. Crowley's loss immediately highlighted power struggles within the caucus. Pelosi, whose main job is to keep the party pointing forward, did not want to give anyone the idea that the victory of Ocasio-Cortez meant anything bigger than itself. It was not a sign of a general leftward tilt. It was not a sign that the Establishment was losing its grip. It was not a sign of anything. "Nobody's district is representative of somebody else's district," Pelosi said at the time. The victory over Crowley "should not be viewed as something that stands for everything else."

The Republican Party leadership, on the other hand, regarded the election of Ocasio-Cortez as a joyous occasion, as if a beautifully wrapped political weapon had landed serendipitously in their gray-suited laps. Everything her supporters adored about her could be inverted to do damage; her political allies could be polluted by association with her and the positions she held. Her femininity could implicate all Democrats as having the qualities misogynists attribute to women, including stupidity, childishness, insanity, naïveté, incompetence, and unreliability. Her Latina identity could be used to stoke racist and xenophobic fears. And her embrace of the socialist label was the best feature of all, for it seemed to give weight to the Republican argument that the Democrats in Congress were just a bunch of radicals intent on depriving regular people of their hard-earned freedoms. The hate campaign began at once. Donald Trump tweeted about her primary win within minutes of its announcement, and Mitch McConnell made use of her the following day. "The energy in the Democratic Party is self-avowed socialist," he said, describing it as eager to abolish ICE and let immigrants overrun American borders. Democrats like Ocasio-Cortez are "a real drag on the party in terms of appealing to American voters who I don't think want us to turn into a European socialist country." McConnell didn't say the immigrants in question were Spanish speaking like Ocasio-Cortez, but he didn't have to.

Ocasio-Cortez has always been most relaxed with press beyond the Beltway, and in a video interview with the hip-hop radio station Hot 97 a couple of weeks after her win, she looked sunny and rested, as if she had just returned from vacation. Rumors had started to circulate online, suggesting that she was somehow a rich kid, having grown up in Westchester (true) and attended Brown (false), and that she was a communist, anti-Semitic ally of George Soros (all false). The Obamafication of Ocasio-Cortez, the campaign to conceptually blur together race and privilege and elitism and communism and exoticism, and in so doing build an effigy monster that the Republican base could chase and burn, had begun. In the interview, Ocasio-Cortez refused to dignify these stories with a response. "Alt-right is gonna alt-right," she said with a shrug. "I'm not going to waste energy trying to clarify whatever lizard-person theories that they have."

She did want to clear something up, though. Having refused to cover her campaign at all, the mainstream media was now publishing stories explaining that she won because she was Latina in a majority-minority district. This offended Ocasio-Cortez to her core. As if they were saying that she were somehow undeserving. Or that she were representing a fringe group. As if her victory wasn't *earned*. She didn't win because she was Latina, she clarified. "That is incorrect. We won across all demographics," she continued. (Some pollsters dispute this.) "Which is important because then people say"—and by "people" here she meant Pelosi above all—"this can only work in the Bronx. But I believe that . . . when you are actually clear and you stand up for working-class people, that can work in a lot of places. I think it could work in the Midwest."

A close listener might have heard Ocasio-Cortez articulating her great ambition, and it was not to run for president. It was to rebuild the Democratic Party, bruised by years of capitulating centrism and sidelined by Trump, in the image of working people across racial, ethnic, geographical, and generational lines. Her vision was big. It was audacious and probably overly optimistic. It was a future in which the Trump voters and the Bernie voters and the Ocasio-Cortez voters could be persuaded to look past their tribalism and racism to see that their frustrations were connected, that they were being abused in similar ways by the same system. That, together, a New York City waitress and a southern fruit picker and a Rust Belt factory worker and a West Coast gig worker could find their political way forward, and build a coalition bigger and more potent than anything any lobbying firm could pay for. Big business and Establishment power have been right about one thing, Ocasio-Cortez said later. "My candidacy is not an individual venture," she said. "It is representative of an actual working-class movement."

• • •

Justice Democrats couldn't believe it. Their gamble on Ocasio-Cortez was a long shot; they all thought so: a Hail Mary with a backup prayer that they could at least leverage whatever performance she delivered into momentum for their incipient movement. "None of us thought she was going to win," remembers Shahid. It was so risky that Sanders, whose platform and tactics Ocasio-Cortez had adopted—and whose former staffers recruited her and ran her campaign—had not endorsed her.

Having achieved this miracle, Justice Democrats doubled down. They took their candidate national. By the first week of July, the political press—Chris Cillizza at CNN, Paul Krugman at the *Times*—had begun calling her AOC. ("Can we start abbreviating?" Krugman asked.) She sat for photos by Annie Leibovitz for *Vogue*. She spoke to David Remnick for *The New Yorker*. She went on *The Daily Show with Trevor Noah*. And she hit the road, traveling the country to stump for other candidates Justice Democrats endorsed or supported, partial compensation for having abandoned them six months earlier. She went to Michigan and to Kansas, where she met Bernie Sanders in person for the first time. She also went to Missouri to give her friend Cori Bush a boost.

Inside her campaign, some staffers thought the national tour was a bad idea. The summer before the general election, they said, she should stay in her district and do the hard work of establishing herself there. Ocasio-Cortez had won the primary decisively, but within NY-14 there were pockets of resistance and communities where she struggled. She won among younger voters, and she dominated among the people who had voted for Bernie Sanders in 2016, easily taking the gentrifier strongholds of Astoria, certain sections of Jackson Heights, and Sunnyside. She won in the whitest neighborhoods in the district, all of which are in Queens. But Crowley had won in certain heavily Black and Latino neighborhoods in the Bronx, including Parkchester, a distinct encroachment on Ocasio-Cortez's turf. An analysis by the director of the CUNY Center for Urban Research found no correlation between a vote for Ocasio-Cortez and a Hispanic surname.

The Census demographics of any district do not mirror the people who vote in primaries. While it's true that the 700,000 residents of NY-14 are overwhelmingly majority minority and working class, the people who had elected Ocasio-Cortez were a whiter and better-educated subset of these. The analysis of the primary results raised a question that would continue to dog Ocasio-Cortez as she navigated her way through Congress: Who, exactly, did she represent? A smart rookie might take some time to try to woo the Crowley faithful and other Democratic old-timers who made things happen in the district—or at least that's what certain counselors thought.

But Ocasio-Cortez was playing a different game on a different field. She suddenly was a celebrity. In June, the month of her primary win, she had 30,000 followers on Twitter. In July, she had 500,000. When she joined Bernie in deep-red Kansas to support Jim Thompson, who was running in a Democratic primary for a House seat, the Thompson campaign booked a venue with capacity for 1,300 people. It sold out in an hour and the campaign had to scramble to find something else. About 4,000 people attended the rally at the Century II convention center in Wichita, located in a district that in 2016 swung by 20 points for Trump.

Wherever Ocasio-Cortez went, people were lining up for selfies. Her youth, her beauty, her New York City glamour played as well in pro-gun Kansas as it did among Black grassroots activists in Missouri. Her fervent reframing of working-class frustration and millennial dissatisfaction in terms of moral imperatives and human dignity infused a pedantic argument with freshness, vitality, and—that rarest of all political commodities—cool. She continued to insist that her election was no demographic fluke. "Working people in Kansas share the same values as working people everywhere else," she said in Wichita. "Thank you . . . for showing that girls from the Bronx are welcome everywhere."

If Ocasio-Cortez had any feelings about how Justice Democrats had underestimated her and were now overmanaging her; if she felt any bitterness toward Bernie, who had initially withheld his powerful endorsement from her and for whom she was now an opening draw; if she was sometimes too tired to eat or drink water, she did not let it show. She had been raised from girlhood to gut it out, and she relied on that ability now, so that—as in college, when she raised her grade-point average in the aftermath of her father's death—whatever bruised her was stashed away. What she showed the world was her intellect, her ferocity, her facility with language, her idealism, and her earnest interest in other people. Still, Ocasio-Cortez performs differently when she is relaxed. In Kansas, her speeches were rousing but dutiful, as if she were reading from a script. The hugs with Bernie had the bumping, obligatory feeling of distant relatives hugging at a holiday dinner. But when she joined Cori Bush, speaking for her at a local restaurant and canvassing with her on a sweltering day, the hugs were continuous, warm, and real.

As Ocasio-Cortez was figuring out how to calibrate her image, her power, and her message, Justice Democrats had to learn how to manage her. Her righteous anger, they knew, was mostly outward-facing. In private, she is cautious, conflict averse. Some people even say she is shy. ("I'm cattle," she told her body man in Michigan when he asked if she wanted to talk about her schedule. "Just tell me if there's something alarming happening.") But when it came to communications, she was a control freak. Staffers say she was obsessive and that they dreaded showing her fundraising emails because she would rewrite each one completely, bogging down the process, but that if the emails went out without her approval, she would be unhappy. "It's not normal for a candidate to approve every email," Shahid said. "That hypercompetent thing," as he called it, meant that "she wanted to do everything and felt that she could do everything."

Corbin Trent, the Justice Democrats co-founder who ran Ocasio-Cortez's communications team into her first year in Congress, discovered that the best way to handle her on the day before a major speech was to leave her alone. She liked to prepare for high-profile public appearances by inhaling volumes of data and information, sitting alone with a highlighter and piles of printouts; if anyone tried to grab her in the moments before she mounted the steps to a stage, to remind her to mention this, name-check that, or phrase x in y way, her brain would lock. She was best, as was clear to everyone except to her, when she left her notes aside and spoke off the cuff. That's when her political magic—her "authenticity," her "relatability"—shone. Trent told a reporter once that he looked for moments to put her out there when she wasn't expecting it, but she didn't like it one bit.

"The past few weeks have been hard," she told a reporter on her swing that summer through the Midwest. "It's just not a normal human experience I'm going through. There's so many cameras on me out of nowhere. Like, I'm not media trained—"

"We can't say that anymore," Trent interjected. "It's not helpful."

"Okay, sorry, sorry," Ocasio-Cortez responded. "I'm just overwhelmed. I'm a normal person, and people treat me now like I'm this two-dimensional caricature that they project narratives onto. It can be emotionally taxing."

• • •

Politics had never had an influencer before. When Ocasio-Cortez tweeted that she liked Stila Stay All Day liquid lipstick in the color *beso*, it sold out at Sephora nationwide. Rihanna invited her to her Diamond Ball benefit, the kind of party attended by Pharrell in a shorts tuxedo and by Cardi B in a princess dress. (She didn't go.) Michael Carter was at home washing dishes one night when he answered the phone to find Elizabeth Warren on the line. According to

Carter, Governor Cuomo, a Crowley ally, invited Ocasio-Cortez to meet him at a cigar bar in midtown in the middle of the day, apparently stipulating that she couldn't bring staff with her. (The Ocasio-Cortez office disputes this version of the story.) When she arrived, he first asked a series of probing questions, ones meant to test her and seemingly assess how much of a threat she'd be—and then asked her for advice on how to be better liked. "He asked, 'Am I doing a good job? Do people really like me?'" Carter says.

Her impact radiated in all directions; teens and their moms were inspired by her example and creators of fan art iterated her portrait on Instagram. The Democrats running for president hoped somehow to hop on to her stardust trail. Two days after Ocasio-Cortez's primary win, Kirsten Gillibrand was talking about "reimagining" ICE and Elizabeth Warren was suggesting replacing it. Kamala Harris said a "complete overhaul of the agency, mission, culture, operations" of ICE was necessary, though she stopped short of expressing a desire to abolish it.

But the Washington professional class still looked, talked, and operated according to certain rules, and in that sphere, people were less enthralled. In mid-July, Ocasio-Cortez made an appearance on *Firing Line*, the PBS show hosted by Margaret Hoover, the center-right journalist who is a great-granddaughter of President Herbert Hoover. Ocasio-Cortez, who usually exudes supreme self-confidence, sat back in her chair and twisted her ankles, while Hoover leaned in and delicately pulled her answers apart like meat off a bone. The host controlled the conversation in its entirety, forcing Ocasio-Cortez to look soft on the specifics of late-stage capitalism and K-12 education. Clearly unfamiliar with this particular flavor of sugarcoated antagonism, Ocasio-Cortez kept wanting to establish a happy concord instead of sticking up for her positions and herself.

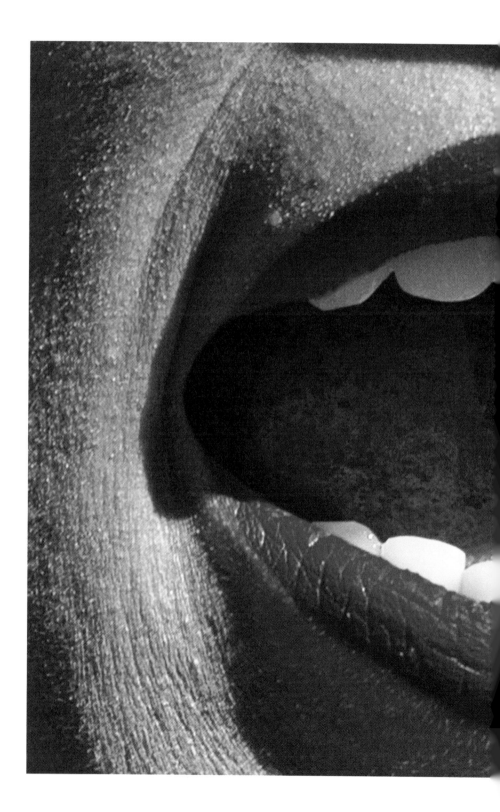

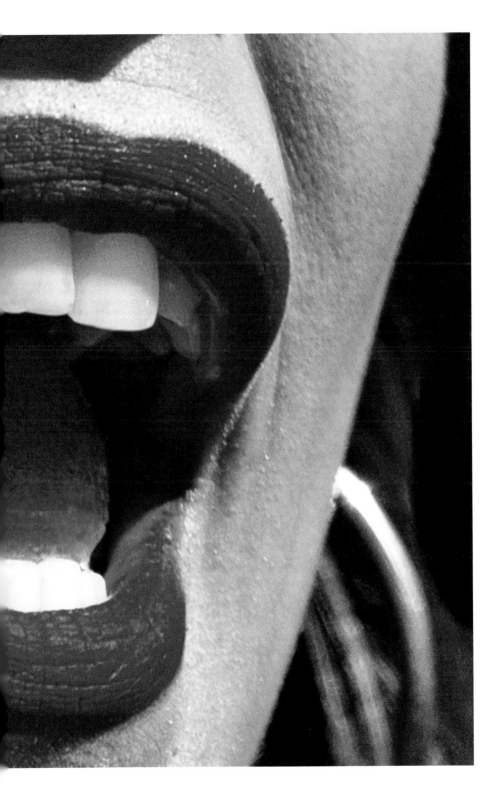

Then Hoover went in for the kill. She mentioned a tweet of Ocasio-Cortez's referring to the killing of Palestinian civilians by Israeli military forces as "a massacre."

"What is your position on Israel?" asked Hoover, straight up.

Ocasio-Cortez said she believed in a two-state solution, followed by something about the "occupation of Palestine" and an "increasing crisis of humanitarian condition."

Hoover dove in. "You used the term 'the occupation of Palestine.' What did you mean by that?" With the use of the word "Palestine," Ocasio-Cortez had walked unwittingly into the minefield of Middle East politics.

"Oh! Um." Here Ocasio-Cortez looked away and remained silent for several beats, as if a teacher had discovered she was unprepared. "I think what I meant is the settlements that are increasing in some of these areas and places where Palestinians are experiencing difficulty in accessing their housing and homes." She looked defeated.

"Do you think you can expand on that?" Hoover asked, smiling.

"Yeah, I think I'd also just—" Ocasio-Cortez smiled and laughed and pushed the air away with the flats of her palms. "I am not the expert at geopolitics on this issue, you know. For me, I'm a firm believer in finding a two-state solution in this issue, and I'm happy to sit down with leaders on both sides of this. For me, I just look at things through a human-rights lens, and I may not use the right words." Again she laughed and waved her hands around as if she were holding a magic wand trying to make the whole set and soundstage disappear.

That was not her only stumble. On *Jimmy Kimmel Live!* about three weeks before the general election in 2018, she seemed a little full of herself, steeped in her own hype, talking about how she was still out canvassing, and when people opened the door, they were just so surprised and delighted to find her standing there. "Sometimes they just lose their m—they're like, 'Wait! You're knocking on my door?' It's like back in the day, when you would knock on the door and carry a big check? People would be like, 'Is this real?'" And then she told a story meant to illustrate her working-class relatability but that came off instead as if she were a New York celebrity bragging about slumming: She had stopped at a Cracker Barrel on her way home from doing an event with Ayanna Pressley—"because we're from the Bronx, [Cracker Barrel] is like exotic to us"—and a woman from Missouri had recognized her and asked her to come say hi to her husband, who was in the restroom. So Ocasio-Cortez and the woman from Missouri waited for the husband outside the men's room while sensor-activated tchotchkes played Christmas music, and when the man exited the restroom, he saw Ocasio-Cortez and said, "Well, I'll be damned." It wasn't a good story, and she didn't deliver it well. She was like a teenager who had just gotten her driver's license and been handed the keys to a very fast car. Accidents were bound to happen.

Still, she put the pedal down, effectively learning and adopting the mind-set of a Silicon Valley nerd. After all, Saikat Chakrabarti and her boyfriend, Riley Roberts, arguably the most influential people in her circle at the time, both had come from that world: They hated business as usual, loved innovation, and believed in unorthodox thinking and disruption—"breaking glass," as the techies say. Justice Democrats appropriated this philosophy and adapted it to electoral politics. They wanted to break government, and Ocasio-Cortez was their hammer. It was a role she took on willingly. The way to animate non-voters, she has said, is to defy the expectation that to win, a politician must be "as close to a saltine cracker as possible."

She wasn't by nature a revolutionary. Her whole life, she'd been a pleaser and a team player. The fluxy discomfort of staking out unpopular positions, of making false starts, of drawing derision and flack—this was "the complete opposite of how I was taught how you pursue success. The way I felt we had to do things was to make sure you knew all the steps in advance. What are you going to do? How are you going to do it? How are you going to pay for it?" she once said. "And if you don't know every single step before you start, then don't start."

But ticking boxes hadn't worked for Ocasio-Cortez. That much was clear. If she was going to take on the pressing problems of a generation, she would need to proceed differently. "We don't have time to wait for someone to descend from the heavens and give us the entire blueprint that's scoped out from step zero to step 100. And we'll figure it out on the way. And we'll find our mistakes, and we'll correct them and we'll iterate on them. But that is what evolution actually looks like."

Defying other people's expectations of her has always given Ocasio-Cortez a sense of freedom. It was a relief to admit to herself that she flat-out needed money, to put her efforts at more conventional success on hold and take a job at a restaurant. And as disappointing as that was, her time in the service industry allowed her to cast her own personal struggle in movement terms. Now, on the brink of obtaining a seat in Congress, she understood that to grow into the politician she aspired to be, she had to shake off the shackles of the dutiful, rules-following girl she once was. "I needed to break the mythology of perfection in people who hold power," she has said.

She easily won the general election and held the victory party—in Queens, this time—at a Latin club called La Boom. Outside, a line snaked down the block. Inside, the room was loud and packed. People were dancing. Alexandra Rojas, now the executive director of Justice Democrats, was speaking with a reporter when she interrupted herself to look around. Her mother was somewhere in the

crowd of well-wishers, and Rojas hoped she was dancing to her favorite song. At one point that night, Waleed Shahid wandered backstage. He found Ocasio-Cortez alone with Roberts, both quiet. Three
weeks earlier, she had turned 29. Shahid had been present for her
transformation from a bartender in beat-up sneakers into this superstar, wearing suffragette white and her trademark red lip. From the
outside, "you get the sense that she is extremely extroverted and loves
the crowd," he said. "I never experienced her in that way. She is private. The people who are close to her are people she's known for a
long time."

Later, as Ocasio-Cortez was giving her victory speech, people in
the audience started to boo. She startled for a moment. Behind her,
the jumbo television set was showing the results of the Senate race
in Texas: Ted Cruz had narrowly beaten Beto O'Rourke. Understanding, Ocasio-Cortez recovered and fluidly went off script. "We are
going to flip that state in our generation. I'll tell you that much right
now," she said. "We should not be scared. There is never any fight
that is too big for us to pick. We proved that this year."

She wasn't bluffing. One week later, she picked a fight with the
richest man in the world. Amazon was proposing to build a new
headquarters in Queens in a deal that would create 25,000 new jobs
and a new public school, not to mention foster widespread neighborhood revitalization. In exchange, it would receive about $3 billion
in tax breaks and subsidies. Governor Cuomo, Carolyn Maloney—who
represented the district in Congress—and the tenants' association in
the housing project nearby loved the deal. Local grassroots activist
groups, including, importantly, Queens DSA, did not. Ocasio-Cortez
didn't seem to care that the proposed headquarters wasn't technically
in her jurisdiction. She summoned her fury and her Twitter hive—
by now a million strong. "Amazon is a billion-dollar company," she

tweeted on November 12. "The idea that it will receive hundreds of millions of dollars in tax breaks at a time when our subway is crumbling and our communities need MORE investment, not less, is extremely concerning to residents here." Blindsided, furious, the project's stakeholders screamed their objections. Urban development doesn't even *work* like that, they said. They called Ocasio-Cortez "an economic illiterate," a neophyte, inexperienced, dumb.[12] (MORE ON THE DOOMED AMAZON DEAL, *SEE PAGE 266.*)

But Ocasio-Cortez was making a different point. How governments spend their money reflects their priorities—"Budgets are moral documents," she says again and again, referencing Martin Luther King—and for New York City to help Jeff Bezos enrich himself further while the wages of the people in NY-14 failed to keep pace with the cost of living, well, that was *unacceptable.* Galvanized by Ocasio-Cortez, local opposition intensified, and Amazon withdrew its bid. "I do think a system that allows billionaires to exist when there are parts of Alabama where people are still getting ringworm because they don't have access to public health is wrong. It's wrong," she said later.

• • •

Ocasio-Cortez is dancing in her kitchen in the Bronx. The song "Q.U.E.E.N.," by Janelle Monáe, is playing—*They call us dirty 'cuz we break all your rules down*—and Ocasio-Cortez is simultaneously wrapping her hair up with the elastic she always wears around her wrist, singing, bopping, and making Instant Pot mac 'n' cheese. Her totally normal brown wood kitchen cabinets are on display, also her totally normal fake-stone counters and jumbo-size grocery-store spices. "There's no special sauce to it," she explains on an Instagram Live recorded just after Election Day 2018. "You've just got to be good at getting things done." The whole scene is so appealingly regular. Here is a congresswoman-elect, not yet 30, enacting what amounts to a live cooking show, apparently for the hell of it. She shows viewers the end result: mac 'n' cheese in bowls dressed up with garnishes. "Looks great," says Roberts in a red T-shirt.

Throughout the summer and fall of 2018, her social-media feeds were blowing up; on the brink of entering Congress, she had nearly 2 million followers on Twitter and 1.2 million on Instagram. In learning to handle these tools, Ocasio-Cortez was discovering how dangerous they were—not just to herself but to her future Democratic colleagues and her party. Political opponents could hijack her feeds and use whatever she said to boost their own profiles and fundraise, too. The previous summer, Ron DeSantis, a Republican member then running for governor of Florida, showed her how this was done. On the stump, he insulted her repeatedly, calling her "this girl, Ocasio-Cortez or whatever she is," adding, "I mean, she's in a totally different universe. It's basically socialism wrapped in ignorance." Ocasio-Cortez rose to the bait. She tweeted, "Rep. DeSantis, it seems you're confused as to 'whatever I am.' I am a Puerto Rican woman. It's strange you don't know what that is, given that ~75,000 Puerto Ricans have relocated to Florida in the 10 mos since Maria. But I'm sure these new FL voters appreciate your comments!" The tweet earned Ocasio-Cortez nearly 50,000 "likes."

DeSantis used this response to serve his own ends, and sent out the text of her tweet in a fundraising email. "50,000 socialists have backed her accusation against me," he wrote. "But I bet I can find 100,000 conservatives who will stand up to the liberal mob's attacks. Will you be one of them?" In one of the narrowest defeats in Florida gubernatorial history, DeSantis won his bid for governor by .04 percent. Ocasio-Cortez couldn't be held singularly responsible for his win, but her words had become a weapon for the other side.

She had to learn to manage her presence online with more finesse, to exploit its potential and build her base while maintaining, as much as possible, the upper hand. In Instagram Live, she found what she needed—a bigger, better, more nuanced iteration of the Standing Rock video diaries. The livestream platform could operate as Ocasio-Cortez's soapbox, but also as a peephole into her life. She could speak at length and extemporaneously on topics of her choice, personal or political, in a venue more intimate than cable news and far more flattering to her intelligence and charisma than the dirty trenches of Twitter.

It helped her increase her reach. Her new job would force her out of campaign mode and into the antechambers and subterranean tunnels of the Capitol. Instagram Live would keep her visible. She could use it to introduce new ideas to her fan base and then—with a big enough audience—to build widespread support for them. This transaction is at the heart of every social-media relationship. Authenticity breeds trust. Trust breeds loyalty, and loyalty leads to action—whether that means buying a handbag or donating money or showing up at a protest or a polling place. Social media, in many ways, *is* community organizing, but at an algorithmic scale. "Before technology, someone would go into a library, read bell hooks, read Noam Chomsky, or whatever, and then like you have conversations at a dinner table, and it's like five people, right?" Ocasio-Cortez has said. "And you organize five people. But then, guess what? Like you read that same thing, or you hear someone articulate it in a podcast, and then you tweet it and you IG it and then, all of a sudden, your whole block is like, *What?*"

Intuitively, she understood something else. People love their idols to appear normal—the starlet with the paper takeout cup, the glamour-puss with a cranky baby. "Relatability" is the grail of marketing, media, and politics, and in Congress, although members strain for it, any semblance of personal normalcy is vanishingly rare. Ocasio-Cortez *was*, in fact, incredibly normal, looking and talking like anybody's college roommate, a person who did yoga and applied press-on nails on the train. But her livestreams showed that she also understood how the *performance* of normalcy could boost her brand. The tireless door knocker could be cast on social media as a reality-television heroine: unpolished but produced, real but stage-managed, transparent but walled off. In control.

She may have been surprised by the volume of attention she drew, but the nature of that attention—equal parts terror and adulation— would have been familiar to her as a woman working and traveling in the world. So instead of trying to defend her particular blend of ambition and femininity, Ocasio-Cortez doubled down. Unlike Hillary Clinton, awkwardly baking cookies to assure her public she was woman enough, Ocasio-Cortez was comfortable making gender a part of her story—not as something to be spun, explained, or defended but as an incontrovertible fact. She embraced contradictions that others saw in her by insisting they were no contradictions at all.

It was no accident that on her first viral livestream, Ocasio-Cortez was cooking college-dorm fare. Years working in the restaurant industry had made her knowledgeable about food; starting in her childhood with the backyard family pig roasts, she had come to understand mealtime, nothing fancy, as an essential ritual in community building. She believed, as she has said, "in the power of food to bring people together." Even still, there was a transgressive element at play. A male politician would never cook on TV. A white female politician might refrain as well, fearing to look too mommy-blogger-ish. Part of the thrill of the video is in seeing a 29-year-old Latina appropriate a kitchen job as a performance of power. She was turning culture's expectations of and stereotypes about Latinas upside down. She wasn't going to serve or scrub for money: She was cooking because it gave her pleasure to do so. She was going to Congress.

• • •

Ocasio-Cortez approached her freshman orientation with the excitement of an eager kid. She called it "Congress camp," and she video-blogged it, marveling like a tourist over all the arcane oddities of her new world. She picked up a "swag bag" containing her new tablet and cell phone, both loaded up with government firewalls, and received her government-issued ID and a face book—literally, bound and printed on paper—with headshots of all her freshman colleagues, as well as a step-by-step manual about how to open a congressional office. But before she immersed herself in the scheduled four days of meet-and-greets, tours, tutorials, and group photos, she had something to do.

Sunrise Movement, a nascent group of young environmentalist activists, was planning a sit-in in Nancy Pelosi's office on Day One of orientation. With dozens of new progressive members elected during the midterms, Sunrise hoped to pressure Pelosi—herself an environmentalist—to make climate change a public priority, even if Trump and the obstructionist Republican Senate were certain to block any bills. Sunrise reached out to the Ocasio-Cortez team, asking for whatever kind of visibility or support she could give. They were hoping at least for one of her high-octane tweets.

The group was stunned when Ocasio-Cortez said yes. She would do better than support their protest. She would join it. Internally, her staff had the jitters. To storm the office of the future Speaker (already embattled by factions within the Democratic caucus intent on toppling her) and challenge her authority on what was, for all intents and purposes, the first day of school—this was an audacious move. On the one hand, it would put the Democratic Establishment on notice: Ocasio-Cortez was not coming to Congress to play. But it was perhaps self-defeating to start out on the wrong side of Pelosi, who controlled committee assignments and could smooth or impede any member's ascent. What kind of new girl gets invited to the party and insults the host?

Waleed Shahid was in London a week or so before the protest when he was woken up by a call from Chakrabarti. Was it reckless? Political suicide? "The way he asked me the question was like he wanted me to talk him out of it," Shahid remembers. Of all the members of the Justice Democrats inner circle, he says, "I tend to be more risk averse." But Shahid knew Sunrise, and he had worked for more conventional politicians his whole career. "I said, 'I think it would be good for her to do it.'" They stayed on the phone a little while longer, but there really wasn't much more to say.

No one expected what came next. Ocasio-Cortez arrived in Washington early in the morning on November 12—the day before orientation and the protest (and the same day she lobbed the Amazon tweet). She had won the general election less than a week before. Upon arriving at her hotel, she did laundry. "The thing that most people don't tell you about running for Congress is that your clothes are stinky all the time because you never have time to do laundry. Congressional life getting off to a glamorous start," she said, in a whisper, as she pushed quarters into the machine on a video she titled "Congress Camp I." Then she went off to gather with fellow new members at a meeting of the Congressional Progressive Caucus. Her friend Ayanna Pressley was there, as were Rashida Tlaib, from Michigan, and Ilhan Omar, from Minnesota, all of whom had been endorsed by Justice Democrats. The four women had their picture

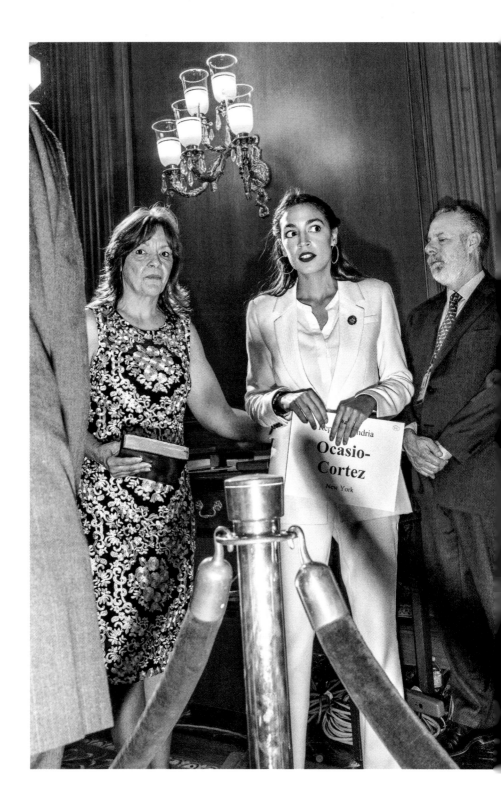

January 3, 2019: Ocasio-Cortez waits in the wings during a mock swearing-in ceremony at the U.S. Capitol.

taken that day, sitting together at a long conference table, scratch pads, pens, and mics before them. Ocasio-Cortez posted the photo on Instagram. She tagged it "Squad." She couldn't have known she was doing the political equivalent of branding a band.

In the midst of this momentous and tightly scheduled day, she kept her commitment to Sunrise. That night, she dropped by a church where the activists were training and planning to sleep on the floor. The group was on a pizza break when Ocasio-Cortez walked in with Rashida Tlaib. Marcela Mulholland, one of the organizers there, gaped. "They come into the fucking church to talk to us about the action we're doing the next day, and we're like, *Oh my God, what the fuck is going on?* This was when you couldn't believe that someone like this existed. Especially in Sunrise, she was like a god for us." It was one of the first nights Ocasio-Cortez ever spent in D.C., "and what does she do after a long-ass day on Capitol Hill? She comes to this church to talk to these 17-year-olds about how important it is to be involved in politics. I get goose bumps now because you don't see elected officials doing that," said Mulholland. Ocasio-Cortez stood up on a little table "and gave the most fucking incredible speech to us, getting us fired up, talking to us about how important it was to have a left and social movements, and I'll never forget this one thing she said. The gist was 'There's no position more powerful in politics than the position of someone who doesn't give a fuck,'" Mulholland continued.

• • •

The next day, Ocasio-Cortez was extremely late to the sit-in. Scores of young activists were crushed into Pelosi's office, cross-legged on the floor, waiting, holding signs that said *Green Jobs for All* and *We Have 12 Years. What's Your Plan?*

Protest organizers had been anxious that she wasn't coming.

Ocasio-Cortez, aware of the stakes, was refining her public remarks. "Oh my goodness, I could have thrown up that morning, I was so nervous," she said.

She did make an appearance, finally—for a photo op, really—walking through the crowd on the floor, handing out high fives, and then standing in the center of the room for just a few minutes, praising the protesters neutrally for "putting themselves and their bodies on the line." It didn't actually matter what she said. "Obviously," Mulholland remembered, "every fucking reporter on the Hill is, like, 'There's nothing juicier than AOC joining a sit-in in the Speaker's office.' I don't even know. We were all speechless."

Most heart-stopping, though, was her virtuosic performance of political doublespeak in the aftermath. Ocasio-Cortez deftly expressed appropriate deference to Pelosi even as she antagonized her, telling a reporter that "we need to tell her that we've got her back in showing and pursuing the most progressive energy agenda that this country has ever seen." Then she did what she came to do. She pushed the whole business out through her Twitter feed—"they asked me to join them, and I did," she wrote—drawing the focus of her million-plus followers to the Sunrise movement and the problem of climate change. And she took the opportunity to remind her followers that climate change is an existential threat. After all this, Pelosi had no choice but to tweet how she was "inspired."

Still, there was something breathless and wide-eyed about Ocasio-Cortez in those early days, an aura of Dorothy arriving, finally, at Oz. This awe must not be so unusual among newly elected members who find themselves catapulted out of local lives and into the gilded halls with access to governing power. What was unique, in this case, was her impulse to bring everyone along. Other politicians, presuming they are entitled to their gains, enter the Capitol and shut the door behind them. Ocasio-Cortez showed her fans everything with her phone. The old Supreme Court chamber. Thomas Jefferson's copy of Plato's *Republic*. The marbled balconies. Even the snacks in the designated freshman lounge. The expectation, Ocasio-Cortez explained, was that the newbies would get so lost wandering around the Capitol complex that they might never be able to find the cafeteria. "Welcome to Hogwarts," she wrote in a caption.

•••

In December, she officially changed her Twitter handle to @AOC. She was sworn in on January 3. The photos from that day show Pelosi in magenta, Ocasio-Cortez in white, and Blanca, Gabriel, and Riley Roberts smiling broadly. But the sit-in had announced her intention: to lead against the insiders from the inside. On her first day, she voted "no" on a long-established budgetary rule, saying it hamstrung visionary legislation. Only two Democrats joined her. Then—after making the Sunrise protest a viral news event—she declined Pelosi's invitation to sit on a new climate committee. Appointed to the Finance Committee, a high-status post for a new member, she made an additional, unsuccessful bid for a seat on the even more powerful Ways and Means Committee. Near the end of January— three weeks into her first term—she voted "no" on an appropriations bill designed to end a partial government shutdown because it designated money for the Department of Homeland Security, including ICE. This time, she was alone.

Her Democratic colleagues were by turns bemused, exasperated, and incensed. And they were exerting all kinds of pressure on her. "You literally have 400-something-odd people saying, 'What are you doing?'" she said later. "I got stopped so many times to change my vote . . . They were big mad. *Real* mad." Forty-one new

Democrats, from states such as Michigan, Pennsylvania, Virginia, and Texas, had won the House by flipping their districts from red to blue, running on moderate pro-defense or pro-business platforms; these members were not served by any perceived alliance to a democratic-socialist bomb-thrower with a hot feed, and Republican lawmakers had already shown that they would do everything they could to portray all Democrats as radicals sympathetic to her. Many avoided being photographed with Ocasio-Cortez, fearing the picture would wind up in a campaign ad. Katie Hill, who entered Congress with her and resigned amid a scandal, observed these dynamics. "There is and will always be a tension between the progressives who come from these safe districts and feel like it's their job to push the envelope and people who are fighting to keep their seats and to keep the majority," she says.

The presence of Trump and the ultranationalist wing of the GOP exacerbated this tension. The Democratic leadership felt it was in an existential war. This was the time for sticking together. Pelosi presided over the caucus like a strict grandma. Representatives might squabble in private, but they should not appear in disarray out in public.

But Ocasio-Cortez kept flouting convention in the halls of power, an upstart attitude that looked to some of the old-timers like disrespect. She continued to distance herself from her party, explaining to an interviewer that she preferred the label "democratic socialist" because "to be completely honest, I don't know what it means to be 'just' a Democrat." Her careless shrug at party allegiance—"Oh God," she said later, "in any other country, Joe Biden and I would not be in the same party, but in America, we are"—infuriated the Democratic leaders and centrists, who wished that she would grow up and play ball.

What really irked her congressional colleagues, though, was the sustained presence and influence of Justice Democrats. Ocasio-Cortez had arrived in Washington with Chakrabarti and Trent on the payroll as chief of staff and communications director, respectively. These self-avowed disrupters, now wearing staff badges, were widely seen as infiltrators, while their boss was cast sometimes as an impressionable child in the thrall to arrogant ideologues and other times as a rebellious teen who had no sense of decorum. Either way, Ocasio-Cortez's decision to reward Justice Democrats with legitimacy was seen as a failure to comprehend the difference between a campaign and a job. It was one thing to be an outsider candidate calling for a totally different kind of representation in Congress. It was quite another to be a sworn legislator threatening colleagues and peers—the people with whom you sat on committees and ate lunch—with career extinction. "We gotta primary folks," Chakrabarti famously said in a Justice Democrats call after Ocasio-Cortez had won the general election. Then, a month after her swearing in, Justice Democrats released a video asking "everyday people" to consider themselves plausible candidates to challenge sitting Democrats in primary races in 2020. Ocasio-Cortez starred in it. "What is even the difference between a Democrat and a Republican?" she asked.

It was all intentional, all strategic, Ocasio-Cortez insisted. In her vision, politics is a collective endeavor, she has said; you don't "rely on one person to do everything." So Chakrabarti and Trent continued to operate in public as surrogates; they were, in effect, double agents, working for the government while planning to dismantle it. After Ocasio-Cortez's win, Justice Democrats had apparently put a target on the back of the more centrist Hakeem Jeffries, a fellow New Yorker who had ascended to become leader of the House Democratic

Caucus after Crowley went down—though they later walked back from that edge. They didn't primary Jeffries, and Ocasio-Cortez denied that he was ever a target. While some Democratic members griped to the press and expressed terror of Ocasio-Cortez's Twitter feed, others, like Nydia Velázquez, quietly advised her to take the long view. "Washington is a political animal where a lot of the work that you want to accomplish depends on relationships," Velázquez told Politico. But Ocasio-Cortez didn't seem to care. She seemed hell-bent on breaking the rules.

In a Martin Luther King Jr. Day conversation with Ta-Nehisi Coates at the Riverside Church in New York City, she spoke about moving "the Overton window." Named after the late public-policy analyst Joseph Overton, it refers to the range of policies that Americans find acceptable. In the view of Ocasio-Cortez, Trump and his Freedom Caucus, and before that the accommodationist Democrats, had moved the Overton window so far right that policies once regarded as reasonable and even desirable, such as health care for all or a path to citizenship for undocumented immigrants, had become symbols of a so-called radical, mutinous left. Her fundamental job, as she saw it, was to move the national conversation by calling out abuses of power and refusing to cede to norms simply because they were there. She would do this by bringing a movement mind-set to Congress—she even paid her interns a $15 minimum wage—and she would do it by aiming her Twitter feed at the perpetrators of inequality, corruption, and injustice and inviting her activist army to come along. By January 2019, she had 1.7 million Twitter followers. The following month she had a million more.

Onstage at Riverside Church, Coates confessed his mixed feelings about her use of social media. He worried that, on Twitter, the discourse sank to a lowest-common-denominator level. Ocasio-Cortez

*May 23, 2019:
Ocasio-Cortez
attends a
briefing held by
the Power 4
Puerto Rico
coalition.*

pushed back. Social media worked like a megaphone to amplify the concerns of millions of people who were not being heard through regular channels. It was a movement tool. "When we have a majority Democratic Party that comes to the table and asks for exactly what it wants, and then you have a Republican Party that argues in bad faith and drags us all the way backwards, what we get in our democracy is the average of those two things."

"And people valorize that average," Coates interjected. "It's good to be average."

Ocasio-Cortez concurred. This conversation was taking place in the midst of the partial government shutdown and followed the fracas over her "no" vote on appropriations. "This idea that we should be *compromising* and giving $5 billion to an unstable person"—the audience erupted in applause at this reference to Trump—"and say, 'Let's just incarcerate a few more kids this year.' No. The answer is no."

Coates wondered aloud how she decided when to clap back on Twitter. "What is the Ocasio-Cortez standard?" he asked. Ocasio-Cortez laughed, her mood lightening, the righteous rebel morphing into the charmer. There was no litmus test, she said. She made a Venn diagram with her fingers. "Whoever's coming at me, in my mentions, with a blue check, when I haven't eaten in three hours, is who gets chosen," she said. Then she grew serious again. It was always about seeing and seizing an opportunity to move the needle. "It's not just reflexive self-defense. I'm trying to dismantle some of the frames of misogyny, classism, racism that we've just allowed to go on," she said.

The following night, on his show, Stephen Colbert raised the topic of the intramural tensions that defined her first month in Congress, asking Ocasio-Cortez point-blank how many fucks she gave about the criticism of her by certain members of Congress and the calls for her to settle down and go slow. Ocasio-Cortez turned away from the camera as if she were rummaging around in an imaginary handbag. Then she came up with her thumb and forefinger in a big fat *O*. She was smiling broadly. "Zero."

• • •

On the morning of February 7, 2019, an overcast day in Washington, D.C., she was on a grassy plaza in front of the Capitol Building, wearing a moss-green blazer and doling out hugs to at least half a dozen fellow legislators, each hug preceded by a cheerful, high-pitched "Heeeyyyy!" ("One of my problems, when I'm trying to be polite to someone, I feel like my voice goes up two octaves," she once said.) This was a gigantic moment for her. In Washington, people talk about politicians in terms of "show horses" or "workhorses"—the former often a denigrating term for women and people of color who seek the limelight—and Ocasio-Cortez was out to prove that she could be both. She was staking out policy turf and making good on her promise to deliver alternatives to the paralytic incrementalism that had dogged party politics for a generation. Together with Massachusetts senator Ed Markey, a gray-haired lefty of the old school, Ocasio-Cortez was holding a press conference to announce the Green New Deal. The term "Green New Deal" had been floating around leftist politics for a dozen years, used to describe iterations of proposals that combined climate-change solutions with labor and infrastructure improvements. By the time Ocasio-Cortez had joined the sit-in in Pelosi's office, Sunrise and a coalition of other climate activists were building an extremely ambitious, updated version.

Markey spoke first, essentially warming up for Ocasio-Cortez, a symbolic acknowledgment of her superior power. She had been a federal legislator for just over a month. He was a 40-year-plus member of Congress. When Ocasio-Cortez took the mic, she did so against a backdrop entirely of white men, all wearing the same self-satisfied expressions of pols who had the good sense to attach themselves early to an actual comet.

Just when it seemed Ocasio-Cortez couldn't become any more visible, she did. The previous day, February 6, she had been in the House Chamber, and, in a dramatic five-minute performance in her role as a member of the House Committee on Oversight and Reform, she had demonstrated—in eviscerating, point-by-point detail—all the ways in which it was legal for corporations and lobbyists to entirely fund political campaigns, creating elected representatives beholden to their interests and willing to make laws profitable to them. She walked a panel of stodgy campaign-finance experts through a series of hypotheticals. "I'm gonna be the bad guy," she began, and she concluded by implicating Trump. If it's "super-legal" for a member of Congress to be owned by corporate interests, "it's even easier for the president of the United States."

"That's right," one witness agreed. Again, that little smile, the comprehension on the face of a career legal ethicist that he had become the foil in a historic encounter with a historic figure and was relishing the moment. A clip of her performance that day was viewed more than 40 million times, making it arguably the most-watched political video ever.

The Green New Deal press conference did not feature that kind of stagecraft. Ocasio-Cortez came across as studied and nervous—the stakes were so high. In her remarks, she compared the Green New Deal in scope and ambition to FDR's New Deal: a game-changing program that would revive Democracy itself and establish environmental, economic, and social priorities for generations to come. The Green New Deal set goals of zero carbon emissions by 2050, which it would achieve by overhauling industry and infrastructure, creating new jobs, technology, and expertise. It would thus avert climate cataclysm and assure for the future clean air, water, and access to nature. But just as industry lobbyists slip perks and pork into bills, so Ocasio-Cortez and Markey slid their social-justice priorities into the Green New Deal: All the job creation they envisioned, all the innovation and rebuilding projects, would include benchmarks to rectify economic, social, and racial inequity. By fixing the climate, they would also fix wealth gaps and racism. "Today, I think, is a really big day for our economy, the labor movement, the social-justice movement, Indigenous peoples, and people all over the United States of America," Ocasio-Cortez said. "Because today is the day that we truly embark on the comprehensive agenda of economic, social, and racial justice in the United States of America. That's what this agenda is all about."[13] (MORE ON THE MAKING OF THE GREEN NEW DEAL, SEE PAGE 305.)

Ocasio-Cortez has compared Congress to high school, in that the freshmen are expected not to strive above their station. They "don't get to have anything nice," she has said. Like apprentices, their role is to co-sponsor legislation, not to draft it; they get "scooted" aside while senior members step in and claim credit for their ideas—"They can take your lunch money, pretty much," she has said. In releasing the Green New Deal, Ocasio-Cortez knew she was violating this protocol, but believed that her visibility and popularity gave her the latitude to waive these unwritten rules. "We can be way more effective early on because we've been backed by a movement," she said.

But Congress is, in fact, like high school. And within its halls, the Democratic leadership saw the Green New Deal as a massive strategic misfire: too ambitious and idealistic and short on specifics. Why waste political capital—and deploy Congress's only true celebrity—on

a resolution that was not even a bill and, given the Republican stranglehold on the Senate, had no hope of leading to legislation or making any real-life impact? The Democratic leadership did not see the
Green New Deal as Ocasio-Cortez and her allies did, as a set of goals
to inspire and galvanize the left. They saw it as a target the right
could ridicule. And as if she were in high school, Ocasio-Cortez received a snub later that day from Pelosi, the arbiter of how things
are done. When reporters asked Pelosi what she thought of the
climate-change plan, Pelosi pretended not to know its name. "The
Green Dream or whatever" is what she called it. She had nothing
more to say.

• • •

By April, Ocasio-Cortez still had no furniture in her D.C. apartment.
Also, no Wi-Fi. She was so busy she almost never knew what day
it was—"Saturday feels like Friday and whatnot," she said—and she
was barely eating. So at around 9:30 p.m., on "April something" (it
was the 3rd), Ocasio-Cortez turned on Instagram Live and invited
people to join her for a chat. Sometimes Ocasio-Cortez uses Instagram to make a point. This time, it seemed she was actually lonely.

It had been an extremely rough few months. "There are real consequences," Ocasio-Cortez has said about getting on Pelosi's wrong
side. "It could mean that I don't ascend to leadership in a committee,
that people don't give me a chance, like all these little things that
could kind of hurt your career."

After Pelosi's dismissal of the Green New Deal, the rollout had
gone from bad to worse. Someone in the Ocasio-Cortez office had
mistakenly released drafts of a Green New Deal FAQ, sent out to
media and posted online, that proposed government support for
people "unwilling to work," as well as the hypothetical long-term

goals of eliminating air travel and "farting cows." It was as if Ocasio-Cortez had decided to throw the Republicans a catered party with Champagne. "I think it is very important for the Democrats to press forward with their Green New Deal," Trump tweeted, exuberantly, and "permanently eliminate all Planes, Cars, Cows, Oil, Gas & the Military—even if no other country would do the same. Brilliant!" Roseanne Barr posted a video on YouTube calling Ocasio-Cortez a "bug-eyed bitch." Tucker Carlson called her a "screechy moron."

Ocasio-Cortez was always great on her livestreams, but on April 3, she showed herself not just as normal but as vulnerable—a woman alone at home and thinking her thoughts after a hard time at work—and in so doing amassed even more power. Trump's popularity was based in his bellicosity, his sadistic arrogance, his insistence on alternate realities. His was a deeply unexamined life. Ocasio-Cortez went the other way. On this night, and again during another session assembling Ikea furniture in July, she shone a bright light on her own complicated, multifaceted self.[14] *(MORE ON THE IKEA LIVESTREAM, SEE PAGE 276.)*

In that video, Ocasio-Cortez looks thin. Her trousers sag. She is wearing her glasses, and her hair is up in a sloppy, just-about-to-wash-my face bun. She is wearing an old moto jacket and is sitting on the floor of her unfurnished apartment eating a bowl of popcorn and drinking a glass of wine. For dessert, she has a small pack of fruit snacks, sent to her in bulk by Roberts's mother. She has no agenda, nothing in particular to get off her chest. It really is as if she were exhausted and wanting to talk. "I'm *alone* today," she says pointedly at the camera, as if speaking directly to Roberts, who is elsewhere, about his absence. "I've been living, like, a completely depraved lifestyle," she says. "I've been sleeping on a mattress on the floor, but it's like"—here she gestures with her hands—"the *mattress,* and then under the mattress is, like, the plastic wrap that the mattress came in. I'm spilling all the secrets right now."

There had been not one moment to shop for furniture, even online. "My time to go furniture shopping is, like, 11:30 p.m. to 2 a.m., so." She pauses. "It's been a little bit of a struggle bus." Another pause. *"Anyhoo."*

But the Ikea furniture is there, in boxes, leaning against the wall, and Ocasio-Cortez launches in, like your best friend, placing the pieces before her in order, looking at the directions, and assessing the steps, delighted at the tiny Allen wrench that comes with the kit, eating handfuls of popcorn and fielding questions at the same time about how she stays grounded amid all the hate. One Republican colleague had recently told the press he'd "swipe right" on working with her. "There's so much nonsense and craziness and personal insults and bullying and concern-trolling and this-isn't-realistic," she says, paraphrasing a conversation she had earlier in the day, but working alongside civil-rights heroes like John Lewis and Elijah Cummings was perspective-giving. They faced so much worse. And so, she claims, the way she handles it is to draw strength from their experience and then regard her own actions and behavior through the eyes of her future grandchildren. She asks herself if they'd look at her life and find that she did everything that she could. And if the answer is yes, "it really takes a lot of the pressure off." And if that means she winds up being a one-term congresswoman, well then, "so what? So. What."

The end table is finished. "Boom! I did it!" she says, placing the circular tabletop into the frame.

The desk is harder because it's much bigger and she doesn't have tools, although one viewer suggests she use a butter knife, and she laughs and says she might just do that. It's around ten o'clock. She has finished her popcorn—a special recipe with a little ground pepper—"like Pop Secret. But gourmet."

What's your opinion of capital punishment, one viewer asks.

"I'm against it," she says, her mouth full of fruit snacks.

Mets or Yankees?

"Bro," says the Bronx-born Ocasio-Cortez with a little eye roll. "Come on, now."

And then a viewer asks the question that makes her go nuts. Ocasio-Cortez is usually very contained. She's a polite person. Even her fury, while palpable, is regulated. But it's late and she's tired.

Why do the Republicans hate you so much?

Crouched on the floor, with one knee under her chin, she explains. The reason they hate her so much—spewing negativity, as she puts it, "like that girl in *The Exorcist* that's, like, vomiting pea soup"—is that she confronts them directly on their moral failings. The wave of her anger begins to rise, and in front of 8,000 live viewers she rides it, addressing her invisible critics—Republican, Democratic, the people who made a mockery of her Green New Deal. "I'm here to tell you that maybe Q2 profits are not more important than our grandchildren. That's what I'm here to say. So you can do whatever you want. You can troll me in the short term. You can rake me over the coals. You can make me look like, whatever, a *joke* in front of all society. Just know that that's a short-term reality . . . And whether I'm here or whether I'm not here, the truth and the facts stay the same, brotha."

She rises from her spot on the floor, agitated, and walks away from the camera to the large cardboard box leaning against the wall. But she turns back again. She's not done.

"And guess what! I'm 29! I'm the youngest woman to ever be elected to the United States Congress. I have plenty of time to learn.

And I'm not afraid to make mistakes and iterate in public, either. And, frankly, if the mistakes that I'm making are just a one-off rhetorical thing, you correct it, acknowledge it, and move on. At least I'm not trying to cage children at the border and inject them with drugs. That's not a *mistake*. That's a deliberate policy . . . That's just hatred. That's just cruelty. That's just wrong."

The honeymoon was most definitely over. A couple of weeks after that livestream, in the session with students at John Jay College of Criminal Justice in New York, Ocasio-Cortez talked about how surreal her life had become. She had just been on the cover of *Time* magazine. She had been on the cover of *Rolling Stone*. She had gone to SXSW and attracted a bigger audience than Elizabeth Warren or Amy Klobuchar, both of whom were running for president. "Has anyone heard of the term *impostor syndrome*?" she asked. "Raise your hand if you've heard of impostor syndrome. Yeah. That's like my life. You know? It really is what I feel so often every day. I don't belong here. This magazine cover is fake. I don't know why these people are following me around."

But mostly, in that session, she talked about how discouraged and exhausted she was much of the time. She talked about how, before her primary win, an older female politician had advised her to grow rhinoceros skin. "Ninety-nine percent of it feels like, 'I don't know if this is working.' Ninety-nine percent of it feels like you're tired." She paraphrased lines from *Homecoming*, the Beyoncé documentary that had just dropped: "No one sees what the dirty work looks like. No one sees what the sacrifice looks like." And then, in practically the same breath, she changed mood and seemed to reassure herself, invoking Teddy Roosevelt's famous description of the "man in the arena . . . whose face is marred with dirt and sweat and blood who decides to valiantly try again and again." She was putting together the pieces of what it meant to do this job. She was gathering strength for the next big fight.

• • •

In March, four months after the "Squad" photo was taken, Rep. Ilhan Omar was speaking in California at a meeting of the Council on American-Islamic Relations, a Muslim organization resembling the Anti-Defamation League. Born in Somalia and naturalized as an American citizen, Omar is an observant Muslim.

A terrorist had recently opened fire at two mosques in New Zealand, killing more than 50 people, and in her remarks, Omar uttered the phrases that henceforth would dog her political career. For "far too long, we have lived with the discomfort of being a second-class citizen, and, frankly, I'm tired of it, and every single Muslim in this country should be tired of it," she said. "CAIR was founded after 9/11 because they recognized that some people did something and that all of us were starting to lose access to our civil liberties." In the same speech, she defended her record of critiquing certain Muslim countries for their human-rights abuses. "I know as an American, as an American member of Congress, I have to make sure I am living up to the ideals of fighting for liberty and justice." (Fact-checkers later pointed out that CAIR was founded long before 9/11.)

An Australian imam and television personality named Mohammad Tawhidi picked out a phrase from the speech—"some people did something"—and tweeted it, noting that Omar had failed to call the 9/11 attackers "terrorists." A Texas GOP member of Congress picked up on Tawhidi's tweet and retweeted it, and an international assault on Omar was launched.

One Friday evening in April 2019, the president of the United States, Donald Trump, whose reelection campaign was building strength, tweeted a video of clips of Omar's speech edited together with clips of the Twin Towers exploding on 9/11. He wrote, "We will never forget!" Omar—Black, female, Muslim—had been receiving

June 21, 2019: Ocasio-Cortez reads a memo in her office at the Capitol.

death threats at least since her election to Congress, but now they dramatically increased. On Twitter, direct threats to Omar's life surged into the hundreds; more general references to killing her—by lynching, dragging, or shooting, typically preceded by phrases like "I hope" and "Somebody should"—were exponentially more numerous. These tweets originated mostly with middle-aged white men and women who included with their posts American-flag emoji. A cybersecurity expert interviewed by the Washington *Post* at the time said that Trump incited this violence indirectly. "Rather than directly call for specific acts of violence, hate groups can maintain plausible deniability by merely suggesting that someone is a subhuman traitor, an enemy of the people," he said. "They know that some random person somewhere who's just on the edge of a mental breakdown will see it, and they'll take matters into their own hands." Omar made a statement connecting Trump's tweet to the rise in threats against her life. Nancy Pelosi beefed up Omar's security detail.

At this point, the Squad both was and was not an actual entity. Female, brown-skinned, progressive, outspoken, working class—their commonalities seemed to signify something important, even cool, a meaningful shift in the cultural moment; the fact that the clique included the celebrity Ocasio-Cortez added to the frisson.

But the distinctions among the individual members of the Squad were mostly lost on the press. They were of different races, cultures, and ethnicities. They had different political priorities, strengths, and temperaments. Within the group, the dynamics were complex: Ocasio-Cortez and Pressley had a warm, deep, and preexisting friendship. Tlaib, from the enormous working-class Arab American community outside Detroit and the eldest of 14 children, was a member of DSA. Pressley, who had the most political experience and the most conventional trajectory—political internships followed by a seat on the Boston City Council—was more of an insider, while Omar was the only immigrant in the group. They mostly voted together, except when they didn't. "I always felt like the Squad got lumped together. They were friends because it was a safe space," reflects Katie Hill. "I do believe they became real friends, but it didn't start that way. It was more of, like, 'Well, I guess we're all in the same boat, so we might as well become friends.'"[15] *(MORE ON THE SQUAD, SEE PAGE 278.)*

The experience of being different together did bond them. And then the real-life horror of being targeted by hate groups emboldened by Trump fortified that bond. Ocasio-Cortez stood up for Omar first. No one understood the vile hatred directed at Omar better than she did. The younger members of the Squad, they also stood in for the combination of youth, beauty, femininity, and foreignness that has always and forever stimulated the most predatory impulses of certain white men, a craving for violence mixed with the flavor of sex.

The previous week, a Republican fund-raising email had called Ocasio-Cortez "a domestic terrorist." She'd had it. "This is not a normal level of political debate or rhetoric. As wild as it can get sometimes, this is something beyond what is normal," she told reporters on April 11. Trump, she pointed out as plainly as she could, was inciting "violence against progressive women of color."

She wasn't done. Where was the support of the party for one of their own? The next day, she took her outrage to Twitter. Omar's life is in danger, she reminded her followers, by then numbering more than 3 million. "For our colleagues to be silent is to be complicit in the outright, dangerous targeting of a member of Congress." Then she quoted the famous speech by Lutheran pastor Martin Niemöller, given just after the Holocaust, which begins, "First they came for the socialists and I did not speak out—because I was not a socialist." She tweeted this at 7:39 p.m. on the evening of April 12. At this juncture, in the spring of 2019, the Democratic presidential-primary candidates were jockeying for position. At around 8 p.m., Bernie Sanders tweeted his support for Omar. By 8:30, Elizabeth Warren had, too. Later that night, Pete Buttigieg got on board, and at midnight, Ayanna Pressley tweeted, "My sister in service @IlhanMN is on my heart tonight. The occupant of the @WhiteHouse is putting her, her family, her team & Muslim Americans across the country in jeopardy. It's unconscionable and I'm furious."

• • •

This was the context in which the conflagration over the border bill erupted in the summer of 2019, with Ocasio-Cortez and the Squad already primed for a fight, incandescently angry over the way Trump was campaigning on their backs while their centrist colleagues sat in mostly self-interested silence.

Ocasio-Cortez had been making a loud moral argument against Trump's immigration policies since she ran against Crowley on #AbolishICE. The growing crisis on the border represented, for her, a whole universe of intersecting injustices, all of which affected her district disproportionately. According to Census data, which undercounts undocumented immigrants, more than 45 percent of the residents of NY-14 are foreign-born and a quarter are not U.S. citizens. This meant that a large portion of her constituents were living in terror of being picked up and sent back to their countries of origin; many people had relatives elsewhere financially dependent on them or with plans to move to the U.S. But "ICE was stealing people off the streets. It was really fucked up," remembers Tia Keenan, who worked on Ocasio-Cortez's primary campaign. Within families, immigration status was not a clear-cut thing. Documented people cohabited with undocumented people, who cohabited with American-born citizens, many regularly in touch with family members abroad. The fear of being snatched up, hauled off, and separated from one another was real and perpetual.

So motivating was this issue for Ocasio-Cortez that a year earlier, the weekend before her primary election in 2018, she had left her district and traveled down to Tornillo, Texas, where she joined a small group of grassroots activists protesting family separation. Wearing all white, she stood in front of a tall chain-link fence and banged her hand on it. "Free the children!" she shouted.

Since arriving in Congress, the situation had worsened. Children were still routinely being taken from the adults who accompanied them to the border with no plans for reunion. Migrants were held in overcrowded cells—in some cases 155 people in a space designated for 35—with little food and scant bathing facilities. Reports from human-rights workers filtered back that the refugees were sick, filthy, and terrified, heartbroken at being separated from familiar faces and desperate for news, while guards yelled at them and ignored their most basic needs. For Ocasio-Cortez, who was personally attracting the cruel fire of Trump's racist and xenophobic rhetoric, only a short distance existed between her own life and that of the caged humans at the border. The detention centers were run by private prison companies, so the children in the cages were, in a very real sense, their product. As at Standing Rock, the corporate-run government machine was—once again, as it had for centuries—trampling the human rights of poor and brown-skinned people to turn a profit and amass power.

At the beginning of May, Trump asked for funds to address the border crisis, including more than a billion dollars for border operations, including ICE. That very same month, a minor-league baseball team in California called the Fresno Grizzlies played a patriotic video during a game, splicing an image of Ocasio-Cortez together with ones of Kim Jong Un and Fidel Castro while the soothing, actorly voice of Ronald Reagan warned of "enemies of freedom." "I've had mornings," Ocasio-Cortez tweeted, "where I wake up & the 1st thing I do w/ my coffee is review photos of the men (it's always men) who want to kill me." (The Grizzlies apologized.)

Provoked did not begin to describe how Ocasio-Cortez felt that late spring and early summer of 2019, and she returned to Instagram Live to say so. Her youth worked in her favor here; the outrage she expressed was so pure—so unpolluted by maturity, weariness, or compromise—it was nearly translucent. Sitting on her couch and wearing a black T-shirt with white letters that read "Rematriate The Land," she started. "The United States is running concentration camps on our southern border," she said. "And that is exactly what they are. They are concentration camps. And if that doesn't bother you—" She pauses, having momentarily run out of words. Then she shrugs and uses both hands to sweep away the imaginary people in her mind who are not troubled by the caging of children. She cannot spend even a thought on them. "Okay, whatever, I want to talk to the people that are concerned enough with humanity to say that 'Never again' means something. And that the fact that concentration camps are now an institutionalized practice in the home of the free is extraordinarily disturbing." This is not just a crisis for immigrant communities, she continued. "This is a crisis for ourselves." Here she taps her heart with the flat of her hand. When asked for her point of view on the camps, Omar said, "I am 100 percent with Alex."

A lot of back-and-forth among pundits and scholars followed about whether the detention camps were, in fact, like concentration camps, and whether it was blasphemous to say so, but the livestream had the desired effect. The media published a torrent of stories about the conditions at the border, all underscoring the ghastly treatment of migrants, which gave Ocasio-Cortez, the Squad, and the Congressional Progressive Caucus cover to make some meaningful demands. It was the end of June, just before the Fourth of July break, and a $4.6 billion aid package was on the table with bipartisan support. But progressives hoped to negotiate over the uses of that money and attach some restrictions. They wanted more humanitarian aid, accountability for human-rights abuses and enforcement of consequences for perpetrators, and less funding for ICE. With popular sentiment on the border crisis leaning their way, the progressives were hopeful for some influence.

But the tensions between the progressives and the centrists were high, and Ocasio-Cortez deployed a stratagem that summer that she would use henceforth in every fractious and consequential political fight. She stuck her flag in the high moral ground and simply stood by it, like an explorer claiming fresh terrain. In this way, she forced her moderate colleagues into one of two unflattering poses. They were either heartless—deaf and blind to the lived realities of migrants, Indigenous people, working mothers, and neglected children—or they were colluders with the system. For Ocasio-Cortez, there was no in between. But for any Democrat in a red or purple district, an appearance of softness on immigration could cost them their seat. Katie Hill was there at the time. "I remember talking to [Illinois Democratic member] Lauren Underwood," she said, "and we were just, like, 'I feel really bad for AOC,' because people didn't talk to her necessarily when they had a problem with her. I think people were afraid of her, really I do. I think they were afraid of getting in her Twitter crosshairs, and they were just intimidated by her. She was like, 'I'm not trying to hurt the party. I'm not trying to hurt these people in their reelections. That's not my goal, and I want to be a team player, but people need to see my side of things, too.'" When Pelosi announced at the end of June that the Democrats would agree to the version of the bill proposed by Mitch McConnell and the Republicans, Ocasio-Cortez and the Squad appeared blindsided. "Hell no," she tweeted.

Shortly after, she did an interview with Jake Tapper on CNN. "Those are strong words against Speaker Pelosi," Tapper said.

Ocasio-Cortez nodded. She didn't disagree: Pelosi caved. "We didn't even bother to negotiate," she said. "Here we are the House of Representatives, and we are a House majority, and we need to act like it."

Then her chief of staff, Saikat Chakrabarti, violated congressional protocol once again. He, too, was angry and not accustomed to taking a back seat. From his own Twitter account, he flamed the centrist Democrats as right-wing collaborators, comparing them to the mid-century defenders of segregation and Jim Crow. The New Democrats and the Blue Dogs, he tweeted, "seem hell bent to do to black and brown people today what the old Southern Democrats did in the 40s." On the House floor, only four Democrats voted "no" on the border-aid bill. The Squad, in solidarity, was making a point.

• • •

Battered and still seething, Ocasio-Cortez kept her plans to travel with a delegation of about a dozen members of Congress to the camps on the Texas border the weekend before the Fourth of July. Pressley and Tlaib would be going too. They had been in Congress for only six months.

On the morning of their departure, Ocasio-Cortez woke up to a story by an investigative reporter at ProPublica. It revealed the existence of a private Facebook group, with a membership of about

10,000 current and former employees of U.S. Customs and Border Protection, that published posts mocking detainees and even joking about their deaths. A link to a news story about a 16-year-old who died in custody was accompanied by an Elmo GIF that said "Oh well." The group targeted Ocasio-Cortez personally. In advance of the congressional trip, one poster suggested starting a GoFundMe to reward the Border agent "brave enough" to hurl burritos at "these bitches," as the poster called Ocasio-Cortez and Veronica Escobar, a member from Texas. There were obscene and violent fake photos of Ocasio-Cortez performing oral sex—in one on a detainee, in another on Trump.

Before arriving at the camps, Ocasio-Cortez went on Twitter. "How on earth can CBP's culture be trusted to care for refugees humanely?" she wrote.

With the government delegation, she left the media scrum on the sidewalk and was escorted inside. Most of the representatives handed over their cell phones, and though they were cautioned not to speak to the migrants, she and a small group that included Pressley and Representative Joaquin Castro, from San Antonio, stepped into a cell. The guards were watching, and Ocasio-Cortez later said she did not feel safe.[16] *(MORE ON THE TRIP TO THE BORDER, SEE PAGE 289.)*

At the end of the visit, Pressley had to pull Ocasio-Cortez off the floor and out of the room. Later, at a press conference outside the facility before a hostile, shouting crowd, Ocasio-Cortez called the treatment of migrants by the U.S. government "unconscionable," while hecklers shouted "Go home!" When Tlaib stood up to the mic, the hecklers grew more raucous, trying to drown her out. "We don't want Sharia law here!" someone yelled.

"What I learned today, in seeing the eyes of a father of a 14-year-old, is that it's not about children only. It's also about the fathers and the mothers," Tlaib said, hoarse, nearly crying, while Ocasio-Cortez stepped forward and touched her back. "I will outwork your hate," Tlaib continued. "I will out-love your hate. I will always put my country first."

Then Pressley stood up. If Ocasio-Cortez has charisma, Pressley has gravitas. "This is bigger than a funding debate—" she started to call out.

"That's right," interjected Ocasio-Cortez in response, while the crowd continued to yell.

"Or about any speeches that we give here or on the floor of the House of Representatives. This is about the preservation of our humanity. And this is about seeing every single person there as a member of your own family. I am *tired* of the health and the safety and the humanity and the full freedoms of Black and brown children being *negotiated*—"

"Yes," said Ocasio-Cortez, nodding.

"And *compromised*. And moderated." Ocasio-Cortez closed her eyes, as if she were in church.

• • •

Less than a week later, on July 6, Maureen Dowd published an interview with Nancy Pelosi in the New York *Times*. She and Pelosi had met over omelets at a restaurant in San Francisco, Pelosi's home district. In what may have been a rare (but rather large) political miscalculation, Pelosi dropped a few choice words for Ocasio-Cortez and the Squad. "All these people have their public whatever and their Twitter world," she said, after eating a chocolate candy. "But . . . they're four people and that's how many votes they got."

The Beltway chorus erupted at this, an instance of one of the most senior members of Congress throwing shade at the most junior in an assertion of her dominance, which, in this case, was questionable. Ocasio-Cortez immediately reached for her feeds. "That 'public whatever' is called public sentiment," she clapped back to 68,000 likes, "and wielding the power to shift it is how we actually achieve meaningful change in this country."

Omar piled on. "You know they're just salty about WHO is wielding the power to shift 'public sentiment' these days, sis." She got 14,000 likes.

Then Kellyanne Conway, seeing a political opportunity, took a moment to widen the rift between Pelosi and the Squad. She went on Fox News and gleefully called the bickering a "huge catfight" and a "meow moment," leading Pressley to call out Conway on Twitter as "Distraction Becky." When asked what he thought about the Squad, Hakeem Jeffries, disinclined to be sympathetic to Ocasio-Cortez ever since Justice Democrats had apparently come for him, responded with one word: "Who?"

Pelosi had had enough. Behind closed doors, she instructed the warring factions to keep their disagreements private. "You got a complaint?" she said. "You come and talk to me about it. But do not tweet about our members and expect us to think that that is just okay." It was a big meeting, and Ocasio-Cortez sat near the back of the room. Pelosi didn't name any names, but it was clear whom she was talking about. "I remember looking over at her," Katie Hill says. "And she's got a good poker face, but I was watching her, I was watching for it. You can see, like, the jaw. And I remember she left during it. You felt the tension very much in the air, that people were watching, waiting for a fight. There were so many times when I was like, *Wow, she deserves so much respect,* because she was not going to have a public fight that was going to make it into the news, so she just left. If I were her, I would have been fucking furious."

Pelosi, it became clear, was done with Chakrabarti in particular, though she denies her ire was directed at him. With their constant threat of primary challenges, Justice Democrats had made few friends in Congress, and notably in the Congressional Black Caucus, where Chakrabarti had shown an arrogant insensitivity to the senior members, who had fought long and hard for their constituents, not by taking potshots but through tactical diplomacy and incremental gains. When Chakrabarti lobbed his "Southern Democrats" tweet into the midst of the border-bill fight, he had singled out Representative Sharice Davids, a Native American member from Kansas, who had flipped a red district. Pelosi wanted Ocasio-Cortez to rein in her chief of staff: Chakrabarti's tweet was "totally inappropriate," she told a reporter. "I've never seen anything like it." After the Pelosi scolding, the official House Democrats Twitter account—operated by Jeffries—raised the Davids issue again. "Keep her name out of your mouth," read one tweet.

Ocasio-Cortez had rarely felt so isolated—strafed in public from all sides, trying to manage a staff with an independent agenda, and carrying the real anguish and responsibility that the trip to the border had raised in her. During congressional testimony by a mother whose child, Mariee, died in custody on the border, she openly wept. "Next month she would have been 3 years old," the mother said, through a translator. In front of the world, Ocasio-Cortez covered her eyes with her hand and then with tissues, but really there was nowhere to hide.

Ironically, and very unintentionally, it was Trump who mended the divisions within the Democratic Caucus. Endeavoring to exploit them, he jumped into the conflict mouth first. "Why don't they go back and help fix the totally broken and crime infested places from which they came," he tweeted about the Squad, instigating a new surge of attacks, death threats, and hate. Suddenly, Pelosi had an opening, a way to smooth things over with the first-termers while redirecting the anger of their Twitter supporters (collectively, the Squad had more than 5 million) away from her and the moderate compromises that had inflamed those on her left. At a press conference, Pelosi stood up behind all four members of the Squad and introduced a resolution on the House floor calling Trump's tweets racist. And Ocasio-Cortez, about to go on her summer vacation, a road trip with Riley Roberts to visit the giant sequoias out West, reached out to Pelosi's office for a one-on-one. "I don't think there was ever any hatchet" to bury, Pelosi said after the meeting. But when Congress resumed in September, both Chakrabarti and Corbin Trent—the Bernie guys who first asked Ocasio-Cortez to the dance—were gone.

•••

There is popularity. And there is power. Before her first year in Congress was over, Ocasio-Cortez had accrued both. Her social-media feeds were like trained lightning, destroying and illuminating at her command. Ever mindful of her ratios—always fine-tuning her posts to engender more love than hate—she reigned over her social-media hive more like Beyoncé or Rihanna than a politician. And like a celebrity who stokes a standom, she must have been mindful of the risk: All that love could turn on her in an instant. But Ocasio-Cortez shrewdly saw the utility of her feeds beyond raising her own profile, and because of that, she became an even more desirable ally—and a more feared opponent.

In the winter of 2019, she interrogated the Trump fixer Michael Cohen in such an exacting and disciplined way that she prompted him to give up information that would become essential to future prosecutions of the president. Then, in the fall, she gently dismembered Mark Zuckerberg, taking five minutes and 35 seconds in a congressional hearing to expose the Facebook CEO as defensive and entitled: out of touch with his own leadership, unaware of important details and dates, and disconnected from the political catastrophe resulting from the Cambridge Analytica scandal, in which the Trump campaign enlisted the company to mine Facebook data and help sway the 2016 election. "It's good to see you, Mr. Zuckerberg," she said softly to begin. Quickly she homed in on Zuckerberg's relationship with Peter Thiel, the right-wing billionaire who is on the Facebook board. When did he and Thiel first talk about Cambridge Analytica? Zuckerberg said he didn't know.

"You don't know? This was the largest data scandal with respect to your company that had catastrophic impacts on the 2016 election. You *don't know*?" Then she concluded by arguing that, heading into the 2020 cycle, Zuckerberg still had not put sufficient controls on the dissemination of political misinformation, was continuing to profit from the profiling of users, and failed to oversee the veracity of ads. No one in Congress understood the inner workings of the Facebook-advertising machinery better than she. Zuckerberg was reduced to blustering that "lying is bad." One YouTube version of the video was viewed more than 800,000 times.[17] *(MORE ON* AOC'S WITNESS-GRILLING TACTICS, *SEE PAGE 298.)*

• • •

In the first six months of 2019, while her Green New Deal was foundering and her colleagues were snarking behind her back, she raised nearly $2 million, all in small-dollar donations—in an off-year. (This was more than any of her colleagues on the Finance Committee, some of whom were supported by banks.) Then, as the fight over the border erupted and Trump turned his violent, trollish attention to the Squad, she raised even more. In the final quarter of the year, she raised another $2 million. For the year ended December 31, 2019,

Ocasio-Cortez had raised $5.3 million. For comparison, a congressional incumbent usually raises about $2.7 million in each two-year cycle.

Ocasio-Cortez has always said that true power means not giving a fuck. Her operation's fat bank account gave her that kind of freedom. It protected her seat, assuming she wanted to keep it. It made prospective opponents think twice about running against her and forced established politicians at higher levels of government—most notably Chuck Schumer, the senior senator from New York—to start worrying about how they might fend her off.

But her ability to raise money online also gave her a fairy-godmother quality, for she could swoop in and save someone's job or support a cause or a candidate she deemed deserving. (This was always a political calculus, too. Did the object of her beneficence want to be known in public as such?) In the spring of her freshman year, the DCCC, the Democratic Party outfit that provides support and strategy to congressional campaigns, announced it would refuse to work with any strategist or consultant who also worked for primary challengers, a policy that outraged progressives who saw pressuring the Old Guard as part of their mission. This group included Ocasio-Cortez and Justice Democrats.

Ocasio-Cortez called for a boycott of the DCCC on Twitter. The new rule was "extremely divisive & harmful to the party," she wrote. "My recommendation, if you're a small-dollar donor: pause your donations to DCCC & give directly to swing candidates instead." Then she named names: California representatives Mike Levin and Katie Porter could use a boost. So could Lauren Underwood of Illinois. In the thread, she included direct links to their campaigns' donor pages. The next night, in advance of the first-quarter federal fundraising deadline, she raised $50,000 for three swing-district

Democrats—Levin, Katie Hill, and Jahana Hayes—in several hours. (In 2020, the DCCC rescinded the punitive policy, but it was too late. Among operatives on the left, being on the DCCC blacklist had become a badge of progressive cred.)

So it was perhaps not in the least bit surprising that as the field for the Democratic presidential primary started to take shape, in the spring and summer of 2019, many of the contenders were vying for her attention, hoping to attract a retweet or a nod. Beto O'Rourke called her a "phenomenal leader." Joe Biden said she was "smart as hell."

Elizabeth Warren and Bernie Sanders both wanted her endorsement. The ideological fit was obvious, as was the need. Warren and Sanders both read as old, white, and wonky (though their wonkiness held different valences). Both knew how badly they could use a push from a young woman of color who was also a celebrity and an arbiter of cool.

Warren courted her, overtly and early, and in May 2019, the two appeared together in a video critiquing the series finale of *Game of Thrones*. Warren, a *GOT* fan, clearly hoped Ocasio-Cortez's nerdy freshness would redound to her. They sat on chairs against a black background, each wearing a colorful blazer.

"I was just really . . . meh," Warren said, looking hopefully over at Ocasio-Cortez as if she'd just been invited to join the popular kids' table.

"I feel like we were getting so close to having this ending with just women running the world," said Ocasio-Cortez, smiling broadly.

"Exactly!"

"And then the last two episodes—"

"One goes crazy—"

"And it's like, *Oh! They're too emotional. The end*," says Ocasio-Cortez, shrugging with her whole body.

"Yeah, exactly." Warren and Ocasio-Cortez harrumphed in intergenerational accord. Warren posted the video on her Senate page, where it got 18,000 likes—not in the Ocasio-Cortez stratosphere but respectable for a 69-year-old professor at Harvard Law.

Warren's approach to politics is and always has been to communicate constantly. Stories abound of people—reporters, staffers, ordinary citizens—picking up the phone to find Elizabeth Warren on the other end, dropping a compliment or asking advice. Now Warren aimed this charm offensive at Ocasio-Cortez, inviting her in for private talks and writing a laudatory essay about her for *Time* magazine. She also co-sponsored legislation with Ocasio-Cortez to direct Defense Department funds to clean up toxic waste spilled by the military in Puerto Rico.

Meanwhile, Ocasio-Cortez kept her cards close to the vest. She liked Warren, she told reporters. She liked Sanders. She was thinking about an endorsement, maybe. Biden was too "middle of the road." Next question, please.

Sanders and Ocasio-Corez worked together on a predatory lending bill, but he remained aloof, and, privately, her staff was irked. If he wanted her help, he didn't show it, an odd stance for a 77-year-old runner-up whose 2016 effort was assailed for being inaccessible to people of color and women. Partially, this was a matter of personal style. Sanders dislikes the "hokey-fenokey" aspects of politics, explained Faiz Shakir, the manager of his 2020 campaign, "the wining and dining and calling people on their birthday, that kind of thing . . . For all of his wonderful strengths, Senator Sanders will concede to you one of his not-so-strong suits tends to be picking up the phone."

But also, with the departure of Chakrabarti and Trent—both members of Bernie's original crew—the old back channels between the

Sanders and Ocasio-Cortez offices had narrowed. And the new peo-ple in charge at Ocasio-Cortez headquarters had a more insider style. Lauren Hitt, the new director of communications, had formerly worked for the moderate Democratic governor of Colorado John Hickenlooper (who made a brief run for president), among others. Ariel Eckblad, the new chief of staff, was a professor at Georgetown Law and had been an aide to Kamala Harris. These staff changes "were a really good move on her part," reflects Katie Hill. They gave Ocasio-Cortez more autonomy, a chance to develop a mature polit-ical identity and to build relationships on the Hill beyond Justice Democrats. But it also meant that she was no longer wearing the wristband that gained her backstage access to Bernie's world.

In July 2019, Warren was ahead of Sanders, and it was clear that Sanders needed a boost. At a campaign summit in Vermont that sum-mer, Shakir impressed upon him the importance of courting Ocasio-Cortez: "If we were going to be the progressive standard-bearer, we wanted her to be with us," Shakir said. Sanders was per-suaded to call Ocasio-Cortez directly and, in an extremely rare gesture, he invited her to dinner at his house in Vermont.

She arrived at the Burlington airport with one staffer. Shakir drove them to the Sanders place, where a low stone wall stood between the street and the front lawn, the small pale-yellow four-bedroom house beyond. The meeting between Ocasio-Cortez and Sanders and his wife, Jane O'Meara Sanders, lasted three or four hours, including a simple dinner. They talked about Ocasio-Cortez's upbringing. They talked about Roberts, who wasn't there, with Sanders expressing interest in an almost parental way. They touched on the issues but didn't debate them. Ocasio-Cortez had run on Bernie's platform, after all. Health care for all; aggressive action on climate change; student-debt relief—for each, these were foundational. It must have been gratifying, and also possibly alarming, for Sanders to encounter this young acolyte who possessed such richness in everything he lacked: vitality, cool, sex appeal. Shakir reflects on something he once heard: "Bernie plus Cardi B equals AOC." And for her part, Ocasio-Cortez wasn't genuflecting. She was interested. "The chemistry between them sparked; it was obvious," Shakir says. "It was like, *She's one of us. She really believes in this stuff.* It wasn't just some prestige thing. It was, *This is my intellectual and emotional home. This is where I come from.* You saw that at the jump."

Ocasio-Cortez had arrived in Vermont with one big question. How did Sanders plan to win? The campaigner who had once critiqued Joe Crowley's rose-hued mailers didn't want to hear highfalutin' visions or theories. She wanted to see numbers of voters and a path to victory. She dug into Sanders's digital-messaging plans, and she questioned, in particular, their ability to attract older Black voters and other people of color. She knew this issue, of whether class frustration could move voters of widely divergent ages, races, and ethnicities to cohere into one powerful working-class bloc, was the trickiest to solve and also the most urgent. Her experience in the primary, as well as her more recent tangles with the Congressional Black Caucus, had been instructive. Older generations of African Americans and Latinos were not always inspired by the brash theatrics of a youth movement. How could Bernie broaden his base to include people who had been turned off before? "She knew that we were investing in digital ad spending," Shakir recalls. "She wanted to know more about it. Alienated voters— how do we get people of color who aren't already on our side? How do we persuade them? How do you get African Americans to vote for your agenda? This is a key we have to unlock."

In general, the evening went well, and before saying good night, Sanders suggested she stay the next morning and meet him for breakfast at Penny Cluse, a café in Burlington. Ocasio-Cortez agreed, and she changed her flight.

The following day, Sanders and Ocasio-Cortez walked down the street together in small-town Vermont, and "it was madness," Shakir recalls. In Washington, D.C., Ocasio-Cortez was followed everywhere by a scrum of reporters, their hands holding phones sticking out of the jumble like crab's legs, the lights of television cameras unremitting. This was not that. Regular people stopped, gaped, and whispered. Each seemed to magnify the allure of the other, creating a heat hotter than the sum of their celebrity; Ocasio-Cortez and Sanders instantly understood how all this energy could be directed at their causes for the good. "Each of them watching how much excitement the other generated in real time gave a glimpse into the partnership's possibilities," Shakir recalls. At Penny Cluse, Sanders ordered his usual: buckwheat pancakes with blueberries. Ocasio-Cortez had scrambled eggs, rye toast, and home fries. They took photos with fellow diners and staff. And then she was off.

Still, a reasonable question lingered. Why should she make any endorsement with the convention a long nine months away? She clearly had the upper hand. The dynamics had changed in the 18 months since her fight against Crowley. Now Sanders—and Warren, for that matter—needed her more than she needed them. Why not wait three months, or six, for the field to narrow rather than risk the chance that whoever she endorsed would make an embarrassing misstep and drag her down? *"If I do go with Bernie, will there be anything I regret?"* is how Shakir framed her state of mind as she left Vermont.

Ocasio-Cortez doesn't gripe. Her usual mode is to stay outwardly positive, to convert public disappointments and frustrations into political leverage, and to nurse personal hurts on her own. Like a pro athlete, she is extremely disciplined about this. Still, there must have been some residual bitterness, even resentment, in recalling how Justice Democrats built its brand on her winning campaign while its inspiration and guide, Bernie Sanders, did not deign to endorse her. Sanders frequently aligned with her politically, but her important relationships in Congress were with women—and especially women of color. The Squad, but also Barbara Lee, Pramila Jayapal, Katie Hill, Katie Porter, Susan Wilde, and Lauren Underwood. The fantasy she shared with Warren of "women running the world" was real, as was her exasperation that, in the world she inhabited, white men still ran everything. All ambitious people eventually consider how useful their mentors can continue to be.

Then, on October 1, Bernie Sanders had a heart attack. He was at a fundraiser in Las Vegas when the chest pain began. He asked to sit down. His staff took him to an urgent-care center, and from there he was sent to a hospital, where he immediately underwent surgery for a blocked artery. Two stents were placed in his heart. For three days, his campaign didn't speak to the press. Inside the campaign, the heart attack had divided staffers into two camps, the true believers and the political careerists, and Shakir worried in particular about where Ocasio-Cortez would land. "I didn't know what to really expect," admits Shakir. It would have been understandable for her to quietly back away.

The senator was still recuperating in the Las Vegas hospital when Shakir got a text from Ocasio-Cortez saying she'd like to speak with him. Sanders was sitting up in a chair waiting for a visit from Harry Reid when Shakir handed him the phone. Ocasio-Cortez and Sanders spoke for a while, and then Sanders smiled and he pumped his fist. He handed the phone back. "She's going to be with us," he said.

It made no political sense, not really. To endorse a 78-year-old man recovering from heart surgery is all downside. Sanders could have died. He could have failed to summon the physical stamina and mental acuity needed to run a respectable presidential race, leaving Ocasio-Cortez in the position of a lame-duck supporter. But her commitment to Bernie's platform, and her understanding of him as an iconic, historic political figure—these were real to her, and they meant something. Her sense of story, her flair for apprehending the dramatic, fit the moment. Ocasio-Cortez resurrected the Sanders presidential campaign. There's no other way to say it. Who better to step in and resuscitate the ailing ideologue than she, the face of the next generation and the heir—whether he designed it or not—to his legacy?

On October 19, Ocasio-Cortez was standing up for Bernie before a screaming crowd of 26,000 in Queens—near where he was raised and her own district. She had just turned 30. "You all like my haircut? It got a lot of attention last week. *Damn*," she commenced, deflating the previous day's viral critique of her $300 cut-and-color by embracing it. And all that vitality—together with the crimson lipstick and the hoop earrings—accrued to Sanders, who had been in the hospital fewer than three weeks before.

Ocasio-Cortez pivoted quickly. She talked about being a waitress in Manhattan. "It wasn't until I heard of a man by the name of Bernie Sanders that I began to question and assert and recognize my inherent value as a human being that deserves health care, housing, education, and a living wage." The crowd roared. And when Sanders came up to take the mic, she called him her *tío* and he shouted, "I am back!" In a photo taken that day, Sanders holds Ocasio-Cortez's hand aloft like a prizefight winner. But it was reasonable to wonder, looking at the scene, whether this was his victory or hers.

• • •

Since the departure of Chakrabarti and Trent, Ocasio-Cortez had been signaling her willingness to play more of an insider's game. The shift was subtle, and in the fall of 2019, she went on *All In With Chris Hayes* to introduce the new iteration of herself. She would continue to hold the line on issues, as she had always done. "My personal political strategy—and this is what I've practiced—is to come in with the boldest vision possible. Because the political reality hits the fan on the floor of the House. So let that happen down the road," she said.

"Don't do it ahead of time, is what you're saying," Hayes said.

"Yeah, don't bargain with and negotiate with yourself ahead of time. And don't kind of be overly cynical about this political moment because what we have right now, frankly, with Donald Trump in the White House is a unique moment to create a mass movement of Americans to push for everything that we want and all that we deserve."

She was beginning to see the value of pragmatic and political friendships. Working in Congress, she told Hayes, is like being crushed in a vise. Bills come before members just 48 hours prior to a vote, and "we're talking about sometimes pieces of legislation that are thousands of pages long, and then you say, 'Wait. Wait! *This* is a really big problem. *That's* a really big problem,' and they say, 'Well, are you on our side or not?'" she said. "There's a real intense pressure to conform."

Life becomes a whole lot easier, she was discovering, with friends and allies on the inside. It's hard to tolerate the pressure when every colleague is also a sworn enemy. "I don't like using the word *civility* in politics because I think it's a term to police how people talk," Ocasio-Cortez said, smiling. "But people know my political positions when I walk in there. And what's great is they know exactly how I feel and who I am, and so that they know not to come to me with certain things."

"It probably saves you some conversation," Hayes said, laughing.

"It saves me a ton of time. A ton of time. But they also are willing to reach out to me on unusual things, but they feel like it would fit with the consistency of my values," said Ocasio-Cortez.

As part of her adjustment, Ocasio-Cortez largely stopped weighing in on primary races, a full reversal of how she approached Congress when she entered a year earlier. But now she was an incumbent herself, running to keep her seat, and though her main primary challenger did not threaten her—Michelle Caruso-Cabrera, a former television host and erstwhile Republican, who argued that Ocasio-Cortez was stoking her own fame at the expense of her district—an awareness of some of her colleagues' tough races and, perhaps, her demoralizing fights with centrists in red districts over the summer held her back. In a show of loyalty, she backed her ally, the incumbent Ed Markey, for Senate in his primary challenge against Pelosi's choice, Joe Kennedy III. And in the House, Justice Democrats supported eight congressional challengers in the 2020 cycle. Ocasio-Cortez backed three. These were entirely noncontroversial. Marie Newman was primarying the much-reviled, anti-abortion representative Dan Lipinski in Chicago. Ocasio-Cortez joined Barack Obama and Joe Biden, among others, in backing her. In Texas, which Ocasio-Cortez has long had in her sights as a flippable state, she joined Warren and Sanders in endorsing Jessica Cisneros in her race against Henry Cuellar, who received an A rating from the NRA. With just weeks to go before the New York primary, Ocasio-Cortez announced her support for Jamaal Bowman, who was running against the 30-year veteran Eliot Engel. (Newman and Bowman won in the end. Cisneros lost by a hair.)

Most notably, Ocasio-Cortez did not endorse Cori Bush, the candidate she had met and bonded with down in Kentucky way back in the spring of 2017, when the trees were just blooming and Justice Democrats was putting together its first, scrappy slate. After her own primary win in the summer of 2018, Ocasio-Cortez had stumped for Bush, knocked on doors for her, made speeches, called her "sister" on Twitter. Bush had posted a photo of herself and Ocasio-Cortez on the street in St. Louis, arms entwined, wearing matching grape-colored campaign T-shirts and looking very much like kids at summer camp, together with the headline to a local news story: "Alexandria Ocasio-Cortez and Cori Bush Are Punk AF." Bush lost that year to the ten-term incumbent, Lacy Clay.

In the 2020 cycle, Bush was challenging Clay again, and even though she was endorsed by Sanders, Justice Democrats, and Sunrise—even though her campaign manager, Isra Allison, was the very same person who reached out to Ocasio-Cortez by phone after Standing Rock to see if she would be interested in running for office—Ocasio-Cortez stayed mute.

It was clear that Ocasio-Cortez was trying to mend fences, but this, too, was a struggle. Friendship alleviated isolation, but created the indebtedness that animated the favor economy of Congress. People looked at her and saw "a huge amassing of influence or power or money or what have you," she said in an interview in the winter of 2020. But "my personal experience does not feel that way—it can feel very lonely," she said. "I think my ambition right now is to be a little less lonely in Congress."

•••

Less than two months before the Bernie endorsement, having returned to the Bronx from her West Coast vacation, Ocasio-Cortez went online

January 26, 2020: Ocasio-Cortez dances on the stage ahead of a rally for Bernie Sanders in Sioux City, Iowa.

to catch her fans up on the final months of her first year in office. Just home from work, still wearing her dress, she looked exactly like what she was: a woman with a big job and no time to deal. She hadn't been able to get to the grocery store, she said, so she had stopped by the bodega, where she picked up regular milk instead of the oat milk she preferred. She would be making mac 'n' cheese again, but this time no-frills and straight out of the box. The connection was more important than the food, she reminded viewers. "What? Am I not going to reach out and talk to people?" she asked.

On this night, she went where no politician had ever gone before. She talked about babies—about wanting them and having them sometime in the future, about what she envisioned, her anxieties and hopes. By airing the dilemmas of young women her age, she (in a cooking video, wedged between job and sleep) neutralized an old, fetishized, and fraught conversation about what women should want and how they should speak about wanting (or not wanting) it.

She had already confessed, on an earlier livestream, her reservations about bringing children into a future meaningfully threatened by climate change. "There's a scientific consensus that the lives of children are going to be very difficult," she said then. Now the question from a viewer came up again: How can a person have a normal, forward-looking life with the planet in danger?

"I think about the kind of family that I want to plan," she said sympathetically, as the macaroni boiled away in a pot. "And I've already known my entire life that, one day, I'd love to adopt children." But even with hypothetical children, Ocasio-Cortez was already downgrading her dreams: "I know that I want to perhaps have one less child than I thought I would maybe have," she said. "If I can even have a child, biologically. I don't know. Just—you know. I haven't tried." She laughed in an embarrassed sort of way. "I don't think older generations sometimes really understand how much we're taking this into account for the future. How scary it can be." Later on, she told an interviewer that she was thinking about freezing her eggs.

To say she is a feminist is to understate the facts. Ocasio-Cortez is the first politician in history to live fully out loud while female. And the degradations of womanhood are personal to her. She has been upfront about the gross men in the restaurant, shrewd about Crowley's instinctive condescension, and sisterly in the face of Trump's opportunistic misogyny. Even before being officially elected to Congress, she was an infuriated opponent of Brett Kavanaugh's appointment to the Supreme Court. "Sexual assault," she said, so kinetic she was practically dancing to a beat only she could hear, "is not a crime of passion. It is about the abuse of power. And that is precisely why it is one of the most serious, serious allegations anyone who cares to be a public servant can be accused of . . . It is always women who are marginalized. It is the young. It is the interns. It is the immigrant. It is the trans. They are always most at risk because society listens to them the least. And that is why a man believes that an elite education, a high income, and his rich friends can get away with sexual assault."

In the 2016 primary against Clinton, Sanders had roused the passion of the millennial left, but he struggled to stoke much enthusiasm among many women and people of color. This was the very problem Ocasio-Cortez had apparently been enlisted to address this time around. So it must have been enraging to read, in January 2020, while she was out trying to help Sanders in Iowa, reports stating that Sanders had previously told Elizabeth Warren that a woman could never win.

And then, the same month, Sanders did a long interview with the former UFC host and comedian Joe Rogan, whose podcast gets millions of listeners. Afterward, Rogan said he would probably vote for Sanders, and the Sanders campaign proudly promoted this statement online. The problem was, Rogan attracts a particular crowd. His guests are overwhelmingly men, and his listeners are, too. White and libertarian-leaning, there are philosophical overlaps both with Trump voters and with the crude and fervent Bernie bros who formed the most motivated part of the Sanders base and from whom the candidate was now ostensibly trying to distance himself. Rogan can be intelligent, but also moronic, and his humor can be bigoted. He has made fun of gender-neutral pronouns and once called a Black neighborhood *"Planet of the Apes."*

Demands from progressive groups swiftly came that Sanders retract or repudiate Rogan's semi-endorsement, and though Ocasio-Cortez said nothing publicly, she was apparently among them. News stories, denied by both camps, reported tensions, with Sanders grumping that she failed or forgot to mention his name in a speech and Ocasio-Cortez staffers pressuring Sanders to do something about Rogan. Sanders stood fast—in addition to courting older people of color and women, he was trying to pull some Trump voters to his side. But after that episode, getting Ocasio-Cortez up to New Hampshire was "like pulling teeth," an unnamed source told the HuffPost. (Shakir denies that the relationship grew fraught at the time, blaming the news accounts on leaks by insiders "who got jealous and upset over a relationship that was growing stronger.") They disagreed publicly about whether Medicare for All was a starting point or non-negotiable. Ocasio-Cortez took the former position. "The worst-case scenario? We compromise deeply, and we end up getting a public option. Is that a nightmare? I don't think so." Bernie went on *Anderson Cooper 360* to roll that back. His Medicare for All bill, he said, was "already a compromise."

Then Ocasio-Cortez made another appearance on *The View*, seemingly to promote Sanders in advance of Super Tuesday to its audience of middle-aged women. She came out on message, with a focus on women's issues. "When we talk about big government, we don't talk about big government injecting themselves into the bodies of women and gender-nonconforming people for anti-choice policies," she said. Ultimately, though, she had a hard time sticking up for her candidate. Meghan McCain, the group's conservative, called her own encounters with Bernie bros online "the most violent, the most misogynistic, the most sexist, the most harmful" she had ever had. "He has a real problem, and I don't think he's doing enough to tamper it down."

Ocasio-Cortez nodded, trying to steer the question toward internet toxicity in general. "It nearly always concentrates on women," she said, "people of color, queer people. We experience the brunt of it."

But McCain persisted. "Do you think he's done enough to try to stop it?" she asked. Everyone watching knew, of course, that Ocasio-Cortez had been a target of near-constant violence online— not from Bernie bros but from their counterparts on the right, recently fielding a Twitter post in which a crowd of frattish-looking young white men wearing "Team Mitch" T-shirts were shown grabbing and groping a cardboard cutout of her. "Break me off a piece of that," the caption read. Ocasio-Cortez had reposted the tweet, directing a question at the Senate majority leader. "Just wanted to clarify: are you paying for young men to practice groping & choking members of Congress w/ your payroll, or is this just the standard culture of #TeamMitch?"

Ocasio-Cortez, who relentlessly calls out abuses of male power, found she couldn't do her job as a surrogate for Bernie. She evaded and spun until Whoopi Goldberg stepped in and gave her a safe place to land.

"He's got to do more," Goldberg said assertively. "He's got to stand up and say it every day if he needs to—"

"Yeah," Ocasio-Cortez agreed.

"Stop this. We're not accepting it."

"For sure," said Ocasio-Cortez.

• • •

The final stages of the Democratic primary were subsumed by the emergence of COVID-19, a monstrous multiphase catastrophe, more global than a world war, with incalculable traumatic consequences. COVID allowed Trump and his club of high-level deniers to create more political chaos, but for Ocasio-Cortez, the crisis was not about optics. It was local. Early in the pandemic, the Zip Code with the highest number of COVID infections nationally was in NY-14. When the city released its first death count, two of the top five Zip Codes were in NY-14. Elmhurst Hospital, a public facility in Queens serving a largely Asian and Latino population, was tagged by the press as the epicenter of the epicenter. It was in NY-14. Its emergency department, one area converted into a makeshift ICU, was crowded with so many patients that medical staff could not navigate between beds. An 18-wheeler idled outside the hospital as a temporary morgue. Ocasio-Cortez was holed up in the Bronx with Roberts and their new French-bulldog puppy, Deco.

Whatever modulations of her political persona Ocasio-Cortez had adopted she now cast aside. She was screaming. She could not stop screaming, and she screamed louder about COVID—and sooner than most of her colleagues, and with more intensity—than she had ever screamed about anything before. She saw the pandemic with clear eyes for what it was: a viral death machine, algorithmic in its infection rates. In college, as a premed student, Ocasio-Cortez had been

---

interested in the systemic problem of health disparities among neighborhoods. Now, in her district, people were dying at higher rates than anywhere else in the country because of the very conditions that she had entered politics to crusade against.

Her constituents were those she called "everyday people": working-class Black and brown people and the immigrants who drove the city buses and taxis, who operated the subways, who delivered food, and cared for children and the elderly, who worked as cashiers, bartenders, dishwashers, and doormen, who encountered dozens, sometimes hundreds of people each day and then came home to small apartments crowded with extended family—grandparents, cousins, children, friends—making them both extremely vulnerable to contracting the virus and extremely likely to spread it.

As early as March 22, when New York shut down, she was issuing warnings—that Trump would cost lives unless he invoked the Defense Production Act, a wartime measure that federalizes the manufacture and distributions of war supplies. There were nearly 10,000 known cases in New York City; 63 people had died. At the time, that seemed like a lot, but Ocasio-Cortez had a feeling that it would get worse. Hospitals were short on face masks, gloves, ventilators, and beds, she said one day on CNN, appearing unflappable. "We cannot wait until people start really dying in large numbers to start this production" of medical equipment. "We need to start production right now to get ready for the surge that is coming in two to three weeks."

Two days later, she was back on *All In With Chris Hayes*, talking about the $2 trillion relief bill on the table. She was "very concerned" about the shape of the bill, she said, which contained insufficient provisions for working people. She wanted meatier stimulus checks, paid sick leave, and mortgage and rent moratoriums. She wanted restrictions put on the corporate recipients of federal money, so they couldn't invest it to increase their wealth or receive it without agreeing to worker protections, such as extensions of health benefits and commitments to refrain from layoffs. She expressed concern about the small-business owners—the storefronts and food trucks in NY-14, the mom-and-pop shops, like the one her father owned—who, even if the relief bill were passed, wouldn't see meaningful help for months. "What we risk if we don't get this right—*if we do not get this right*—we risk small businesses across the country shutting down and big businesses experiencing a total payday with lack of accountability," she said. "And that will create a generational issue. If we think income inequality is bad now, we really need to make sure that we get this right to prevent the worst possible outcome."

Three days later, the Senate passed the bill and Ocasio-Cortez was venting on Twitter. "This is a frightening amount of public money to have given a corrupt admin w/0 accountability."

On the day of the House vote, Ocasio-Cortez stood up in the chamber, again wearing all white. She looked like a prophet or a medium tapping a deep well of popular fury. She had something to say for the record. Ocasio-Cortez can be sassy in her anger, and she can be steely, but she is rarely as agitated and emotional as she was on that day, her hands and arms waving as if they were independent of her. What infuriated her as much as the insufficient help the Senate was offering the working people of NY-14—who stood, in her mind, for working people everywhere—was that she and the other progressive dissenters in Congress were being cornered, given an impossible choice: either further enrich the companies that least need enriching or fail to help the people who most need help.

She had one minute. "I represent one of the hardest-hit communities in the hardest-hit city in this country," she said. "Thirteen dead in a night in Elmhurst hospital alone. Our community's reality is this country's future if we don't do anything. Hospital workers do not have protective equipment, we don't have the necessary ventilators, but we have to go into this vote eyes wide open. What did the Senate majority fight for? One of the largest corporate bailouts with as few strings as possible in American history. Shameful! The greed of that fight is wrong. For crumbs! For our families. And the option that we have is to either let them suffer with nothing or to allow this greed and billions of dollars, which will be leveraged into trillions of dollars to contribute to the largest income-inequality gap in our future. There should be *shame* about what was fought for in this bill and the choices that we have to make. And I yield."

Ocasio-Cortez voted "no" on the bill, again the only Democratic member to do so, and she voted "no" on supplementary funds the following month—again all alone, after a number of her progressive colleagues indicated they might join her. In her district, she was fundraising for food pantries and making deliveries herself, masked and hauling groceries up stairs, and she made an Instagram video insisting on health care for all. She speaks frequently about a conversation she had with Barbara Lee before entering Congress, when she asked the 11-term representative from California how she found the fortitude after 9/11 to vote "no" on the Authorization for Use of Military Force Act—the single "no" vote—because she believed it gave the president too much power to wage war. Ocasio-Cortez took Lee's response to heart. "You really have to pick your corner and to stand on it, and eventually everyone tends to come around to you," Lee said.

But in the moment, as a human, "I was just, like, heartbroken," she told an interviewer. "Our brains are just designed to experience a lot of excruciating pain at the idea of being alone," she continued. "When you cast those lonely votes, you feel like your colleagues

respect you less, and that you are choosing to marginalize yourself."
On the day of the vote, "I walked home in the rain," she said. "I was
very in my feelings, big time, and I felt very discouraged."

• • •

Bernie Sanders folded up his campaign on April 8, 2020, making
the announcement via a remote feed from his home in Vermont. He
was grateful to all the volunteers, the donors, the texters, the
phone-bankers, the surrogates, he said, but a path to victory did not
exist. He called winning "virtually impossible." Sanders understood
that his most ardent supporters would want him to keep fighting, he
said, but under the circumstances, with COVID mushrooming and
the president incompetent, he could not in good conscience keep
battling on. He would focus in the Senate on trying to get Americans
help, and he would continue to collect delegates in order to exert
leverage at the convention in August. In the video, he didn't hesitate.
He threw his support behind Biden, whom he called "a decent man."

The emergence of Biden as the nominee added a new degree of
difficulty to Ocasio-Cortez's already heart-stopping high-wire act.
She didn't think much of him at the time yet had no option but to
back him. She found him "middle of the road" on climate, said he
had "work to do" with women and that, in general, the idea of him
running didn't "particularly animate" her. Biden was the kind of
politician she had entered Congress to unseat, a centrist who preached
calm and unity, for whom bipartisan agreement was the highest goal,
whose very existence seemed predicated on keeping everything cool.
"What are you supposed to answer Trump with?" she once asked.
"Settle down?"

This was a real question, and it would plague her through the
summer of 2020, as COVID hospitalizations and deaths rose in

NY-14; as federal relief for families ran dry; as the murder of George Floyd propelled millions out of quarantine to march; and as one of the most consequential presidential elections in U.S. history loomed. If ever there were a moment to back revolution, this would be it, and yet Ocasio-Cortez had a different brief. She—who started in politics as an outside agitator—was an elected official who needed to ensure a Joe Biden win. The moment Bernie Sanders stepped out of the race, the pressure to the left of Ocasio-Cortez mounted. How would she hold Biden to account?

Biden reached out to Ocasio-Cortez, and on May 13 he announced she would help lead his climate-change task force. Her partner would be a septuagenarian aristocrat, the former secretary of State and presidential candidate John Kerry. She said yes.

Two weeks later, on May 26, the day after the murder by police of George Floyd, she tweeted "#GeorgeFloyd should be alive . . . The status quo is killing us." Four days after that, walking through the city at a brisk pace with a surgical mask dangling from her right ear, she had a thing or two to say on Instagram Live to the people who were calling for an end to the "unrest" in New York City. The past few nights had been tense and violent. Protesters had broken store windows, while police used batons and tear gas and rubber bullets on civilians, corralled them behind barriers, pushed them down into the street, and, in at least one case, drove vehicles through the crowd.

Ocasio-Cortez wanted to point out a few things about structural inequality for the edification of those who called for calm. Poverty is violence, she said. Lack of access to housing is violence. Denial of health care is violence. The people who were calling for peace had better also be working to remediate these realities. "If you don't call for those things and you're asking for the end of unrest, all you're asking for is the continuation of quiet oppression. I just can't. I *can't* with folks that are saying we need to stop this unrest—we need to stop violence—as though charging someone a thousand dollars a month for insulin that they need to survive isn't violent." Three days later, she was handing out masks at a protest in Queens.

Throughout the summer, Ocasio-Cortez used the hashtag #defundthepolice, a battle cry for the young protesters in solidarity with Black Lives Matter. For Ocasio-Cortez, it was also an extension of her belief in budgets as moral documents. As she put it on morning TV to George Stephanopoulos, "The New York City Police Department has a $6 billion a year budget. That is more than we spend on youth, housing, health care, and homelessness combined."

But #defund was also a provocation. Up in Yorktown Heights, those who knew Ocasio-Cortez as a child felt betrayed. "My husband was a cop," says Lisa Stamatelos, her Girl Scout troop leader. "She had no problem being in this cop's house, and eating this cop's food growing up." Joe Biden didn't like #defund and said he preferred a reform approach rather than a dismantling. In a Gallup poll that summer, 61 percent of Black people said they didn't want the police to spend less time in their neighborhoods. They wanted the police to protect them equally, to regard their safety as their job. The centrist Democrats in the House running for reelection in red districts reviled #defund, and they feared it. Ocasio-Cortez's vocal support of it was putting their political lives at risk, they felt, and possibly those of every Democrat in the House. Trump was tweeting #defund as proof that every Democrat was a "radical."

Even within the progressive left, there was some hand-wringing over her use of #defund. Ocasio-Cortez, they said, had to take more responsibility for her celebrity. She had to recognize that her words and actions attracted more press than those of any one of her peers. Why didn't she use her visibility to promote policies that might be less bold than #defund but were in reality more popular and addressed inequality in specific ways that might meaningfully change people's lives? "She has this bill, the Loan Shark Prevention Act"—co-sponsored with Sanders—"which would literally protect so many people from predatory lending practices," says Marcela Mulholland, the political director of Data for Progress, who had been at the Sunrise protest 18 months earlier. "I wish she was relentless in talking about policies like that, which will then help progressives and Dems build a stronger electoral case." But Ocasio-Cortez did not retreat from #defund.

Then, in July, Ocasio-Cortez shared the policy recommendations from the Biden climate-change task force on Twitter. The environmental platform of the centrist, civility-loving 77-year-old Democratic nominee for president looked and sounded a whole lot like the Green New Deal. It was far more aggressive even than what Bernie Sanders had proposed in 2015. It called for carbon-free power by 2035. It included government-funded infrastructure investment, millions of new jobs, and, within all this, quantitative benchmarks for racial and economic equity. In her tweet, Ocasio-Cortez—who 17 months earlier had struggled to get anyone other than a few stalwart progressives to consider the Green New Deal seriously—took credit. She had done it. She had moved the Overton window. "Among the notable gains: we shaved *15 years* off Biden's previous target for 100% clean energy," she said.[18] *(MORE ON* HOW THE GREEN NEW DEAL CHANGED EVERYTHING, *SEE PAGE 305.)*

When, later, a reporter noted on Twitter that Biden's plan looked a lot like the Green New Deal without the baggage of the Green New Deal—"some political sleight of hand," he wrote—Ocasio-Cortez responded with a wink emoji. "It's almost as if we helped shape the platform," she wrote.

• • •

What are the metaphors for Ocasio-Cortez's political performance during the hot, horrible, historic summer of 2020? A trapeze artist over a shark tank. A climber without a rope. The higher she ascended, the more fatal the risk of her fall—yet she kept strengthening herself.

On July 20, Florida Republican representative Ted Yoho called Ocasio-Cortez a "fucking bitch" on the steps of the Capitol. This was bad, impolite, but the epithet wasn't what pissed her off. After all, she had been called a "fucking bitch," among other such "little comments," a million times before at the restaurant, on the subway, on the streets of New York. She had thrown guys like Ted Yoho out of her bar. After the incident, "I honestly thought I was going to pack it up and go home," she said later. "It's just another day, right?"

No, what pissed her off was Yoho's non-apology, which he later made on the floor of the House. Like a boy caught throwing spitballs in school, he read from a script so quickly and in such a perfunctory monotone that his insincerity radiated off him. He denied he said "fucking bitch." Maybe his remarks had been misconstrued, he said. He implied that, in any case, whatever he said was owed to his passion for causes and his political disagreements with Ocasio-Cortez, whom he didn't specifically name. And he said that, as a father of daughters and a husband to a wife, "I'm very cognizant of my language." Ocasio-Cortez took to the podium the next day. She wanted her remarks, as a matter of personal privilege, to be read into the congressional record for posterity's sake. She had reflected on this matter, she said, and she hoped to make herself very clear. The ordinary, everyday degradation of women was one kind of problem, and for elected officials, including her own colleagues and the president of the United States, to use insulting, violent, and humiliating language was *not acceptable*. But this wasn't what she was here to speak about, and she wasn't going to stay up late waiting for a sincere apology from Ted Yoho, who seemed disinclined to offer one. "What I do have an issue with," she continued, "is using women, our wives and daughters, as shields and excuses for poor behavior. Mr. Yoho mentioned that he has a wife and two daughters. I am two years younger than Mr. Yoho's youngest daughter." Here, Ocasio-Cortez paused, and when she continued, her voice shook. "I am someone's daughter too. My father, thankfully, is not alive to see how Mr. Yoho treated *his* daughter. My mother got to see Mr. Yoho's disrespect on the floor of this House, towards me, on television. And I am here because I have to show my parents that I am *their* daughter. And that they did not raise me to accept abuse from men." No politician has ever described, as succinctly or with so much righteousness, the universal experience of being female.[19] *(MORE ON* AOC'S YOHO SPEECH, *SEE PAGE 309.)*

The Biden camp wasn't sure it wanted Ocasio-Cortez to speak at the Democratic convention. With #defund and #AbolishICE, she was, from an optics point of view, problematic. The convention was to be a showcase for the conversion stories of such Republican leaders as President George W. Bush and former Ohio governor John Kasich, who were abandoning party for the sake of country. Sanders would open the proceedings for the progressive side. "I know the Biden campaign had some hesitation," remembers Faiz Shakir. "Now you're going to put them both up on the stage in a major way and give her more exposure?" Shakir says it was Sanders who made the case for Ocasio-Cortez. "We had to aggressively demand it, and we did, and they gave in." She got fewer than two minutes, prerecorded, and she didn't mention Joe Biden's name.

As Sanders predicted, his most ardent supporters rejected a Biden candidacy. The hashtag #NeverBiden trended on Twitter, and in some of those realms, Ocasio-Cortez was being compared to Obama, an Establishment stooge posing as a progressive. It was these voters, along with others more receptive to her—the young, the alienated, the cynical, and the despairing—whom she addressed after the convention on September 18, the night of Supreme Court Justice Ruth Bader Ginsburg's death.

For so many Americans, the aged and ailing Ginsburg had been a bulwark against the horrors of the Trump era, her tiny body and her enormous intellect evidence that values such as rationality, humanism, and compassion could be deployed for good. Her loss felt like the last straw. And this was the thing Ocasio-Cortez went on IG Live to talk about. Despair was something she understood. Also grief and mistrust of politics and politicians. "If you're a person that's saying, 'I don't know what to do right now,' don't worry. We've got you. We will support you. We will help you figure out what to do." But, she added, if young people wanted anything to change, they had to vote. They had to check their registration, make sure it was valid, and go vote. They had to make a list of five people and tell them to vote. They had to call, and write, and tweet, and protest, and join grassroots and community organizations, and vote. This year, and this fight against authoritarianism, was too important to opt out. "We got to leave it all on the field," she said. "Now is not the moment for cynicism, now is not the moment for hopelessness, now is not the moment to give up. We do not give up." She spoke in paragraphs, without preparation, as if she were right there in the kitchen with each of her 5.6 million viewers, one-on-one.

"What I'm here to say is that this year—this election—voting for someone, voting for Joe Biden is not about whether you agree with him. It's a vote to let our democracy live another day." A vote for Biden was a step in the direction of protecting immigrants and the victims of police violence, trans people and McDonald's employees who aren't earning a living wage. "I'm not here to ask you to say that any one politician is the answer because no one politician is the answer. No one president is the answer. You. Are. The answer."[20] *(MORE ON* THE RBG LIVESTREAM, *SEE PAGE 314.)* The following month, Ocasio-Cortez doubled down on her call to young voters by playing "Among Us" on Twitch.

In the final tally, 52 to 55 percent of American ages 18 to 29 voted in the 2020 election, compared to 42 to 44 percent in 2016. Eighty-seven percent of Black voters in that age group voted for Biden, 83 percent of Asians, and 73 percent of Latinos. Among white youth, Biden's share was lower: 51 percent.

In the aftermath, centrist Democrats in Congress blamed Ocasio-Cortez for the loss of 13 House seats by campaigning on socialism and #defund. "We need to not ever use the word *socialist* or *socialism* ever again," Representative Abigail Spanberger said on a call. Spanberger had barely squeaked by to win her seat. "We will get fucking torn apart in 2022."

Ocasio-Cortez pushed back, saying she was tired of working with people who were hostile to her politics. And she blamed the party for being technologically challenged. "Republicans levied very effective rhetorical attacks against our party. That, I believe, is absolutely true," she said. But the Democratic Party had become too out of touch to mount effective counterattacks. "Our digital campaigning is very weak," she said. "The Democratic Party is still campaigning largely as though it's 2005. And I know a lot of us don't want to hear this, but 2005 was 15 years ago." Trump won in 2016, she pointed out, because of his proficiency on Twitter.

• • •

Heading into the New Year, the activist left was watching Ocasio-Cortez with caution. She had attained her prominence by promising them allegiance. Then she made good on those promises by entering Congress with a symbolic rebellion—the Sunrise sit-in at Pelosi's office. But by the winter of 2021, she was a second-term congress-woman holding the dubious distinction of having created some day-light between herself and Sanders and for working in her way as a Biden surrogate. What could she—would she—do to prove she wasn't like every other politician, co-opted by the incrementalism she had vowed to fight against?

A small collection of visible leftist activists, including Briahna Joy Gray, who ran communications for Sanders in 2020, and the come-dian Jimmy Dore, called for Ocasio-Cortez and the Squad to threaten a "no" vote on Pelosi as Speaker unless Pelosi forced a vote on Medi-care for All. In the midst of the pandemic, with (at that point) more than 300,000 Americans dead, these activists saw a strategic oppor-tunity to draw the attention of the country to the issue, and to the gap, as Gray put it, between what Americans wanted and what their politicians were willing to do. The idea was to enter the 117th Con-gress with another high-profile revolt and push the national conver-sation further left. Other members of this leftist alliance, including the NFL running back Justin Jackson, joined the calls to turn up the pressure. "Power concedes nothing without a demand," Jackson tweeted, quoting Frederick Douglass.

Ocasio-Cortez said no way. Political realities were different now. With Trump in charge, all she—or any other Democratic legislator—could do was raise her voice in protest while building numbers, force, and arguments in exile to mount a future counterattack. But now, with Biden in the Oval Office and Democrats poised to take over Congress, there was the hope of getting stuff done, even if there were still not enough votes in the House to pass Medicare for All. She used the phrase "opportunity cost." "So you issue threats, hold your vote, and lose. Then what?" she tweeted. She preferred to hold her fire for the fight over the $15 federal minimum wage and other attainable goals. In the furthest circles of the left, young people rolled their eyes. The hashtag #fraudsquad began to circulate.

Was she winning or losing? With the Democrats in charge of both Houses of Congress and the White House, it became harder to tell. The left insisted on ideological purity, that she set the standard, morally, for how government should be. She should continue to deploy her communication skills in the service of the long game. "If you want AOC to flex some power, it's not going to come from playing the inside game," says Briahna Joy Gray, in an interview. "There are costs to playing the inside game. There are sacrifices that have to be made."

Being a legislator, especially amid the multiple, cascading crises that have beset the nation in the past decade, and especially as a person so young, is *hard*, Gray concedes. "It must weigh on her shoulders heavily, especially because she is a member of her community in a way that not every legislator is. And every day, she has people calling and coming into her office, and she looks at people in the face who are dealing with horrible tragedies that she has an ability to weigh in on or alleviate." With real power comes the ability to fix things for people in the moment and set principle aside. The test of that power, for an empath like Ocasio-Cortez, comes not in hobnobbing with the rich and influential but in encountering human grief and loss in individual cases. Gray continues, "The more you have those kinds of exposures, the easier it is to say, 'It's worth making the compromise because I changed this life, and this life is not an abstraction.' What you see less acutely is a longer arc of history and the extent to which constantly failing to uphold a kind of litmus test for the party and the kinds of policies we should be fighting for prevents the arc from bending in a direction that ultimately is going to impact many, many more lives. You're saying, *I'm going to potentially jeopardize the health or safety or comfort of someone today in the hope that this game of political chicken is going to pay off five or ten years from now.* And you don't know if it's going to pay off."

When, several weeks after Biden's inauguration, the fight for the $15 minimum wage came up as part of his $1.9 trillion COVID-relief bill, it became collateral damage in politics as usual. Biden had run on raising the wage, but as the bill came to the floor, he said that it might not pass muster with Senate budgetary rules—an indication that he would not fight for the provision, which happened to be a deal-breaker for Republicans and some Democrats. As Biden predicted, the Senate parliamentarian excluded the provision, and the Squad, who had insisted on $15 but declined to hold Pelosi hostage, had to choose. Kick the fight for $15 down the road or vote "no" on the new bill. "It wasn't helpful that there was a signaling from the administration that $15 might not stay in there," Omar said later.

Ocasio-Cortez went on Twitter and called for the parliamentarian to be fired or overruled. She also declared she would never compromise on $15. "'Oooooh, AOC,'" she said later, "'*por que* you don't compromise?' $15 *is* the compromise." But she voted for the bill. And then she went on Instagram Live to celebrate it. "You know what? Let's take our wins when we can get them. It's ok to say when good things happen. We don't have to be a negative Nancy all the time," she said. "This is major. Major."

If, a year earlier, when she was walking home in the rain feeling the excruciating isolation of her "no" votes, she had been able to craft a COVID relief bill from the ground up, it would have borne some resemblance to this one. There were $1,400 stimulus checks for almost every American and extra cash for single mothers with children.

"While it's less money" than the $2,000 checks progressives wanted, "more people are going to get it," she said. "We played a little hardball with those conservative Democrats in the Senate." There were retirement protections for union workers, extension and expansion of unemployment benefits, aid for Native Americans and for Black farmers, infrastructure investment and infusions of cash to municipalities. There was rent relief, mortgage relief, COBRA relief, and student-debt relief—a provision "that feels like an Easter egg, which I think gives us some hope" that student-debt cancellation might turn into reality: "Someone's paving the path. Progressives are looking out for you."

Ocasio-Cortez was especially proud of a provision she personally fought for that gave direct help to her constituents in NY-14: up to $9,000 to cover funeral expenses for each COVID death. "I lost my dad when I was about 18 years old," she said on the livestream. "My family couldn't afford it, and we spent years—years—just trying to dig ourselves out." During the apex of COVID in NY-14, morgues and hospitals were so overrun that bodies had to be stored in refrigerator trucks, and the families of the dead received bills for the storage. "Keep your receipts. Keep your documentation," Ocasio-Cortez said. "No one should ever have to pay for that. That is not your fault."

Minimum wage, health care for all—these would have to be fights for another day. "Do I think that our party should be this conservative? No, I don't. But it is what it is right now."

• • •

A couple of weeks before Christmas 2020, after Joe Biden won the election but before Trump conceded his loss, on the fourth anniversary of her trip to Standing Rock, Ocasio-Cortez made another impromptu social media appearance. It had been a while since she'd

*January 7, 2021:
Ocasio-Cortez bows her
head during a closing
prayer of a joint
session of Congress to
confirm Electoral
College votes.*

cooked for people, and she had the ingredients for salmon pasta on hand. In a bit of fashion forecasting, her sweatshirt said "Tax the Rich." She put on water to boil, but on this night, cooking wasn't really on her mind. She was preoccupied with the way the right had co-opted the word *radical,* so that the things they wanted were perceived to be regular and the things she wanted were on the dangerous fringe. "If I was, like, a clean-cut white dude saying we should cancel student-loan relief, it would be seen as like automatically more normal," she said, indicating a short, groomed haircut with her hand. How had America gotten to a place where it was normal to regard it as the government's duty to bail out "billionaires and people with ten helipads and, you know—whatever—then leaving their inheritance so their cat can have a butler?" She pointed to her T-shirt. "How about we *Tax. The. Rich?*"

They are questions always asked of an era's immense talents: When did they realize how influential they had become, and how did they understand their responsibility? In just two and a half years, Ocasio-Cortez had become a force field, massive, eternally in the nation's leftward peripheral vision and making any political calculation impossible without first considering her and her contingent. She wields her celebrity and her ability to unleash the fury of a leftist generation like a warrior, proving her strength with a shrug. In February 2021, she humiliated her nemesis Ted Cruz after the nation discovered his plans to vacation at a Mexican resort when the Texas power grid failed and his constituents were freezing to death. She held what amounted to an anti-Cruz fundraiser online on behalf of the people in Texas, and from her home about 1,700 miles away raised $5 million in three days. Then, to put a point on it, she flew down to Texas herself and handed out food.

As she attains her maturity, she faces complaints, apart from her ability or willingness to stay ideologically pure. In NY-14, her celebrity is seen as a double-edged sword. On the one hand, yes, her visibility redounds to her district, so that the problems and solutions there can receive national attention. Contrary to Pelosi's initial critique that Ocasio-Cortez's triumph over Crowley did not represent some larger shift in the country, the people of NY-14 have become, because of Ocasio-Cortez's constant invocation of them, representative of working people everywhere. And the residents of NY-14 mostly claim their star with pride. But her massive celebrity is an impediment to approachability, and that's felt on the ground. "When she first got elected, she was so much more accessible, and things escalated quickly," says Andrew Sokolof Diaz, who runs a tenants organization in Queens. "She had to change her whole home style. She couldn't stay in places too long. She's had countless threats against her, and that immediately changed how she was able to be present." A district rep who is too huge to be local is a different problem from Crowley, but the resulting sense of practical absence can feel the same.

On the Hill, the rap is that the Ocasio-Cortez office is in disarray—beset by staff changes, impossible to get a quick answer from or to schedule anything with. This is the downside of being a celebrity who is constantly in demand. Since the departure of Chakrabarti and Trent, widely celebrated as a positive move ("I think that let her really come into her own," Katie Hill says), Hill staffers have been unsure of who's helping Ocasio-Cortez make decisions.

But Faiz Shakir, who ran the Sanders campaign in 2020, believes this is temporary, part of an organic maturation process. Ocasio-Cortez is "the future president, to be honest," he says. She's got "real power here. If she gives a thumbs-up or thumbs-down, it can surely change the course of history. She can be a hell of a lot more powerful and stronger in the years ahead. She can move the dial, change political outcomes." The next step, he says, is to assert her influence beyond demanding change. She needs to make it. "Does she popularize the campaign for climate change, or does she actually enact a policy proposal that changes our energy and environmental future?" To do that, she needs to get off what Shakir calls "the Twitter machine" and build relationships. She needs to get on the phone.

She's getting there. Nydia Velázquez, the representative from New York City who initially counseled her to make friends in Congress or risk the consequences, has been watching her progress. Together, she and Ocasio-Cortez have been working on the Puerto Rico Self-Determination Act. Throughout the spring of 2021, they regularly scheduled 15 or 20 minutes in Velázquez's office, and Ocasio-Cortez always stayed much longer than that. "It's not about issues," Velázquez reflects. "It's about us." A colleague recently approached Velázquez to ask: "How is my relationship with her? Can she be trusted?" Velázquez said "yes."

The nattering advice, the guidance, critiques, and helpful suggestions—they matter, but, of course, they also don't matter. Ocasio-Cortez could drive herself nuts evaluating all the different tactics people want her to consider, all the refinements they wish she would make. It's natural that people desire her to be better, or different, or hew more closely to the lines they draw.

But the truth is that she is already a powerhouse, unprecedented in her origin story and revolutionary in her practice. From the instant she entered Congress, her colleagues sought to emulate her methods, not the other way around, particularly when it came to reaching younger voters.[21] *(MORE ON AOC'S CLOUT AMONG TEENS, SEE PAGE 316.)* She wasn't in office for three weeks before she held a seminar for them on how to build a social-media following. "Be yourself," she said. And "really write your own tweets so that people know it's you talking."

Such political innovations may seem small, but they are ground-breaking, like individual components of a revolutionary new engine or the chemical combinations in a life-saving drug. Her impact can be measured in her origin story, in how she looks and talks, in what she chooses to wear and how she cuts her hair. It can be proved in the digital platforms she masters to communicate most effectively to her myriad of audiences. But without the human, breathing person of Ocasio-Cortez herself—the cells in her body, the beating of her heart, the sharpness of her mind, and her relentless, seething insistence on casting policies as moral necessities—these adaptations might be regarded in retrospect as temporary fashions. It was Ocasio-Cortez who ultimately collected the fractious progressive left under her command.

Without Ocasio-Cortez, there would be fewer women and fewer people of color in Congress. The millennial generation and its successors would not define their fidelity to progressive causes in relation to her. The Squad, ever expanding, would not exist, and the broader Congressional Progressive Caucus would not be a power bloc to be reckoned with in the legislative arena, with the ability to deliver or withhold the votes to pass a bill or tank it. Without Ocasio-Cortez, Pramila Jayapal, the CPC chair, would not be a household name.

The ascent of Ocasio-Cortez does not mean that progressives will ultimately win the big legislative battles, of course, or that their idealistic vision will prevail. America is in an existential war with itself over its present identity and its future survival, and beyond certain left-leaning villages (and even within them), many progressive priorities—and their messengers—continue to terrify moderates and send them fleeing to the other side. No matter how passionately Ocasio-Cortez articulates and maintains her positions, some inside her party—and most outside it—may always regard her as a threat to their safety, their security, and their wealth. So even if she can acquire a taste for diplomacy and compromise—if she wants to or believes it can serve her causes—she will always be fodder for the opposition. The making of legislation is an essentially dirty, unprincipled game unsuited to empaths or perfectionists. But among her other attributes, Ocasio-Cortez possesses the mettle required to lose, again and again, to be humiliated and infuriated in public and nevertheless to stick to her principles in the face of overwhelming and often cruel opposition. The Trump years, for better and worse, seem to have hardened her. Since Ocasio-Cortez entered Congress when she was 29 years old, so many of her priorities, once deemed "radical," have become the stipulated nonnegotiables of the mainstream left. Biden's climate-change plan resembles the Green New Deal in almost every way but its name. Cities all over America are rethinking the way they protect, punish, and deploy the police. Two-thirds of Americans support a $15 minimum wage, and in his first hundred days, Biden raised the wage to $15 for all federal employees. And in what was perhaps the most extraordinary, but certainly not the last, display of the scope of her influence, in the fall of 2021, Biden, the quintessential white-guy moderate, threw his support behind Ocasio-Cortez and the CPC in their battle to join a roads-and-bridges bill with a slate of climate remedies and social protections for poor and working families, which they planned to pay for by raising taxes on the rich.

Ocasio-Cortez is sensitive, and she wears the scars of political warfare in public. Over the years, her IG Lives have become anodyne: Her backdrops are neutral, her location obscure; her delivery is brittle and careful, as if someone is whispering warnings in her ear. These are safety precautions, to be sure, but also a protective adaptation, a disinclination to expose herself, her emotionalism, and her kitchen spices to the critics and the fans. The vulnerability and authenticity that catapulted her to celebrity have become, by necessity, a more manufactured, managed thing. And yet she cannot completely insulate herself or her public from the anguish of the choices she has to make, and so after she voted "present" on a vote to fund the Israeli military, abandoning her sisters in the Squad and the constituents who were counting on her strong and righteous "no," she stood in the congressional chamber and she wept.

She often insists she does not know her plans for the future. She might not stay in electoral politics at all. "I'm serious when I tell people the odds of me running for higher office and the odds of me just going off trying to start a homestead somewhere—they're probably the same." This is the not-giving-a-fuck that she talks about, the deep source of her power. And people who know her say that it's true: Her ambition does not trend in the usual directions. Yet watching her rip into Zuckerberg or dismantle Yoho, or observing her on her living-room couch anguishing over detainees at the border, it's evident that not caring is only half of the truth. She does care—deeply—which is why she doesn't eat or drink enough sometimes and what people respond to in her, why they idolize, follow, and fear her. The way Ocasio-Cortez plays it, politics has meaning. It is not a cynical game. She maneuvers through her everyday on a tightrope, caring and not caring just enough to keep her balance and not fall to bits.

• • •

Fragility and mortality are part of any story of ascent, and Ocasio-Cortez wanted to tell people how it really was the day that she thought she was going to die. She wanted to say that on January 6, 2021, on a Wednesday when she was just doing her job, racist mobs entered the Capitol Building and hunted her as if she were prey. In a political screed and personal catharsis unlike anything American politics had ever seen, she went on Instagram Live on February 2 and spoke for 89 minutes. The background behind her was gray—it gave nothing away, not even the city or state she was in.[22] *(MORE ON THE CAPITOL INSURRECTION, SEE PAGE 320.)*

On the morning of the 6th, Ocasio-Cortez said, she had been feeling good. Their job that day was purely procedural—to ratify the state-by-state results of the general election, the last step before ushering Biden into office. She carpooled with Ayanna Pressley, arriving at the Capitol a little past nine. Things were slow, everyone operating in the pandemic with a scaled-back staff, and Ocasio-Cortez figured she would use her time productively. She got her second dose of the COVID vaccine, took some video with plans to upload it later, and then started scrolling through takeout menus to see if she could order in a nice lunch for the lone staffer who had pulled office duty that day.

No one on Capitol Hill was more familiar with the threatening and violent impulses of the Trump-enabled nationalist right, but somehow, for some reason, Ocasio-Cortez was feeling calm that morning, after a week of mounting anxiety. Friends and colleagues had been texting her, warning her of the Trump supporters who were expected to descend on Washington to protest the ratification of the election results. She would be an obvious target. But Capitol security had assured members that it had it in hand.

A few days earlier, Ocasio-Cortez had encountered a group of Trump loyalists milling around her car—"all these people with, like, these huge flagpoles with the spear tips and whatnot"—and again in the grocery store where she went to buy a matcha tea and get her parking ticket validated. "It literally felt like people were looking at me in the grocery store, deciding what they were going to do. Like,

Are we going to do something right now? I could see the calculations going on behind their eyes. It was a hundred percent like when you're in a bodega at one o'clock in the morning and you don't know if someone's about to get jumped. It felt like that."

What even some of her closest friends didn't know, because she had never told them, was that Ocasio-Cortez had been a victim of sexual assault. This was that old habit, which came up in her descriptions of her grief at the death of her father, of locking pain away while pushing relentlessly forward and then being hijacked by hurt in the aftermath. And so, as she was sitting in her office, scrolling menus on her phone, with the pro-Trump crowds gathering outside the walls of the Capitol and her firsthand knowledge of their predilection for violence, the anxieties of the previous week compounded with the old, hidden trauma. And that's when she heard a huge and terrifying thud on the door. "Like someone was trying to break the door down. There were no voices. There were no yells. No one saying who they were." Her staffer looked at her and said, "Hide."

She had appeared vulnerable before, but on this livestream she stripped herself bare, as if she needed the world to know what it was like to be a democratically elected member of Congress, hiding in her office bathroom and afraid for her life. She wanted her audience to see, and to grasp as viscerally as she did in this moment, that the nation had been assaulted by Trump, his cronies, and his mob in exactly the same way—and with the same language, defenses, and denials—with which men have historically abused and assaulted women forever. Her monologue could have been called a trauma dump, but she deflected that critique by facing it down. "I'm in a job where people are constantly calling me untruthful or that I'm exaggerating," she said on the livestream, but "I'm not going to let it happen to me again. I'm not going to let it happen to the other people who've been victimized by this situation again. And I'm not going to let this happen to our country. Ever."

What happened next was like a scene from "a zombie movie or something." Ocasio-Cortez hid in her bathroom as a white man entered her office, bellowing "Where is she?" He turned out to be a police officer, but she didn't realize that at first, and when she finally came out of hiding he was hostile before instructing her to join her peers in another location without specifying where. Ocasio-Cortez and her staffer then ran through the vacant halls and tunnels of the Capitol, she in high heels, as the mob encroached—she could hear them screaming outside—looking for some safe haven but determined not to gather with other members of Congress who might be sympathetic to the insurgents and reveal her location.

Ocasio-Cortez described running down a long, empty hallway with nowhere to hide, "fully expecting one of these insurrectionists to turn the corner with a gun," when she saw her colleague Katie Porter entering her office after grabbing some coffee. Ocasio-Cortez pounded on Porter's door, and Porter invited Ocasio-Cortez in, giving her some gym clothes and sneakers to change into, so that if Ocasio-Cortez had to run for her life, she could. Ocasio-Cortez, in shock and terrified, started "opening every closet, I'm opening every nook, I'm opening, like, every cranny, looking for where I'm going to hide when they get into this office," while staffers pushed furniture up against the door. Porter said later that she was surprised to see Ocasio-Cortez unraveling; she usually came across so poised.

"Don't worry," Porter said. "I'm a mom. I've got everything here we need. We could live for, like, a month in this office."

"I just hope I get to be a mom," Ocasio-Cortez responded. "I hope I don't die today."

Her terror stayed with her all day, until police had secured the building and the mob had been dispersed, and for hours after that, even when she finally connected with Ayanna Pressley, who gave her some food. Her colleagues were tweeting that they were safe, they were okay, but Ocasio-Cortez's feeds were silent. Her mind kept circling back to the bathroom and her belief that the man who entered her office would find her and kill her. "Maybe it was four seconds, maybe it was five seconds, maybe it was ten seconds. It felt like my brain was able to have so many thoughts in that moment," she said. And then that familiar feeling settled upon her, like grace. The caring. And the detachment from caring. "I really just felt like, you know, if this is the plan for me, then people will be able to take it from here." She is speaking to her phone, with more than 6 million people watching, and she is weeping. "I had a lot of thoughts, but that was the thought I had about you all. I felt that I—if this was the journey that my life was taking—I felt that things were going to be okay, and that, you know, I had fulfilled my purpose."

And...

Bernie Sanders . . . The Boyfriend . . . A Graphic
Trip to the Border . . . The American Left . . . Dunks . . .
Instagram Feeds . . . and more.

1

Puerto Rico:

A Child
of
Borinquén

〜〜〜

By

ANDREA GONZÁLEZ-RAMÍREZ

To be Puerto Rican is to be an amal-
gam of contradictions; to be
fiercely protective and proud of a
national identity that is complicated by a
painful legacy of colonization. Alexandria
Ocasio-Cortez has often spoken of living
between two worlds: the Bronx and Westchester, the edge of poverty and financial
stability, her work as a grassroots organizer

and now inside government. But she is also a child of *Borinquén*, and her relationship to the oldest colony in the world might be the most paradoxical part of her private and professional identity. "I am a third-generation Bronxite. I am a Latina, I am a *boricua*," Ocasio-Cortez said when she launched her congressional bid. "I am a descendant of Taíno Indians. I am a descendant of African slaves. I am proud to be an American, but we have to rise to that promise."

Both the United States and Puerto Rico are impossible homelands. Many Puerto Ricans born outside the archipelago like Ocasio-Cortez grow up with their hearts split in two, loving both the land of the free and its colony—never fully belonging to either. *Diásporriqueños* experience the pain of being perceived as an outsider despite how connected one might be to their ancestral home, and are simultaneously othered in the U.S. regardless of how deeply their roots run Stateside. *El español masticao* of Ocasio-Cortez—her imperfect Spanish—sets her immediately apart from island-born *boricuas*, while her critics often tell her to go back to where she came from. "A lot of my life was defined by my experiences in the island," she said in an interview with Puerto Rican newspaper *El Nuevo Día*, "and having an identity, not only as a Latina but also a *boricua*, is something very special and unique." If you know where to look, that influence is as clear in her life as her oft-touted working-class background or progressive credentials: It's reflected in how she refuses to whitewash her name, going by both her father and mother's surnames; in how she avoids the euphemisms that her congressional colleagues use to describe Puerto Rico's colonial status; in how she wears a pin of the Puerto Rican flag next to her American one; and most famously how, on the day she was sworn in as the 14th District's congresswoman, Ocasio-Cortez showed up to Capitol Hill dressed head-to-toe in suffragette white, with thick gold hoops and lips the color of red *carmesí*—the uniform of scores of Puerto Rican women before her. "The youngest woman to ever serve in Congress is a *boricua*," said Democratic congressman Darren Soto, the first Puerto Rican to represent Florida in Congress. "That's historic."

• • •

Her paternal grandparents, Sergio Ocasio Sr. and Thamar Neirida Ocasio, left their home in the northern town of Arecibo, Puerto Rico, to try their luck in *La Gran Manzana* in the mid-20th century. Their story of *brincar el charco*—leap across the pond—is a story so common it has been captured in Puerto Rican lore from "La Carreta" to *West Side Story* to *La Guagua Aérea*. "New York City was always the magnet. It was always the main Puerto Rican settlement in the U.S.," said Dr. Carlos Vargas-Ramos, a social scientist who works at CUNY's Center for Puerto Rican Studies.

The Ocasios settled in the South Bronx, where in 1959 their son Sergio was born. He came of age as the Nuyorican identity began to take shape, a time of radical politics and the community activism of the Young Lords, of explicit discrimination against *boricuas*, and of the Bronx, with its large Puerto Rican and Black population, literally on fire. "The children of those migrants from the post–World War II generation were reacting to the conditions they experienced as second-class citizens in the United States. They were trying to figure out, 'Why is it that I'm not getting equal treatment? Why is it that my culture is degraded?'" Vargas-Ramos said. As a result, Stateside-born *boricuas* held on even tighter to their culture and traditions, flying the Puerto Rican flag every chance they could. "These became symbols of resistance," Vargas-Ramos added.

Sergio grew up traveling to Puerto Rico frequently, and it was on one of those trips that he met Blanca Cortez. The 20-somethings quickly fell in love

and married in Sergio's family home of Arecibo. Blanca, who didn't speak English, soon joined Sergio in the Bronx, and on October 13, 1989, their daughter, Alexandria, was born, followed a few years later by their son, Gabriel.

"I grew up with a very strong sense of patriotism. A very strong sense of *we are American*," she told *Latino USA*. "I also was raised, 'You're *boricua*, like through and through.'" On Thanksgiving, the family served turkey and *pernil*, the classic special-occasion dish of roasted pork. The salsa of Celia Cruz and Héctor Lavoe blasted through the speakers at family parties, and often the adults played dominoes as the night drew to a close. Ocasio-Cortez grew up celebrating *el Día de los Tres Reyes Magos* with the same gusto she welcomed Santa Claus, and singing "Sana, Sana" as a good-luck charm.

Despite their financial woes, Sergio and Blanca made sure to travel together to the island every year with their children—taking in the marvel that once was the Arecibo Observatory; spending time in the tourist areas of Vieques, even as parts of the island town were still being bombed by the U.S. Navy; and enjoying hot, humid afternoons in the rainforest El Yunque. When needed, the children were sent ahead to the Caribbean, partly a way to outsource childcare they couldn't afford in the summertime. It is a familiar pilgrimage for children of the diaspora: Ocasio-Cortez's summer days were spent running downhill with her cousins in the sweltering heat before sitting down for big family dinners of *arroz con habichuelas*. As a young adult, Ocasio-Cortez still made the point of visiting at least once a year. "You know you're in Puerto Rico when you ride your cousin's horse in flip flops," she tweeted in 2011. An activity in rural Puerto Rico that is as natural as breathing air.

The experience proved formative in other ways, too. During those summers, Ocasio-Cortez would attend Pentecostal service with her extended family, a world away from the Catholic faith in which she was raised in New York. "We'd be in this van, kind of on these careening muddy roads to get to the top of the mountain and a small, kind of tucked-away church," she said in an interview with Dr. Cornel West and Professor Tricia Rose.

Ocasio-Cortez's focus on community organizing, too, mirrors the activism of *boricua* women throughout history. "Puerto Rican women, and Latinas in general, have expanded what we consider politics. Canvassing on the street, knocking on doors, going to community meetings, union involvement," said Julie Torres, an assistant professor of women's and ethnic studies at the University of Colorado. A young Ocasio-Cortez learned this type of advocacy from her parents. Though Sergio and Blanca were not outwardly political, they would often welcome the cashiers from the local Dunkin' Donuts into their Westchester home, and serve *cafecitos* while talking about how to help one another and the community at large. "They were always about leaning in to people. And the politics comes second," she told *Latino USA*. "That's how I practice, as well. Even though I feel very strongly about my beliefs, my number one job is to care about people."

One way that she expresses that care is by speaking out, loudly. "Puerto Rican women have also done activism as everyday refusals—quiet or outspoken challenges—to advocate for their families and communities," said Torres. And Ocasio-Cortez has more than tapped into the outspokenness of the *mujeres* before her, firing back at her critics on Twitter and at times calling out her congressional colleagues for everything from negligence to cowardice. And she's not alone.

Her Squad—with Representatives Ayanna Pressley, Ilhan Omar, and Rashida Tlaib—looks like the multiracial, multiethnic alliances that Puerto

Rican activists have forged with Black activists for generations. It is reminiscent of the affinity between the Young Lords and the Black Panthers and others over the past 50 years.

But despite all that, Ocasio-Cortez has also faced questions on whether she's *boricua* enough.

Island-born Puerto Ricans often use one's fluency in Spanish as a standard of authentic *puertorriqueñidad*, and Ocasio-Cortez's dominion of the language is far from perfect: She has a *gringa* accent, and mixes up her singular and plural tenses as often as she incorrectly swaps the gender of many words. Nevertheless, she has not shied away from frequently speaking Spanish in public, "Growing up, Spanish was my first language . . . but like many 1st generation Latinx Americans, I have to continuously work at it & improve," she tweeted after an interview with Spanish-language channel Univision.

More than these personal conflicts, Ocasio-Cortez has been harshly criticized for her public-policy stance with regard to Puerto Rico, some even describing it as an overstep. Because of its status as a so-called U.S. territory, Puerto Rico has no voting representation in Congress and no seats in the Senate. Islanders can't even vote for president. This has forced congressional members of Puerto Rican descent to act as surrogate representatives for the archipelago. Some islanders have come to resent that type of intervention, as they believe American-born congresspeople don't really understand their needs as folks who were not raised in Puerto Rico. Regardless, Ocasio-Cortez has tried to embrace her role as part of the unofficial Puerto Rican delegation in Congress focusing on the issues the island is facing, including the debt crisis, political status, and recovery efforts for natural disasters like the recent Hurricane Maria (which affected Ocasio-Cortez's own family). Unlike most Democrats, she has never pronounced herself in favor of statehood—though her family in Puerto Rico told local newspaper *El Nuevo Día* that it is her preferred option. Glimpses of this inclination peek through when she's talked about the need for more federal funding for Puerto Rico, the unjustness of Puerto Rican voters' disenfranchisement, and the island's colonial status— all in synchronicity with the modern pro-statehood movement. But on paper, she has insisted that it's up to the people of Puerto Rico to determine their own fate.

In conjunction with Representative Nydia Velázquez, the first Puerto Rican woman ever elected to Congress,

Ocasio-Cortez introduced the Puerto Rico Self-Determination Act in March 2021. The bill would allow *boricua* voters to create a status convention in which elected delegates would come up with a long-term decolonizing solution for the island's political status. "The principled position—especially for the head of that colonizing power—is to say that people should have a process of self-determination and to not put your thumb on the scale of one direction or another," Ocasio-Cortez told Axios.

It's no surprise that Ocasio-Cortez has developed a close working relationship with Velázquez, who was born in Puerto Rico's southeastern town of Yabucoa and has represented New York in Congress since Ocasio-Cortez was a child. "She brings so much to the table when it comes to their relationship with young people in this country. She and I, we care deeply about Puerto Rico. I'm very proud of her."

For political anthropologist Yarimar Bonilla, the relationship hints at how Ocasio-Cortez's relationship to Puerto Rico has evolved. "In some ways, her attachment to Nydia Velázquez is a way for her to learn how to develop her political stance towards Puerto Rico in connection with someone more rooted in Puerto Rico," she said. When all is said and done, Ocasio-Cortez will be one of the most famous Puerto Rican women in history. There are plenty of ways in which her rise has been chock-full of symbolism, from the David-versus-Goliath nature of her primary upset over Joe Crowley to the almost messianic quality that many liberals have projected on her since. But it's not exactly a surprise that the symbolism of having a *boricua* becoming the youngest woman ever elected to Congress is lost on many.

As recently as 2017, nearly half of Americans didn't even know that Puerto Ricans were U.S. citizens. Her history-making tenure in Congress is at once the embodiment of the so-called American Dream and a hearty "screw you" from the oldest colony in the world. It's an inherent contradiction, and there's nothing more Puerto Rican than that.

2

The Boyfriend

~~~~~

By

JOSH GONDELMAN

I n the 2019 documentary *Knock Down the House*, the public was introduced to Representative Alexandria Ocasio-Cortez's boyfriend. Well, we weren't *introduced* to him per se so much as a few people spotted him across the room and immediately began plying anyone in sight for information about him. "Who Is AOC's Boyfriend?" explainers popped up on magazine websites. And soon after, many off-brand gossip sites, whose unfamiliar names seemed more like strong email passwords than the titles of reputable news outlets, joined the SEO gold rush and aggregated the few available details.

Here's most of what we know: His name is Riley Roberts. He's a web developer. He and Alexandria Ocasio-Cortez met while they were in college at Boston University when they both went to hear the dean speak. After graduating, the two broke up for a little while but have been back together for years and are now cohabitating. In *Knock Down the House*, we see Ocasio-Cortez tell herself, "I can do this." "I know you can," Roberts replies.

Their interactions in the documentary are sweet, and their story is remarkably basic (well, aside from one-half of the couple's rise to national political prominence). Roberts himself seems regular too. He's not a celebrity, nor is he (as far as I know) one of those nauseatingly wealthy non-celebrity types whom you'll see in a photo with Taylor Swift or Rihanna, later finding out from *People* magazine that his grandfather invented cyanide or fracking or whatever and now, as long as he keeps up his CrossFit regimen, he gets to date pop stars. Specifically, Roberts seems Boston Regular. Even though he's

not originally from Massachusetts, with his shaggy red hair and his bushy, because-I-can beard, he seems like a dude you might have seen ten years ago ambling out of Sunset Cantina as one of his friends named Sully bellowed his surname in an unmistakably local accent: *RAWBITS!!!*

Roberts's few moments of screen time in *Knock Down the House* were met, online at least, with a resounding . . . *Him?* . . . which felt unkind to both, well, *him* and to her. Voices from across the internet called their pairing into question and disparaged Roberts's appearance in a way that we are still socially allowed to do with men, but barely. A now-infamous viral tweet likened his appearance to that of a "bin raccoon," which felt especially cruel considering that a raccoon in a trash barrel doesn't even look that different from one in the forest.

The criticism spawned a series of spirited defenses and eventually a tongue-in-cheek post on AOC's Instagram stating that "the internet roasted Riley into getting a haircut/glowup." Outlets from *Refinery29* to the *Daily Mail* covered this makeover, essentially running with the story: "Man Visits Barber." Even the glowup photos featured Roberts in a BU T-shirt, with the university's name printed in typeface reminiscent of the Red Sox logo, which feels like the big reveal in the final scene of a show called *Straight Eye for the Straight Guy.*

After the initial flurry of attention, Roberts has mostly stayed out of the public eye, with the exceptions of two appearances on Representative Ocasio-Cortez's Instagram account. One was the aforementioned glowup. The other was a brief video of him alongside AOC, filmed during an informal Q&A session, in response to a question about "combating racism as a white person." It was blogged about with approval by left-leaning publications and with eye rolls by right-leaning racism factories. After that, Roberts's presence receded to the fringes of Ocasio-Cortez's social-media accounts, the way Jay-Z does when Beyoncé has important Beyoncé work to do.

Roberts is likely afforded a little more privacy as the male partner of a female politician than when the gender roles are reversed. He's subjected to less auxiliary bullshit like the "Wives of House Representatives Flag Day Pie Bake-Off," or whatever its current iteration is. There's less pressure on him to look hot (but modest) in holiday photos or to raise perfect children while heading up a philanthropy initiative to end child trafficking or

eliminate pop-up ads (whichever cause is closer to his heart). He gets to work in web development, a career that is not particularly prestigious or glamorous. Imagine if Dr. Jill Biden had a job doing like . . . business-to-business marketing for a company that sells energy-efficient printers. Actually, I think that would be kind of fun.

Roberts is not, himself, a famous or powerful person. He doesn't seem especially interested in being famous or influential, whether independently or because of his famous and influential girlfriend. He is also not, as far as we know, secretly terrible in a way that compromises his partner's politics; he isn't a vice-president at Amazon, the company Ocasio-Cortez famously sparred with over the location of its new headquarters, which would have made for a modern, if grim, update to *You've Got Mail.* And he's not an Anthony Weiner–type failspouse, more famous for his numerous improprieties and infidelities than his accomplishments at this point. (What did Anthony Weiner do for work again? I want to say celebrity chef?) We don't know *that* much about Riley Roberts, and we don't *need* to.

Given the dearth of information provided, I've been unable to avoid projecting my own thoughts onto Roberts and Ocasio-Cortez. I am always charmed by couples who stay together after one member becomes famous. Doesn't everyone feel that way? I think it's because we like to imagine ourselves acting the same way: remaining loyal, unswayed by the access and opportunity our newfound renown has conferred upon us. It's also nice to see a guy who knows when to stay out of the way and not make himself the center of attention; it's something I should be better at myself. Again, I'm projecting here.

What we do know about Roberts doesn't fit the stereotype of a politician's partner. He doesn't seem focus-grouped or media-trained for state dinners and press conferences. We know he's supportive and encouraging in private. And his expertise, as far as his public image goes, is his elusiveness and restraint. These are both qualities that take strength, but not in the way we think of men as being strong. When a man is quiet, it's traditionally in a stoic, authoritative way, like a rock formation that is also your dad, projecting importance. And when a man is supportive, he's expected to be loud and instructive, like a car alarm that coaches high-school football. But Roberts is, publicly at least, none of these things.

I admire Roberts's tenacious invisibility in large part because I cannot imagine being okay with it. It brings me a lot of joy to see my wife thrive. I'm also chronically plugged in and terminally online, constantly tweeting dumb jokes and even dumber sincere thoughts. My across-the-table whisper comes out at the volume of a TED Talk. And if I'm being honest with myself, I think it would be tough to give all that public persona up in support of my wife's career. And if I'm being even *more* honest with myself (which, yuck, who needs it?), I don't know how much of that need for recognition is inherent to who I am at my core, and how much is just what I'm allowed to get away with as a man. I expect to be able to take up as much social space as I want, regardless of what my wife needs.

Not Riley Roberts though. He's the perfect beta to AOC's alpha—tiptoeing through the public sphere, leaving little evidence of his presence, the social equivalent of a cyclist's carbon footprint. I feel guilty even writing about Riley Roberts; he clearly doesn't want to be written about, and he hasn't done anything to compel me to disrespect his wishes. So I hope from now on we leave him in peace, quietly glowing up in the shine of someone else's star.

3

The Dance
Videos:

"Wait Till They

On January 2, 2019, a
Twitter user posted
a 30-second video of
AOC reenacting the
dance scene from
the movie *The
Breakfast Club*. The
caption read, "Here is
America's favorite
commie know-it-all
acting like the clueless
nitwit she is . . . High
School video of
'Sandy' Ocasio-
Cortez." Though the
video was posted
with the intention of
humiliating AOC, it
had the opposite
effect, making the
Republican scolds
seem out of touch.
The video dated from
her time as an
undergraduate at
Boston College.
    After initially
replying, "You hate

Find Out Congresswomen Dance Too!"

me coz you ain't me, fellas," the next day she posted a response video of herself dancing and lip-syncing outside her congressional office to Edwin Starr's "War." Her accompanying tweet, sent not even 24 hours after being sworn into office, set the tone for the rest of her first term: "I hear the GOP thinks women dancing are scandalous. Wait till they find out Congresswomen dance too! Have a great weekend everyone :)."

4

Bernie Sanders:

First She
Needed Him,
Then He
Needed Her

By

Eric Levitz

I n Wichita, the heart of the Koch
empire, Alexandria Ocasio-Cortez
joined Bernie Sanders in 2018 in
lending support to James Thompson,
who was campaigning to paint the state's
Fourth Congressional District blue. Seeking to assure the crowd that a better

Kansas was possible, AOC recalled how a grade-school history lesson had endeared a 10-year-old girl from the Bronx to their home state. "Kansas was founded in a struggle over the conscience of this nation," she said. The territory could have entered the union as a slave state, but Kansans "chose to be free."

Minutes later, waiting in the wings, AOC watched in disbelief as Sanders named *her* as a reason for believing that Kansas would make that choice again. Her improbable triumph, he declared, had proved that ideas "once considered to be radical are now part of the mainstream."

• • •

A year later, Sanders was in a hospital bed in Nevada, and his second presidential campaign was on life support. At 78, Sanders had faced questions about his fitness for office even before his cardiac episode. After all, the race's other progressive, Elizabeth Warren, was eight years younger than Sanders and polling better with Democratic-primary voters. Surely the Democratic left would now coalesce behind the sprier of its champions.

But the millennial left's standard-bearer would not. While the Warren and Sanders campaigns had both lobbied for AOC's endorsement, she had remained on the sidelines, reluctant to tip the balance of power between two progressive campaigns with disparate strengths. And neither had offered her their endorsement when she had needed it.

Sanders, for his part, had met with AOC in Burlington a few weeks earlier to talk about her priorities. "It just felt like people who just know each other and understand each other," Faiz Shakir, Sanders's campaign manager, told *Politico*. "They have been to some degree within their own caucuses . . . made to feel that they're outsiders looking in. And I think they find common bond in that."

Now, hearing that Sanders was in the hospital, AOC had what she would later describe as a "gut check." The sudden reminder of mortality, she said, threw things "into sharp relief." She wanted "to be part of a mass movement of working-class Americans, and I wanted to be a part of that as quickly as I could."

AOC picked up the phone and dialed Shakir, who passed his phone to Sanders. As the candidate lay in his hospital bed, his former campaign volunteer told him that she was endorsing his candidacy, months before she was expected to pick a side.

"I know what you just went through," she reportedly told Sanders. "But I have so much trust and confidence in you,

*Presidential candidate
and U.S. senator
Bernie Sanders hugs
Representative
Alexandria Ocasio-
Cortez during a
campaign rally in
Ames, Iowa, on
January 25, 2020.*

that you are the one who will fight the fight that I believe in. I'm with you."

AOC had revived Bernie's campaign with a single phone call. When some of his closest aides and allies learned of the endorsement, they burst into tears. Sanders couldn't be old news with the youngest and most dynamic member of Congress on his side. Ocasio-Cortez's endorsement stabilized Sanders's millennial backing when it was at its most precarious. And as the ensuing primary contests would make plain, without the overwhelming support of AOC's demographic, the socialist senator wouldn't have made it much past Iowa.

Yet what made Ocasio-Cortez such an effective emissary to young left-wing Democrats would ultimately cause friction between her and the campaign. Sanders came to Congress from a predominantly white, rural, Republican-friendly state; his political rise involved making tactical alliances with police unions and the National Rifle Association, voicing skepticism about unregulated immigration, and emphasizing issues of class over those of culture. AOC's leftism, by contrast, was shaped by a childhood that gave her a visceral appreciation for the challenges facing marginalized racial groups, and her political base in Queens and the Bronx demanded that she not triangulate on

gun rights, policing, or immigration. The differences came to a head on the stump in Iowa in 2020. Some in the Sanders camp were reportedly irked when AOC made a point of lauding the candidate's commitment to abolishing Immigration and Customs Enforcement, a position the campaign was seeking to downplay. The congresswoman, meanwhile, was reportedly put off by the campaign's decision to tout an endorsement from Joe Rogan, a superstar podcaster with some bigoted remarks in his back catalogue. Shortly thereafter, the campaign began to find AOC less amenable to requests for support on the campaign trail. "It was like pulling teeth to get her to New Hampshire," one source told HuffPost.

Neither AOC nor Sanders ever aired these grievances on the record. And any quarrels did not seem to cause any lasting damage to their alliance. At the Democratic National Convention, AOC was given two minutes in prime time to formally second the nomination of Sanders. The senator's campaign slogan was "Not Me. Us," and the congresswoman spent her 60 seconds paying tribute to "us"—to every overworked bartender, underpaid organizer, undocumented Dreamer, striking teacher, alienated zoomer, and miscellaneous millennial who had helped turn

Sanders's candidacy into a catalyst for a "mass people's movement working to establish . . . guaranteed health care, higher education, living wages, and labor rights for all people in the United States." Then, in mid-sentence, she transitioned from the vernacular of Sandersism to her own generation's more radical dialect, adding, "a movement striving to recognize and repair the wounds of racial injustice, colonization, misogyny, and homophobia."

Whatever frictions may have arisen between Sanders and Ocasio-Cortez on the campaign trail were overwhelmed by the solidarity they felt on Capitol Hill. Congress is a lonely place for those who would rather make "good trouble" than good friends. The more time AOC spent in its halls, the greater her admiration for "Tío Bernie" grew. After all, when Sanders was a House freshman, he didn't have a "Squad" fighting by his side. "Now that I'm on the other side of this, as a member of Congress, and understanding the pressures there are on the inside," AOC told an interviewer, "it's astounded me, frankly, that the senator has been there fighting for me long before I got to the halls of Congress."

Days before the 2020 election, Bernie joined AOC and her fellow Squad members for a strategy session. It was conducted as a live video chat—not only to avoid spreading COVID-19 but to enable everyone involved in the broader movement to attend. Throughout the call, AOC's enthusiasm for her mentor was palpable. "Electing Biden is not the end-all, it is the beginning," Sanders said at one point, framed by an uncharacteristically colorful Zoom background. "And as the result of the work that all of you have done, Biden's proposals in this campaign were a lot stronger than they were in the primary—Alexandria was on the climate task force, did a great job."

The congresswoman beamed.

"All of us, we really thank you for . . . bringing the ruckus on the Democratic Party," AOC told her elder comrade. "Because that was not seen as okay for a very long time . . . and it would result in so many people being ostracized and targeted. You built your whole career enduring that.

"And now that that's been normalized," she continued, "I think it's really completely reset people's political imagination, not only of *what* we can achieve but how we achieve it."

For countless overworked, underpaid millennials on the other side of that livestream, the former bartender's own ruckus-making had accomplished the very same thing.

5

The Dakota Access
Pipeline Trip:

A 1998 Subaru,
a Bag of Hot
Cheetos, and an
Epiphany

By

MICHELLE RUIZ

The morning after Donald Trump won the 2016 election, 27-year-old Alexandria Ocasio-Cortez was one of the millions of New Yorkers who rode the subway in eerie silence. She reported to work as a bartender at Flats Fix, a taqueria in Union Square, and sold

Scenes from a road trip.

more daytime alcohol than ever before. Friends were texting her, despairing about what to do. She told them to get IUDs if they didn't have them yet; to fast-track their applications for citizenship.

"Sandy," as people in her pre-congressional life called her, had been a community organizer for Bernie Sanders in the Bronx. Regulars at the bar came to her not just for margaritas but conversations about "how we could make the world a better place," said Scott Starrett, a frequent lunch patron who later became the designer of Ocasio-Cortez's Cesar Chavez–inspired 2018 campaign poster. "People were starting to think about life a little differently in 2016."

Five weeks after Election Day, as a spirit of resistance bubbled up across the country (throngs had shouted outside Trump's gilded Fifth Avenue penthouse; the first Women's March was in the works), Sandy had made up her mind to join a protest that predated Trump. That December, she posted a "big announcement" on Facebook: She and two friends would drive cross-country from New York City to the North Dakota prairie to protest the construction of the Dakota Access Pipeline.

The $7.5 billion crude-oil behemoth, slated to run 1,712 miles from North Dakota to Illinois, was already mired in controversy. Funded by Texas gas giant Energy Transfer Partners, the pipeline threatened to cut through ground sacred to the Standing Rock Sioux Tribe, potentially endangering their water supply and that of millions of others. What began in early 2016 with a small group of protesters pitching teepees and tents to camp in nonviolent resistance had grown to a grassroots gathering of thousands, including a union of Native nations not seen since the Battle of the Little Big Horn, and "water protectors" from around the country, channeling their fury at climate injustice, corporate greed, and the continuation of the dark American history of desecrating Indigenous land.

223

A little over two years before she stood in front of the U.S. Capitol unveiling the Green New Deal, AOC was a "fracktivist" who saw a connection between Standing Rock and her own underserved, majority-minority hometown. She recalled when New York wanted to introduce fracking in the Bronx and across New York. "I was concerned about the water quality for families and children," she wrote on Facebook, under her then–profile name "Alex OC." Since New York had decided against fracking, she said: "It seems fair that Standing Rock should have the same freedoms."

On December 19, 2016, the day after sharing her plan on Facebook, Ocasio-Cortez left for Standing Rock in a borrowed 1998 Subaru Legacy with Maria Swisher, a fair, blonde co-worker, aspiring actress, and fellow Bernie supporter ("All of our shifts were always very politically dominated," Swisher said), and photographer Josh Pereira, a friend of Swisher whom Ocasio-Cortez met in the car. They set a modest GoFundMe goal of $500 for camp supplies to deliver to Standing Rock to weather the subfreezing winter temperatures ("Can you gift a bundle of wood, a cot, or a sleeping bag?" Ocasio-Cortez asked in a status update) and promised to document the journey—including a planned stop in Flint, Michigan—via then-nascent Facebook Live.

Hours of footage still live on her old page (before it was made private). In the mundane first minutes of the trip out of New York, Sandy rode shotgun, wearing a black puffer coat and an emerald-green beanie with a pom-pom on top, her dark hair wavy underneath. From behind the wheel, Swisher, in black-rimmed glasses and a hoodie, focused on "not killing us," while a bearded Pereira nestled in the back seat. The trio buzzed with wide-eyed energy: Sandy showcased the Legacy's owner's manual, the way *The Price Is Right* models presented soup cans, a city girl marveling at the novelty of driving. There was a glow in the car, both from the sun through the dash and the pure determination to do more than rant on social media.

After working on Bernie's campaign with Swisher that summer, "I started feeling much more motivated to, I think, act," said Ocasio-Cortez, who swallowed and nodded into the camera—Pereira interjects to inform Swisher that she missed an exit. AOC smiles and starts again: "I started feeling more of an impulse to act on what I felt was right." Talking and navigating proved an ongoing struggle: "Every time we turn on Facebook Live, we make a wrong turn," she later said, laughing. "We're working on it, people!"

Vlog viewership was humble, composed mainly of their Facebook friends and AOC's mom, Blanca Ocasio-Cortez, a frequent commenter ("You go, guys"), but they branded it with an official-sounding, network-newsy title, anyway: *The Road to Standing Rock.* "That's when she started doing Facebook videos and talking to the world," Starrett, who lent her a GoPro for the journey, told me of the road trip, "and I think that's where she really found her sea legs. That really opened up something in her spirit and gave her a lot of confidence."

Pereira aptly described their video diary as "reportage-slash-therapy session." They pontificated on white privilege. "I think it's so dumb when people say, 'Oh, like, this country is more sexist than it is racist,'" Ocasio-Cortez mused, glancing out the window into the pitch black of Pennsylvania, clutching a cup of coffee. They traded theories about why Trump won and Hillary didn't—a national pastime in the aftermath of the 2016 election. "I'm sorry, like, I voted for her . . . but we have a problem in this country with elitism," AOC said, a hint of apology in her voice. Hillary, she said, sighing, seeming to choose her words carefully, "didn't try hard enough in Michigan."

On day two, Sandy took the wheel en route to Flint, with her hair pulled back and her slightly cat's-eyed sunglasses pushed on top of her head. "Literally everyone texted me saying, 'You're not gonna be the one that's driving, are you?" AOC smirked, expanses of open road whizzing through the windows. "Everyone's being so rude." They'd crashed with one of her college friends in Cleveland the night before, and, in true midwestern fashion, he welcomed them at 3 a.m. with a plate of Christmas cookies and deep conversation about the power of protest.

Sandy connected their talk to Standing Rock, her eyes darting between the road ahead and the camera's lens. "I've heard, 'This isn't your fight. These people have nothing to do with you'"—make a left, Pereira interrupts, no, a right—"It goes back to this fundamental value, where we are one nation and what happens to some of us happens to all of us," she said, her eyes narrowing with intensity. "When children's water is being contaminated in Flint, it is my business, and when people's lives are in danger because their sovereignty is at risk, in my country, it is my business, because a threat to you is a threat to me and to close my eyes in the face of my neighbor's injustice only opens the door for my injustice." It's a stump speech waiting to happen.

The trio brought standard-issue millennial road-trip tomfoolery, too, including a steady flow of caffeine ("How many Red Bulls does it take to get three millennials to an Indian reservation?" AOC asked. Pereira: "We have 12 in the back."); carpool karaoke to TLC's "No Scrubs" and Bon Jovi's "Livin' on a Prayer" in exchange for donations—AOC shoulder-shimmied and air-drummed gamely. Much of the entertainment was snack-based. Ocasio-Cortez sampled cheese curds for the first time: "I'm getting notes of Lunchables," she said as she tentatively bit into a little pillow with the texture of "two-day-old Play-Doh." The New York *Post* would later comb the footage and release an onslaught of wannabe-gotcha stories packaged as "The AOC Tapes." They contained such smoking guns as: Ocasio-Cortez, who later advocated for occasional meatless meals to combat climate change, once ate a sausage-egg-and-cheese. Once, she says "fuck," and her mom chimes in on Facebook Live: "Hey, watch it."

The trek took an "amazing, heart-opening" turn, as Swisher described it, in Flint, Michigan, a city still smarting from its own water crisis. In late 2015, Flint had declared a public-health emergency, confirming years of complaints from residents: When the city changed its water source from Detroit to the cheaper Flint River in 2014, officials failed to protect the new drinking water from corroded pipes, exposing over 100,000 majority-Black Flint residents, including between 6,000 and 12,000 children, to elevated levels of lead. A civil-rights commission confirmed the glaringly obvious: Systemic racism played a role.

Over coffee and waffles at the Starlite Diner & Coney Island, Ocasio-Cortez, Swisher, and Pereira spent two hours talking with then–Flint Housing Commission leader Frank Woods, trying to make sense of what happened. "There was no real clear answer," Ocasio-Cortez would later say, "except one thing: There were too many people that put themselves, who put corporations, who put lobbyist influence, who put money ahead of the lives of everyday people."

They left Flint electrified, if a little shaken up. The stop felt "totally transformative," AOC said solemnly, as snowy expanses filled the car windows. "Their children are suffering cognitive disorders because their government didn't tell them that their water was poisoned." A link between environmental crisis and job creation—perhaps the very first flickers of the Green New Deal— emerged. "We have water pipelines that need to be put down, proper ones,"

THE DAKOTA ACCESS PIPELINE TRIP

Ocasio-Cortez mused. "How many people can be put to work doing that?"

The government's failure in Flint led to a spirited chat about the outsize role of money in politics. AOC railed against the funds believed to be necessary to run for local office. "The fact that it costs 40 grand to serve your community is wrong," she said, indignant. Two years later, she'd enter Congress with $2 million in donations, more from small donors than any other member. But in 2016, she was just thrilled to double the GoFundMe's meager $500 goal. "You are the wind beneath our wings," she raved to friends watching, before mistakenly crediting the Bette Midler lyric to Barbra Streisand (she's no pop-culture savant, she admitted in another video). They were getting donations from people they *didn't even know.* "We're going viral," AOC squeaked— even though most videos have no more than 800 views, even now, after fans and trolls alike unearthed her old page. "It feels like there's a whole movement of people driving across the country with us."

The next morning, AOC was behind the wheel again, rolling through the darkness near St. Cloud, Minnesota, with Pereira sitting groggily in the passenger side and Swisher snoozing in the back seat. "Sandy is a psycho, and she wants to wake up at like four in the morning and go drive," Swisher teased her the day before. "Sandy's a monster." The previous day, too, they'd been up at the "butt-crack of dawn," AOC said, booking it out of Ohio. Exactly four insomniac friends clocked into the Facebook Live as AOC and Pereira (but mostly AOC) contemplated race and cultural appropriation, inspired by DKNY putting baby hair on the runway.

Growing up Puerto Rican in the Bronx, "we were taught that dressing a certain way is ghetto and you don't show up to a job interview in a nameplate and hoop earrings and baby hair," AOC said. Not if she wanted to be seen as intellectual. It was *interesting*, she said, emphasizing and drawing out the word, that the very same styles had become popular and mainstream-cute. "Why is it that then I wear hoop earrings it's, like"—she changes her tone—"*sassy*, but when Jessica Biel wears hoop earrings, it's elegant?" She wore tiny posts then. To her swearing in two years later, she rocked hoops.

The trio rolled into Standing Rock that night, at golden hour on the winter solstice, driving slowly down a long, dark road to the reservation, flanked by tribal flags. They had pulled over on the way, to look up and wonder at the low, fluffy clouds practically touching the snow—like a scene out of *Fargo*. They were initially thwarted at a checkpoint by men in bulletproof vests wielding semiautomatic weapons—an effort to intimidate and frustrate those trying to get in, AOC assessed. The trio eventually arrived at the Oceti Sakowin protest camp near Cannon Ball, North Dakota, after dark. The closer they got to camp, the more AOC's skin pricked with goose bumps. "I felt like I was driving toward a magnet," she said, "and I was a piece of metal."

They were humbled by an instantly warm welcome: a tent outfitted with wood-burning stoves, cots, and zero-degree sleeping bags. Outside their new "canvas home," a group huddled around the sacred fire (Oceti Sakowin, meaning "Seven Council Fires," is the proper name for the Sioux) at the center of camp. Arriving at night was magical, Swisher said. A flute played in the distance, and the stars were brighter than Swisher had ever seen.

They were on sacred ground now, a commune of "protectors" more than protesters, a distinction made on signs around camp. There were clashes at the nearby front line, with police firing rubber bullets and pepper spray, but the mood at Oceti Sakowin was one of peaceful, "prayerful demonstration," as Ocasio-Cortez described it. "Everyone

wakes up before dawn and gathers together so we can watch the sunrise as a community," she wrote on Instagram. As day breaks, elders lead a water ceremony, where participants offer tobacco at the Missouri River and perform prayer songs. (She'd later advise friends considering a trip to Standing Rock to bring bundles of sage as gifts.) Ocasio-Cortez, Swisher, and Pereira marveled at the prevalence of heart-to-heart hugs over handshakes, and unbroken eye contact that AOC likened to Marina Abramovic's *The Artist Is Present*, the 2010 MoMA performance art, in which she gazed into the eyes of hundreds of visitors. Talking to elders, AOC said on Facebook Live, "felt like it distilled the whole universe."

In many ways, Oceti Sakowin represented the sort of equitable society AOC seeks as a Democratic Socialist. There was no money exchanged at camp. "If you're hungry, you eat and if you're sick, you get taken care of," she said. When her socks got soaked through in the snow, a woman offered her a new pair. Though she, Swisher, and Pereira spent time filming, they also chopped wood, fetched water, filled propane tanks, got generator gas for a guy named Huggy Bear, and attended organizing meetings, including one for women, under "the Dome," a giant yurt-like enclosure.

"There was a spirit in the air . . . that became really powerful and really moving," Dave Archambault II, the tribal chairman of the Standing Rock Indian Reservation at the time of the protests, told me, "occupying that land and showing the country and showing the world that we have a voice." AOC "was understanding the need to be an activist," Archambault said. "What drives her is to try to protect Mother Earth," but not only that: "It is to give a voice to those that don't have a voice."

The *science* in environmental science might have been part of the pull to Standing Rock—Ocasio-Cortez is a lifelong, self-identified nerd who once campaigned to clean the cloudy water of a pond outside her middle school. But so was her Puerto Rican heritage: She knew something, too, about being brown, about being colonized and denied self-determination.

On the way back a couple days later, AOC's voice had turned nasal, and she clutched a balled-up tissue—the potential fallout from days of little sleep, in icy weather. The national media had left Standing Rock, she said. If Christmas hadn't been just days away, Ocasio-Cortez, Swisher, and Pereira wouldn't have left. "Don't tell our boss that," Swisher said with a laugh. Ocasio-Cortez pleaded with friends watching on Facebook Live to keep the camp in mind. "Just bear witness," she said, enunciating each word. "It sounds like nothing, but it is actually everything."

6

The
Mastermind

~~~~~~

By

DAVID FREEDLANDER

Saikat Chakrabarti met Alexandria Ocasio-Cortez for the first time in 2017 at a half-empty Thai restaurant not far from the bar in Union Square where she worked. He and Zack Exley, two veterans of the Bernie Sanders campaign, had just started a new organization called Brand New Congress. The goal of the group was audacious, and befitting of Chakrabarti, a software engineer who had made a fortune in Silicon Valley start-ups: to rewire Congress by recruiting 435 community leaders to run in every congressional district as a single, bipartisan slate, sharing staff, resources, and best practices.

Over dinner, she appeared skeptical of whether this new venture could really work. Chakrabarti wasn't sold on her, either. But as they talked, she displayed a fluency with left-wing economics stemming from her time at Boston University. It was clear, from the start, that she was a talented communicator.

Did Chakrabarti know then what he was in the presence of—a young woman of preternatural political gifts who would go on to become one of the most influential voices of her time? "No, of course not," he told me. Sure, she was impressive, but so were a lot of the potential candidates he was meeting in those days. If his plan to take over Congress failed, Chakrabarti figured, he and Ocasio-Cortez might at least end up as friends or something, the kind of millennial acquaintances who get together once in a while for a game night or a few drinks.

Those who know AOC and Chakrabarti say they are a lot alike. Despite the bombast they deploy on social media, both are introverted, bookish, and interested in others. "Saikat is the kind of guy all of our mothers are disappointed that we didn't become," said Corbin Trent, AOC's former spokesman. But their methods, and their mission, are not the same. A few days after AOC's primary win over Representative Joe Crowley, over beers with a bunch of campaign staffers, Chakrabarti made clear that he had no plans to accompany the congresswoman-elect to Washington. "I would hate it," he told the group. "I want to build a movement."

Over the course of the campaign, however, Chakrabarti had made himself indispensable. "He was the only guy with all the keys, the only guy who knew all the passwords and all the relationships," recalled Waleed Shahid, another campaign staffer. So when AOC asked Chakrabarti to serve as her chief of staff, he went.

Now, as her inauguration approached, staffers held a retreat at a cabin in upstate New York. Interview requests were pouring in from around the world, including *Morning Joe* and *60 Minutes*. Chakrabarti mapped out a diagram of how to handle the onslaught in a way that would amplify her voice. Interviews with *Desus & Mero* and the *Jacobin* podcast were in; interviews with the Beltway press were out.

But Washington proved to be just as preposterous as Chakrabarti had feared.

Weekly meetings in the Speaker's office, attended by all the chiefs of staff, were dedicated to painful minutiae. Was everyone filing their time cards properly? Did they know not to crowd the elevators? Chakrabarti had expected Congress to be filled with mini-Machiavellis. Instead, he found himself surrounded by listless lifers who seemed more concerned with punching out than punching up.

Chakrabarti was also appalled at the start of the term, when committee assignments were being handed out. AOC was eager to get to work on solving the problems her constituents cared about. But someone in the House leadership suggested to Chakrabarti that she take an assignment that would earn her points with her new colleagues: improving how Congress handles its human resources. "No one in our district cares about congressional-recruitment processes," Chakrabarti fumed. "Nobody in Washington wants to get stuff done because nobody wants to touch anything controversial. But guess fucking what? Everything in Congress is controversial, or should be. So nobody takes initiative, and nothing ever happens."

With his contempt for congressional norms, it wasn't long before Chakrabarti committed his first breach of The Way Things Are Done in Washington.

Congressional staffers typically shun the spotlight. But with so many media requests pouring in, Chakrabarti began to appear on cable-news shows in AOC's stead. Suddenly, he was the center of attention. The Washington *Post*, in a long and positive profile, dubbed him "AOC's Chief of Change." The New York *Post*, looking for dirt, contacted someone he had spoken to, once, in his freshman year of college.

"I was just like, *Fuck!*" he recalled. "It was creepy and terrifying." It got worse. Five months into her first term, AOC and the rest of the Squad broke with House Speaker Nancy Pelosi and voted against a border bill that handed Trump $4.5 billion to lock up more migrants. Following the vote, Pelosi belittled the dissenters in the New York *Times*, claiming their following was limited to Twitter.

Chakrabarti, who had become accustomed to speaking for his boss, punched back in a tweet. "All these articles want to claim what a legislative mastermind Pelosi is, but I'm seeing way more strategic smarts from freshman members," he wrote. "Pelosi is just mad that she got outmaneuvered (again) by Republicans."

From there, it went downhill fast. Someone in the House leadership dug up a two-week-old tweet in which Chakrabarti compared Democrats who supported the border bill to southern segregationists. By locking up migrants, he tweeted, they seemed "hell bent to do to black and brown people today what the old Southern Democrats did in the 40s." Although Chakrabarti deleted the tweet, he followed up with another one blasting liberals for "wasting $4.5 billion of taxpayer money to put kids in concentration camps."

Sensing an opportunity to put AOC in her place, Democratic staffers launched a civil war against Chakrabarti on social media. One staffer accused him of using his Twitter account to target Sharice Davids, a Native American lawmaker. Pelosi told the Washington *Post* that colleagues had come to her "almost crying, some very upset and angry" about Chakrabarti's tweets. In a closed-door session with House Democrats, Pelosi ordered them to "think twice" before publicly attacking a fellow member of the majority. "Actually, don't think twice," she snapped. "Think once." AOC, who arrived late for the meeting, said nothing.

A few weeks later, Chakrabarti was out. AOC announced that he would be joining Zack Exley and Corbin Trent at New Consensus, a new think tank dedicated to reimagining America's industrial policy. "Saikat's goal has always been to do whatever he can to help the larger progressive movement," she said, "and I look forward to continuing working with him to do just that."

Chakrabarti wanted to wait until the controversy had died down before leaving, so it wouldn't look like he was being pushed out. But as the palace intrigue dragged on, he figured it was time to go. "Look, Alex," he says he told his boss, "let me leave now and save you some of the bullshit you are going through." Ocasio-Cortez didn't try to persuade him otherwise.

The scuttlebutt in Washington was that Chakrabarti had been forced out after Pelosi privately admonished AOC over the incident. Her opponents were gleeful: Here was the ideological purist seemingly turning her back on her own chief of staff—the man who had recruited her to run for office—for engaging in the same kind of social-media attacks that she routinely employed. Perhaps she was just like everyone else in Washington, willing to sacrifice principle for influence.

Chakrabarti offered a different version of his departure. He had planned on leaving anyway, he told me: His wife was pregnant with their first child, and his experience in Washington had been a dismal one. "You try to do something out of the ordinary, and you have all these people calling you up and yelling at you and making your life miserable," he said. "I wanted to work on stuff that matters. And I ended up getting embroiled in the exact kind of petty bullshit which is politics at its worst."

Chakrabarti was replaced by a veteran staffer who once worked for Kamala Harris. AOC's office is now run with more discipline. She still tangles with House moderates and speaks out, often alone. But the back-and-forth with Pelosi has subsided.

"Sometimes there are folks on the outside that reluctantly come in the inside but want to still be on the outside," AOC said when I asked her about the uproar five months after it happened, referring to Chakrabarti's hesitancy to join her in Washington. She knew from the start that passing a measure like the Green New Deal would require forming a new organization, independent of Washington politics. "I can't rely on lobbyists or [party] polling to inform my position," she said. "We needed to make our own progressive think tanks, so Saikat essentially had to make that for us."

Chakrabarti now lives in San Francisco—about as far from Washington as it is possible to get in the continental United States. (Chakrabarti had been the third employee at Stripe, the payments-processing company valued at $95 billion; friends joke that when

the firm goes public, he'll be able to finance AOC's political revolution himself.) He and AOC don't talk much, save for the occasional texted photo of his baby or her new puppy. "I don't want to sound patronizing, but it is hard not to use the word *proud*," he said. "She is this powerful person who is using her power for something." He hopes, one day, to see a Congress full of AOCs. One, he said, is not enough.

7

The *Vogue*
Video:

WHY BEAUTY IS POLITICAL

"Hello, *Vogue*, Buenos Días!"

— AUGUST 21, 2020 —

*"Some days, I choose to go in with a bare face.
And other days, you know,
when I want to feel glam, I do glam"*

—AOC IN VOGUE'S MAKEUP TUTORIAL

1. On makeup as power:

"Femininity has power, and in politics, there is so much criticism and nitpicking about how women and femme people present ourselves."

2. On makeup as meaning:

"There's this really false idea that if you care about makeup or if your interests are in beauty and fashion, that that's somehow frivolous, but I actually think these are some of the most substantive decisions that we make, and we make them every morning."

3. On makeup as confidence:

"When you're always running around, the best way to look put together is a bold lip. And of course, being Latina, this is very much our culture—I will wear a red lip when I need a boost of confidence."

4. On makeup as radicalism:

"Culture is so predicated on diminishing women and kind of preying on our self-esteem. And so in my opinion, it's quite a radical act—it's almost like a mini-protest—to love yourself."

5. On makeup as individualism:

"They are always trying to tell you, 'You're not the right weight. You're not the right color. You're not the right whatever it is.' And when you stand up and you say, 'You know what, you don't make that decision. I make that decision,' it's very powerful."

6. On makeup as the instrument of patriarchy:

"If waking up in the morning and doing your makeup gives you life, then that is amazing and you should do it. But there are studies that show that women who wear makeup make more money. And so at that point, these decisions stop being about choice. And they start being about patriarchy."

7. On makeup as self-expression:

"I think beauty should be about the person who is applying it."

8. On makeup as a practical matter:

"One of the things that I love about a liquid lipstick is formulas that stay all day, because I really don't have time to be running in and out of the bathroom to be doing touch-ups and all this other stuff."

9. On makeup as pride:

"Look in the mirror and say, 'I'm the bomb. And I will make the world a better place in my own little pocket, because that's what I'm here to do.' You are a blessing to the world. Your talents are a blessing to the world. No matter who you are, there is something that you bring and you need to know that. And that is the best beauty secret of them all."

8

The Authenticity
Paradox:

Like an Open
Book, Turned to
Exactly
the Right Page

~~~~~

By

MOLLY FISCHER

I
n a 1988 essay on political stagecraft
called "Insider Baseball," Joan Didion
described the machinations of making Michael Dukakis look regular. It involved a procedure the TV-news crews
following his campaign referred to as "tarmac arrival with ball tossing." Here is how

it worked: After the Dukakis campaign jet touched down someplace new, the presidential candidate would emerge in shirtsleeves, mitts and a ball would be produced, and, in front of the waiting cameras, Dukakis would play catch with his press secretary. The first recorded ball tossing took place somewhere in Ohio. On that occasion, the campaign realized that only one TV crew had caught it, and so it was immediately restaged. Didion witnessed the play in San Diego.

"Just a regular guy," says one of the jaded cameramen she overhears. "I'd say he was a regular guy," confirms another. Regular-guy behavior duly documented, the cameramen pack up their gear.

To read about this performance today is to be immediately in league with Didion and the cameramen, eye-rolling on the sidelines. "Tarmac arrival with ball tossing" was an effort to convey authenticity—elusive, fetishized, and much debated—a quality that has long vexed American politicians. By the time Alexandria Ocasio-Cortez was running for Congress, the pursuit of authenticity had reached a crescendo. Donald Trump was an untrammeled public id for whom artifice (the hair, the tan) was so blatant that even it could seem like a kind of authenticity. Yet in the years between Dukakis's choreographed

games of catch and the viral campaign ad that showed Ocasio-Cortez applying mascara in her bathroom, the demands of authenticity had evolved. If Dukakis was working with semaphore (DOING SPORTS: *masculine!* SPECIFICALLY BASEBALL: *American!*), Ocasio-Cortez has mastered something more like livestreaming in HD. The tools of the trade have improved, and as they have, a void at the heart of the project has become clear. Strive to be authentic, but authentically—what?

"It's shape-shifting," says historian David Greenberg of authenticity in politics. It can mean "honest" or "spontaneous" or "the salt of the earth." And while related qualities—"integrity," say—are more or less timeless, the notion of authenticity as it's now cultivated emerges only once the public starts imagining politicians as people whom they know. (Abraham Lincoln was born in a log cabin, yes, but nobody wondered whether voters wanted to have a beer with him.)

"Authenticity" is, in part, a question of media skill, the ability to conjure a recognizably human presence through the technology at hand. John F. Kennedy looked into the camera during his first debate against Richard Nixon; in living rooms across America, viewers looked into his eyes. Here, a generational advantage comes into play. During the '90s childhoods of Alexandria Ocasio-Cortez and her peers, being on-camera became an utterly ordinary fact of life. *Knock Down the House*, a documentary about the 2018 midterm primaries, includes home footage of a tiny "Sandy" delivering a pretend newscast. Talking about aliens and approximating a news anchor's cadence, she holds the camera's gaze comfortably. Not every kid who goofed off in front of a camcorder during the Clinton years was destined for public life, but still, it's possible to see the beginnings of the skills that would serve her well. And in the years that followed those home movies, reality TV accustomed her generation to seeing ordinary people as onscreen villains and heroes. A knowing attitude about misleading edits and "narratives," once the province of PR professionals, became a pop-culture commonplace.

Even for the many Americans who are neither politicians nor reality stars, there are more screens than ever on which to see and be seen. Fortunately, it is easier to sound like yourself on the internet if you've spent your formative years practicing, as AOC and her cohort have. But to focus on her knack for a snappy retort on Twitter is to ignore the actual asset on display: not the novelty of the digital tools she uses (*a congresswoman*

playing video games on Twitch!) but the self-presentation such media inculcates. Successfully sounding normal online does not mean pouncing on the right meme. Successfully sounding normal online means constant, intuitive self-editing. Exposure is always selective and strategic—this is a matter less of subterfuge than of etiquette. Certain jokes work on Twitter but not Instagram; certain photos belong on Stories but not the main grid; revealing the occasional rough edge is a gracious touch that puts your followers at ease. Boundaries are to be carefully maintained. Ocasio-Cortez's appearances on Instagram Live are voluble and conversational and offer almost nothing in the way of voyeuristic appeal. Viewers may see her cooking dinner (*in an Instant Pot!*), but they get little identifiable sense of place and few if any glimpses of supporting characters in her personal life. After the Capitol riot, she spent an hour online taking questions and describing what had happened that day. The resulting video (which she later posted to the relative permanence of YouTube) is intensely personal in its account of her fear and anger and starkly impersonal in everything else. She wears a dark turtleneck and sits tightly cropped before a blank white wall. The apparent vulnerability of her candor is possible because she controls its frame. Her audience can focus on only what she wants it to: what she has to say.

Authenticity operates on the level of human presence (can this far-off figure be made to feel like a real person?) but also on the level of biography. The goal here is to seem authentically representative of the America where voters live. A 1976 campaign ad for Jimmy Carter rehearsed a formula that soon took hold: Promising honesty and an outsider's trustworthiness, an avuncular voice describes the presidential candidate as "a man whose roots are founded in the American tradition." We see sepia-toned photographs of small towns, blond children, and the words "U.S. NAVAL ACADEMY." Authentic, in this sense, means straight-talking and straight-shooting. It means farm-working, but it could also mean coal-mining. It means ball-playing, beer-drinking, deer-hunting, truck-driving. Says Erica Seifert, author of *Politics of Authenticity in Presidential Campaigns, 1976–2008*, "What it means to be 'American' and in politics is very, very male." And so the question of authenticity has often served as a cudgel to be used against politicians who were not male—or white, or straight, or born in America, or any of the other characteristics of the

"authentically American" role they were expected to play. For such a candidate, trying to satisfy the given terms is lose-lose: You're inauthentic if you don't, and inauthentic if you do, and the effort is uncomfortable to watch either way.

One of the thrills of watching Ocasio-Cortez is how neatly she sweeps this paradox aside. Because, as much as her media advantage is generational, it's gendered, too. If growing up on social media is good preparation for a career in panopticon-era politics, so is growing up female. In his 1959 book *The Presentation of Self in Everyday Life*, the sociologist Erving Goffman distinguished between "front-stage" and "backstage" behavior: The first is the way we act in front of others; the second is what we do behind the scenes. Even sincerity is a kind of performance, Goffman explains. But no one who has ever been a teenage girl needs Erving Goffman to tell them that daily life is like being on-stage. What was once understood as a liability for women in politics—their gender—has become an asset in Ocasio-Cortez's hands. Being a woman, especially a woman of color, means constantly being asked to recalibrate oneself for different audiences, and seeming authentic in contemporary politics is a matter of doing exactly that, imperceptibly. What you want is a public persona that can take you from day to night, from committee hearings to a picket line with Teamsters, from a conversation with Cornel West to a beauty video for Vogue.com. Success in such a realm cannot be won with a hasty game of tarmac catch. When your voters maintain finstas and have spent years close reading the machinations of Kris Jenner, clumsy gestures only patronize them. All of this is to say: Ocasio-Cortez has found in her identity a kind of communicative power. Already, she has shown she can use that power to reshape what words like *authentic* and *American* might mean.

In July 2020, she spoke on the House floor about an encounter with Florida Representative Ted Yoho on the Capitol steps. Yoho had accosted her a few days before, calling her—within earshot of a reporter—a "fucking bitch." The story made headlines, and Yoho offered a half-apology for his "abrupt manner" without mentioning her by name.

• • •

"All of us," she said—i.e., all women— "have had to deal with this, in some form, some way, some shape at some point in our lives." Rather than casting the encounter as exceptional, a breach of time-honored congressional decorum, etc., she stressed how ordinary it was. "Representative Yoho's comments were not *deeply hurtful* or piercing to me," she said. "I have worked a working-class job. I have waited tables in restaurants. I have ridden the subway. I have walked the streets in New York City."

But then Yoho had offered up the familiar as-a-father-of-daughters formulation in his defense. "And that I could not let go," she said, adding, "I am two years younger than Mr. Yoho's youngest daughter. I am someone's daughter, too." The speech arrived at its emotional climax. "I am here because I have to show my parents that I am their daughter, and that they did not raise me to accept abuse from men."

Her manner throughout combined extemporaneous clarity and emotion, articulate anger and frank vulnerability. It had the hydraulic power of human feeling carefully channeled. Within six hours it became C-Span's most retweeted clip ever. At the end of the video, the C-Span camera pulls back and shows the House Chamber mostly empty. Her audience, wherever you are, was you.

9

The Twitter Wars:

THE ART
OF THE DUNK

"Keep It Coming Jr"

*Come for her if you dare. How the
political communicator of our
time mastered the Twitter clapback.*

By
BROCK COLYAR

DUNKING ON

TED CRUZ

Senator Ted Cruz of Texas takes to Twitter to complain about "snowflakes" in the midst of debates over net neutrality.

Ted Cruz ✔
@tedcruz

Snowflake, believing online propaganda: "OMG w/o net neutrality, the Internet is gone!" Informed observer: "You know, the FCC issued that rule in 2015. The Internet grew up wonderfully free from govt regulation & this restores the status quo ante." Snowflake: "Uh, never mind..."

12/14/17, 9:06 PM

You can almost hear the disbelief in AOC's voice as she mocks the gentleman from Texas for taking a subject as bland as net neutrality and injects it with some culture-wars hysteria.

Alexandria Ocasio-Cortez ✔
@AOC

(1) "Snowflake?" Aren't you a sitting Senator?

(2)

Also, Comcast paid you $36k to write this tweet. Campaign contributions are public record. (3)

Another rhetorical question subtly interrogates Cruz's high-ranking political position and his lack of decorum: something the right is always doing to AOC herself.

AOC always does her research. Dunk achieved.

DUNKING ON

JOHN CARDILLO

Former NYPD officer John Cardillo tweets a photograph of a modest home.

John Cardillo ✓
@johncardillo

This is the Yorktown Heights (very nice area) home @Ocasio2018 grew up in before going off to Ivy League Brown University.

A far cry from the Bronx hood upbringing she's selling.

Jul 1, 2018 · Twitter for iPhone

> **Time to spell it out.**

> **AOC refutes Cardillo's first false claim, that she went to an Ivy League school.**

> **Very AOC, refuting falsehoods by pointing to the obvious.**

> **A simple reminder of her working-class bona fides.**

Alexandria Ocasio-Cortez ✓ @AOC · Jul 1, 2018
Replying to @johncardillo
Hey John,

(2) (3)

(1) 1. I didn't go to Brown or the Ivy League. I went to BU. Try Google.

(4)

2. It is nice. Growing up, it was a good town for working people. My mom scrubbed toilets so I could live here & I grew up seeing how the zip code one is born in determines much of their opportunity.

💬 1.5K   🔁 10.1K   ❤️ 72.7K   ⬆️

Alexandria Ocasio-Cortez ✓ @AOC · Jul 1, 2018
3. Your attempt to strip me of my family, my story, my home, and my identity is exemplary of how scared you are of the power of all four of those things.

(5)

(6)

💬 2.5K   🔁 7.3K   ❤️ 59.8K   ⬆️

> **And once again she circles it back to the real reason the right is afraid of her.**

> **This will become common territory for an AOC dunk: Refuting claims that her childhood, her wardrobe, her accessories, etc. are proof she can't be a socialist. The right is constantly trying to signal a certain inauthenticity for AOC, but one of her strongest charms is the opposite, being authentic.**

DUNKING ON

RON DeSANTIS

Congressman DeSantis calls AOC "this girl . . . or whatever she is."

> **Amanda Terkel** ✓
> @aterkel
>
> GOP Rep. calls Alexandria Ocasio-Cortez "this girl...or
> whatever she is" bit.ly/2v5l3px by @jbendery
>
> GOP Congressman Calls Alexandria Ocasio-Cortez 'This Girl ... Or Whatever S...
> Rep. Ron DeSantis was referring to a full-grown woman who is a New York
> Democratic congressional nominee.
> huffpost.com

Mimicking his language shows just how creepy and patronizing it is.

She murders with fact.

> **Alexandria Ocasio-Cortez** ✓
> @AOC
>
> ① Rep DeSantis, it seems you're confused as to "whatever I am."
>
> ② I am a Puerto Rican woman. It's strange you don't know what that is, given that ③ ~75,000 Puerto Ricans have relocated to Florida in the 10 mos since María.
>
> But I'm sure these new FL voters appreciate your ④ comments!
>
> > 🔵 **Amanda Terkel** ✓ @aterkel · Jul 23, 2018
> > GOP Rep. calls Alexandria Ocasio-Cortez "this girl...or whatever she is"
> > bit.ly/2v5l3px by @jbendery

AOC is never fearful of reminding politicians on the right of the subtle reasons why they dislike her so much: her gender and racial identities, her youth, her working-class background.

Of course, that wouldn't work out so well. He'd be elected governor of the state in 2018.

DUNKING ON

FOX NEWS

Fox airs a segment showing pictures of the Squad and its "radical new democratic ideas," like free college, free health care, the Green New Deal, and abolishing ICE.

This is a dunk AOC begins herself by screenshotting the television.

#SQUAD.

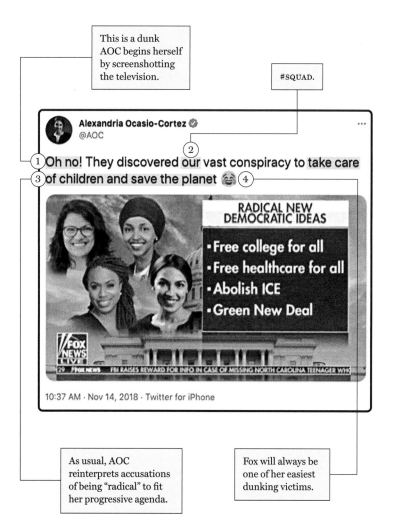

Alexandria Ocasio-Cortez @AOC

② Oh no! They discovered our vast conspiracy to take care of children and save the planet 😂

10:37 AM · Nov 14, 2018 · Twitter for iPhone

As usual, AOC reinterprets accusations of being "radical" to fit her progressive agenda.

Fox will always be one of her easiest dunking victims.

DUNKING ON

DONALD TRUMP JR.

Donald Trump Jr. shares a meme implying that socialists and AOC eat dog meat. AOC doesn't let it slide.

> How best to take down a petty First Son? The way his father does it: an emasculating nickname.

> Before she's even in Congress, AOC is showing she won't let herself get bullied. She'll meet her trolls face-to-face.

Alexandria Ocasio-Cortez ✔
@AOC

(1)
I have noticed that Junior here has a habit of posting nonsense about me whenever the Mueller investigation heats up.

(2)
Please, keep it coming Jr - it's definitely a "very, very large brain" idea to troll a member of a body that will have subpoena power in a month.

(3)
Have fun!

> **The Washington Post** ✔ @washingtonpost · Dec 7, 2018
> Donald Trump Jr. trolls Ocasio-Cortez with meme implying socialists eat dogs
> wapo.st/2RGmYfl

1:54 PM · Dec 7, 2018 · Twitter for iPhone

> Is that a threat? AOC says it isn't: "I don't have power to subpoena anybody. Congress as a body, GOP included, has the power. No indiv. member can issue a subpoena unless they are a Chair (which, as a freshman, I can assure you I will not be). Also must be under purview."

Alexandria Ocasio-Cortez ✔ @AOC · Dec 7, 2018   · · ·
Replying to @AOC
For the GOP crying that this is a "threat" - I don't have power to subpoena anybody.

Congress as a body, GOP included, has the power. No indiv. member can issue a subpoena unless they are a Chair (which, as a freshman, I can assure you I will not be). Also must be under purview.

DUNKING ON

EDDIE SCARRY...

Eddie Scarry, a reporter at the Washington Examiner, *tweeted a photo of AOC's back one day at work, claiming that her wardrobe indicated she couldn't possibly be a "girl who struggles." Put in only slightly less sexist terms, he meant she didn't look like a person hustling to make ends meet.*

Eddie Scarry @eScarry

Hill staffer sent me this pic of Ocasio-Cortez they took just now. I'll tell you something: that jacket and coat don't look like a girl who struggles.

Alexandria Ocasio-Cortez @AOC

If I walked into Congress wearing a sack, they would laugh & take a picture of my backside.

If I walk in with my best sale-rack clothes, they laugh & take a picture of my backside. (1)

Dark hates light - that's why you tune it out.
(2)

Shine bright & keep it pushing. ✨
(3) itter.com/eScarry/status...

This Tweet is u

6:13 PM · Nov 15,

She signs off with a little self-motivation. Very millennial. Very AOC.

Eddie Scarry later deleted the photo, but Ocasio-Cortez was not about to let him off the hook so easily. She tweeted the photo again herself, calling out his misogyny.

Alexandria Ocasio-Cortez @AOC

Replying to @AOC

Oh, does @eScarry think he can delete his misogyny without an apology?

I don't think so. You're a journalist - readers should know your bias.

Eddie Scarry @eScarry

Hill staffer sent me this pic of Ocasio-

...AND LAURA INGRAHAM

Years later, AOC would appear on the cover of Vanity Fair *in $14,000 worth of designer clothing. The clothes were loaned to her by the magazine for the photo shoot, as is often standard procedure with fashion covers, but that didn't stop conservatives like Laura Ingraham from losing their minds.*

Laura Ingraham ✔ @IngrahamAngle · Oct 29, 2020 · · ·
AOC appears in Vanity Fair in outfits worth $14,000 to curse out Trump | Fox News

AOC appears in Vanity Fair in outfits worth $14,000 to curse Trump out
Freshman Democratic congresswoman Alexandria Ocasio Cortez wore thousands of dollars worth of outfits and jewelry for her spread in Vanity ...
🔗 foxnews.com

AOC had a clapback for that, too.

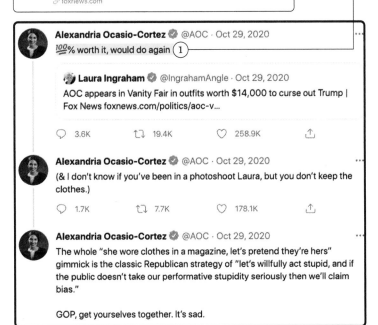

Alexandria Ocasio-Cortez ✔ @AOC · Oct 29, 2020 · · ·
100% worth it, would do again ①

> 🏛 **Laura Ingraham** ✔ @IngrahamAngle · Oct 29, 2020
> AOC appears in Vanity Fair in outfits worth $14,000 to curse out Trump | Fox News foxnews.com/politics/aoc-v...

💬 3.6K   🔁 19.4K   ♡ 258.9K   ⬆

Alexandria Ocasio-Cortez ✔ @AOC · Oct 29, 2020 · · ·
(& I don't know if you've been in a photoshoot Laura, but you don't keep the clothes.)

💬 1.7K   🔁 7.7K   ♡ 178.1K   ⬆

Alexandria Ocasio-Cortez ✔ @AOC · Oct 29, 2020 · · ·
The whole "she wore clothes in a magazine, let's pretend they're hers" gimmick is the classic Republican strategy of "let's willfully act stupid, and if the public doesn't take our performative stupidity seriously then we'll claim bias."

GOP, get yourselves together. It's sad.

DUNKING ON

JUSTIN T. HASKINS

Conservative commentator Justin T. Haskins shares a Fox News article declaring AOC's Green New Deal the "most radical plan offered in decades."

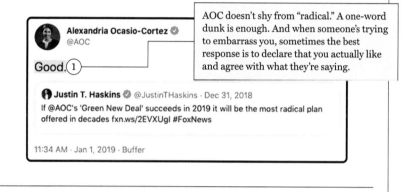

> AOC doesn't shy from "radical." A one-word dunk is enough. And when someone's trying to embarrass you, sometimes the best response is to declare that you actually like and agree with what they're saying.

DUNKING ON

DONALD TRUMP

At an AOC town hall, a woman in the audience makes a rambling comment about "getting rid of the babies" to combat climate changes. Don Jr. seizes the moment to depict AOC as an insane radical, and the president retweets his tweet calling her a "wack job."

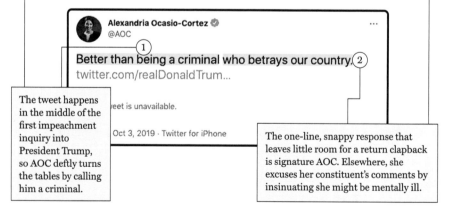

The tweet happens in the middle of the first impeachment inquiry into President Trump, so AOC deftly turns the tables by calling him a criminal.

The one-line, snappy response that leaves little room for a return clapback is signature AOC. Elsewhere, she excuses her constituent's comments by insinuating she might be mentally ill.

DUNKING ON

TOMI LAHREN

When Cardi B and conservative commentator Tomi Lahren start fighting on Twitter, AOC steps in and has Cardi's back.

Notice her smooth reference to her own game. Another key to the clapback? Confidence.

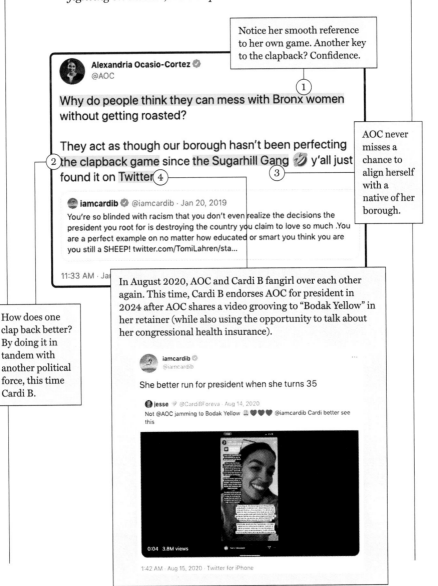

Alexandria Ocasio-Cortez ✓
@AOC

(1)

Why do people think they can mess with Bronx women without getting roasted?

They act as though our borough hasn't been perfecting
(2) the clapback game since the Sugarhill Gang 🎤 y'all just
found it on Twitter (4)
(3)

AOC never misses a chance to align herself with a native of her borough.

iamcardib ✓ @iamcardib · Jan 20, 2019
You're so blinded with racism that you don't even realize the decisions the president you root for is destroying the country you claim to love so much .You are a perfect example on no matter how educated or smart you think you are you still a SHEEP! twitter.com/TomiLahren/sta...

11:33 AM · Ja

How does one clap back better? By doing it in tandem with another political force, this time Cardi B.

In August 2020, AOC and Cardi B fangirl over each other again. This time, Cardi B endorses AOC for president in 2024 after AOC shares a video grooving to "Bodak Yellow" in her retainer (while also using the opportunity to talk about her congressional health insurance).

iamcardib ✓
@iamcardib

She better run for president when she turns 35

jesse ✓ @CardiBForeva · Aug 14, 2020
Not @AOC jamming to Bodak Yellow 🧎 💜💜💜 @iamcardib Cardi better see this

0:04 3.8M views

1:42 AM · Aug 15, 2020 · Twitter for iPhone

10

The American Left:

The Twisty Road from Eugene Victor Debs to Alexandria Ocasio-Cortez

By

TIM SHENK

T he long, often noble, frequently dispiriting history of the American left is filled with activists inspired by dreams of a more just and equitable world. Alexandria Ocasio-Cortez is part of that lineage, the heir to an unbroken line of crusaders and agitators. But her extraordinary success arose from something far less familiar—a subterranean tradition on the left, running all the way back to the country's founding, that focuses not just on ideals but on power. At the core of this vision is a simple but elusive goal: to build a democratic majority committed to radical change.

Well into the nineteenth century, the United States was at the vanguard of a worldwide democratic insurgency. Yes, it was a slaveholding republic clearing a continent of its native population by force. But leftists around the globe couldn't help but be inspired by a nation born in revolution and dedicated—at least in theory—to equality. At home, the egalitarian spirit of the Declaration of Independence breathed life into abolitionism, women's suffrage, and a nascent labor movement.

What America lacked, unlike Europe, was an organized socialist party rooted in the working class and competing in a serious way for electoral power. Two factors conspired to keep socialists out of U.S. party politics. First, the traditional concept of "class" was complicated by the absence of a hereditary aristocracy and the extension of universal suffrage to poor white men. Second, the working class itself was sharply divided along racial, ethnic, and religious lines.

It wasn't until the turn of the twentieth century that socialists emerged as a political force worth fearing. In the wake of the Civil War, as the country industrialized at a breakneck pace, the gap between rich and poor turned into a chasm. During this so-called Gilded Age, the United States experienced the world's most violent class conflict, as hundreds of thousands of striking workers confronted the armed might of the railroads and the steel manufacturers. The Populist Party—a loose coalition of reformers that flourished briefly in the 1890s—tried to harness that energy at the polls but couldn't move beyond its rural base. Socialists rushed to take its place, led by their charismatic spokesman, Eugene Debs.

An Indiana native and onetime Democrat, Debs had been radicalized by his experience organizing a national strike through the American Railway Union. President Grover Cleveland—a Democrat—had ordered federal troops to end the walkout. "In the gleam of every bayonet and the flash of every rifle," Debs later wrote, "the class struggle was revealed."

Debs made his first run for president in 1900. He campaigned five times, peaking in 1912 when he won 6 percent of the popular vote. The Socialist platform dismissed both Republicans and

Democrats as tools of the robber barons and called for public ownership of all large-scale industries. (Its less radical demands included a minimum wage, a progressive income tax, and the abolition of child labor.) While the presidency was the longest of long shots, Socialists were thick on the ground. Not just a movement of the urban working class or of the intelligentsia, Socialists made deep inroads in the Great Plains, where they hosted carnivals and the occasional rodeo. The most popular Socialist paper, the Kansas-based *Appeal to Reason*, had a circulation of more than 700,000 readers.

It didn't last long. A brutal crackdown on domestic dissent during the First World War, followed by the Red Scare triggered by the birth of the Soviet Union, put American socialism on the defensive. By the 1930s, caught between Franklin Roosevelt on one side and a surging communist movement on the other, the party had fallen into a precipitous decline. In 1956, the Socialist presidential nominee received just over 2,000 votes. It was the last time the party fielded its own candidate for the White House.

Yet the collapse of the Socialist Party coincided with an unprecedented success for its agenda. Among the idealistic 20- and 30-somethings who flocked to

Washington in the 1930s to enact the New Deal, the lines separating liberal from socialist were fuzzy at best. New Dealers didn't seize control of the means of production, but they did make enormous strides toward establishing the kind of welfare state long championed by socialists: old-age and unemployment insurance, public housing, a minimum wage, and a massive increase in public works. They also regulated banks, cracked down on monopolies, and encouraged an explosion in unionization. Union members—almost a third of the total workforce—voted for the party of Roosevelt in droves, giving American politics an unaccustomed proletarian edge.

Surveying the political landscape, the small number of remaining socialists saw an opportunity to remake party politics. Led by the brilliant and irascible Max Shachtman, a onetime protégé of Leon Trotsky, they coalesced in the 1950s behind a strategy known as "realignment." According to Shachtman, socialists had collapsed as an electoral force because the labor movement had turned the Democrats into the de facto party of the working class. By burrowing inside the Democrats, socialists believed they could use the party to forge a truly progressive majority. Shachtman and many of his followers, known as

Shachtmanites, took up senior positions in the AFL-CIO, seeking to leverage the power of labor unions to push the Democrats to the left.

The Shachtmanites were soon joined in their project of realignment by a host of '60s radicals, including civil-rights activists and the young organizers who founded Students for a Democratic Society. But the rise of the counterculture produced a deep schism on the left. To old-guard socialists like Shachtman, the baby-boomer radicals threatened to scare off blue-collar Democrats with their antiwar theatrics and glorification of sexual freedom. To college students of the New Left, the Shachtmanite commitment to working within the system looked like capitulation to the bankrupt status quo.

The GOP, meanwhile, seized on the divisions between the union bosses and the hippies. Under Richard Nixon, Republicans rebranded themselves as culture-war populists taking on out-of-touch coastal elites. In 1972, Nixon's "silent majority" dealt a landslide defeat to George McGovern, a darling of the student left reviled by the Shachtmanites. Eight years later, Ronald Reagan consolidated the party's gains, tightening the GOP's hold on the white working class.

Socialists had helped transform American politics, and the results were a disaster for their own cause. The New Deal coalition was in tatters. The future of the left—and of American democracy—would be determined by a single, thorny question: Could Democrats find a way to overcome their differences and forge a durable new majority?

• • •

The short answer was no—or, at least, not yet. To understand why, it helps to look at three figures who made their careers in the shadow of realignment, each of whom contributed significant strands to AOC's political DNA.

The first was Michael Harrington, who moved to New York in 1949 and spent more than a decade toiling in obscurity as a socialist organizer, earning a reputation as one of Shachtman's brightest pupils. After the surprise success of his best-selling 1962 exposé of poverty, *The Other America*, Harrington became the public face of American socialism.

At first, like Shachtman, Harrington was skeptical of the New Left. But over time, he broke with his mentor, coming to see the young radicals as potential partners in a new progressive coalition—if they would renounce "their barely concealed contempt for working people." Harrington thought student activists, along with a growing class of educated professionals, could form a "conscience constituency," a group willing to sacrifice its own economic advantage to advance liberal ideals.

Ex-friends on the left denounced Harrington for, in the scathing words of one critic, attempting "to split the socialist movement" by siding with "the affluent, educated elite." But Harrington was simply seeking to extend Shachtman's strategy beyond the labor movement, making common cause with all progressives in the Democratic Party. "Political realignment," he maintained, "is a precondition for the resurgence of a meaningful Socialist politics."

As the founder of Democratic Socialists of America, Harrington championed a "visionary gradualism" that held up socialism as an ideal while accepting Democrats as the lesser of two evils. The heir to Eugene Debs, he campaigned, enthusiastically, for Bobby and Teddy Kennedy. "I'm a radical," he insisted. "But I want to be on the left wing of the possible."

He was joined there by Bella Abzug, a child of Russian Jewish immigrants who grew up in the South Bronx. As a preteen socialist, she developed a talent for public speaking after studying street-corner lecturers in her neighborhood. By the time she was elected to Congress, in 1970, Abzug had matured into, as Harrington admiringly put it, "a very serious liberal."

There wasn't much that separated Abzug's liberalism from Harrington's socialism. Like Harrington, Abzug saw herself as a bridge between the old left and the new, working to hold together a coalition of, in her words, "the young, the poor and blue-collar workers, the peace movement, the disenfranchised minorities, and concerned women."

Abzug came closer to real power than Harrington ever did, which, in a painful turn, made her an even better illustration of the pitfalls of pragmatism. As one of just over a dozen women in Congress, she was barred from high-profile committees and sex-segregated congressional facilities. "I spend all day figuring out how to beat the machine and knock the crap out of the political power structure," she wrote in her journal. But the power structure knocked back. The causes she was most closely associated with—including universal child care, the Equal Rights Amendment, and gay rights—all went down to defeat. She left the House after just three terms and went on to wage losing campaigns for the Senate, the House, and mayor of New York.

As Harrington and Abzug were prodding Democrats to the left, a third figure was engaged in a similar and far more successful campaign to push Republicans to the right. Newt Gingrich arrived in Congress in 1979. Less concerned with passing bills than with recasting the national debate, he urged Republicans to treat policy disputes as battles for the nation's soul. He signed up 12 like-minded young congressmen, camera-ready firebrands eager to condemn liberals—and, when necessary, squeamish Republicans—as downright un-American. Savvy use of the media gave Gingrich's "squad" of conservative bomb throwers an outsize platform. (A typical innovation: delivering fiery speeches on the floor of the House, knowing that C-Span would not show the empty seats around them.) Over time, Gingrich's tiny base expanded to form the core of the conservative caucus. By the time Republicans won back the House in 1994, the congressional GOP had been remade in Gingrich's image: bold, angry, and—most important—able to win.

AOC's distinctive approach to politics is a unique combination of Harrington's, Abzug's, and, yes, Gingrich's—not because she consciously modeled herself after them, but because she is responding to the world they made. Instead of denouncing a few bad apples on Wall Street, she condemns a broken capitalist system rigged against working people. Instead of criticizing Donald Trump and his Republican enablers, she takes

on the entire political class, including many in her own party. Her proposals are ambitious yet easy to understand, her language rooted in a moral critique of the status quo. She is both more committed to electoral politics than Harrington, who never held office, and much tougher on the Democratic Establishment. In her very first campaign ad, with the spine of Thomas Piketty's *Capital in the Twenty-First Century* visible on her bookshelf, she told voters, "It's time we acknowledged that not all Democrats are the same."

Like the rest of her generation, AOC came of political age at a moment when the economy was reeling from structural transformations championed by both parties. Loaded down with student debt, she graduated into a miserable job market just as Occupy Wall Street was pushing economic inequality to the forefront of the national conversation for the first time in decades. Activists who cut their teeth at Zuccotti Park moved into progressive activism, while Black Lives Matter opened a new chapter in the campaign for racial justice. Then Bernie Sanders turned the attack on the 99 percent into the basis for his 2016 campaign, shocking pundits—and himself—by winning 13 million votes and falling just short of capturing the Democratic nomination.

During college, AOC had worked for Teddy Kennedy and idolized RFK, two old Harrington favorites. Knocking on doors for Sanders immersed her in the broader world of the left. She joined Democratic Socialists of America, the organization Harrington founded, not out of a doctrinal commitment to Marxism, but because its members showed up for the causes she believed in. For her, socialism didn't stand for Soviet commissars or empty grocery shelves. Why would it, when the USSR collapsed while she was still a toddler? Hers was a vernacular socialism, a demand that fundamental human rights—health care, higher education, a job—not be subject to the whims of the market.

She didn't run from socialism, but it wasn't the basis of her appeal. Like Sanders, she has positioned herself as an heir to FDR. Much of her program reads like an attempt to revive the world-conquering spirit of an earlier generation of liberalism: Medicare for All, tuition-free public college, a jobs guarantee, and the Green New Deal. Like other socialists, however, she was no longer willing to work from within a Democratic Party that appeared to have abandoned the spirit of the original New Deal. If liberalism meant Joe Crowley raking in donations from corporate America; if liberalism meant a

Washington Establishment that had lost touch with ordinary people; if liberalism meant technocratic nudging rather than systemic change; if liberalism meant a Democratic leadership that cared more about white-collar suburbanites than the working class—well, if liberalism meant all of that, then Alexandria Ocasio-Cortez was no liberal.

• • •

The coalition that elected AOC was made possible, in large part, by the post-'60s realignment in American politics. She racked up her largest vote totals in white, wealthy, educated precincts— the twenty-first century version of Harrington's "conscience constituency." And like Harrington, she drew on support that went beyond class-first socialism. "DSA played a very important role," she has said. "But so did Black Lives Matter of Greater New York, so did Justice Democrats, so did a lot of labor and tenant organizers, Muslim community organizers, young Jewish organizations." Issues of culture and race were now as central to American socialism as income equality.

In Congress, AOC's tactics have owed as much to Gingrich as to Abzug. Both AOC and Gingrich started out by recruiting allies—a bumper crop of blow-dried white guys for him, the multiracial "Squad" for her. Both focused more on changing the terms of the debate than on the nuances of legislation. Both used clever media strategies to compensate for their junior status; one had C-Span, the other Twitter, Instagram, and Twitch.

Like Gingrich, AOC's goal is nothing less than a radical transformation of her own party. She seeks to make a reality of the enduring socialist dream of an electoral majority built around a united working class. A lifetime after one realignment, she is calling for another. "Republicans have focused on that long-term project for a very long period of time," she argues. "Democrats don't. We think if something is red, it stays red. But you know what? I think if a state like Tennessee or West Virginia can go from blue to red in our lifetime, I think it can go back."

To forge a successful electoral coalition, AOC's ability to navigate the complex realities of racial identity and cultural diversity has buoyed supporters who felt wearied by Bernie's unrelenting focus on the plutocracy. And her undeniable star power has given her a standing that, in the age of Donald Trump, should never be underestimated.

But there are costs to her strategy. Whatever its limits, Sanders's approach— from his rumpled suits to his fixation on income inequality—was tailor-made to creating inroads with white working-class voters who lean to the left on economics and to the right on culture. And while Democrats have become increasingly dependent on affluent suburbanites, not exactly a natural constituency for redistributive economic policy, Republicans have made incremental but steady progress with Black and brown voters. If both parties continue to split the blue-collar vote, it will be hard for Democrats to forge a winning coalition that unites workers of all races.

AOC understands that such a realignment is the only way to convert populist outrage with a broken status quo into lasting change. She is not the first socialist to seek a marriage of radical ideals and pragmatic electoral politics—Harrington's "left wing of the possible." But at the head of a movement attuned to the dangers of both economic and racial inequality, speaking to the crises of a dysfunctional system, she could marshal something even more elusive: the untapped possibilities of American democracy.

259

11

The Movement:

The Campaign Warriors Who Got Her Elected

By

BRIDGET READ

Zack Exley, Brand New Congress founding member: We had this idea that we were going to recruit a new kind of candidate—we were going to catapult off the Bernie movement, generate enough press attention, find all these amazing people. In the summer of 2016, we did a hundred-city tour, where we explained, "We're not looking for the loudmouth activists like us. We're looking for people who are building businesses and serving their communities."

But the same Bernie Bro every meeting would raise his hand. So I was kind of giving up.

Alexandra Rojas, Justice Democrats executive director: We had over 10,000 nominations, and AOC was one of those. Her brother had written hers—he explained his sister's life story and what she had been focused on since moving back to the Bronx. It was pretty simple and straight to the point, just asking us to get on the phone with her.

Saikat Chakrabarti, Brand New Congress founding member: Isra Allison was her big proponent. The rest of us were a little skeptical. Like, what's her X factor? Zack and I met her in person in March of 2017.

Exley: We had dinner with her around the corner from the bar where she worked. She was a totally normal person. She wasn't like part of this weird countercultural left that just hated America and hated regular people and all that stuff. She was just a nice warm person. And she was already on the Green New Deal page, which was so rare and weird. When I heard she had studied economics at Boston University, I was like, "Oh, no," because usually economics majors are totally programmed with neoliberalism. But she had somehow been exposed to this whole other set of ideas. She was just starting out in life; she didn't have that big a résumé or track record. At the end of the night, she took a deep breath and had a lot of excitement, and, we were like, "Okay, we'll think about it and let's talk again."

Rachel Lears, *Knock Down the House* filmmaker: I went to the first meeting of candidates and potential candidates in Kentucky that Brand New Congress and Justice Democrats were convening in April. Cori Bush was also there. I had been popping in with the organizers for several months already at that point—my idea for the film was based on reading about their project of recruiting extraordinary ordinary people from around the country to run on this unified platform. People often ask me, "Did she stand out to you from everyone else at the very beginning?" The answer is sort of yes and no. She definitely impressed me very much with her facility with communication.

Chakrabarti: She still wasn't entirely convinced to run after that. She was scared about the fact that Joe Crowley was so powerful and had millions of dollars and all this stuff. She was wondering, "Is this even really possible?" So she did a drive around the district with Riley for a day. She knew the Bronx, because that's where she grew up, but she didn't know Queens. I think she realized that this is an immigrant working-class community. And part of it was simply logistical, like, "I can imagine myself going across this district." She called me after, and that was when she decided to run.

Jesse Korman, photographer: I knew Sandy when she worked at Coffee Shop. I was there every day, and we became friends. Mind you—I'm a death-metal screamer with no friends in the politics world at all. I just assume when I have a friend who says they're getting into politics, I'm like, "What *Vice* magazine article did you read?" So when she was telling me about why she was running, she knocked me out of my seat. For her to be so passionate about it and explain it in a way that made sense to me and how it directly connected to me, I was blown away.

Exley: The people who showed up to Alexandria's first big meeting at this church in the Bronx were different kinds of people than the remnants of the Bernie movement who had been showing up on our 100-city tour. Middle-aged cranky white people basically, bitter disillusioned lefties . . . At this meeting, they were all different ages, all different races. The group was majority people of color. So many people heard about it from her social media. Alexandria got up, and she was a great speaker. She just had great energy and was really passionate and on fire but, at the same time, totally down to earth and talking in normal language. That's when it was really validating. I thought, *Now it's just a technical matter of whether the campaign is actually going to be able to change the behavior of five or six thousand people.*

Aaron Taube, Democratic Socialists of America: People from DSA had a meeting with Alexandria at some point in the summer or fall of 2017, and it just didn't click. The first time I met her was at one of the campaign's house parties at a nice apartment overlooking Queens Boulevard or something. It's crazy how much has changed between now and then, but it was strange to hear a person running for Congress in my district who will say things like, "The Democratic Party needs more than just not being racist." She talked about all these empty units in Manhattan while there's this huge homelessness crisis. And there was a moment where a baby started crying and she just very seamlessly smiled and waved and acknowledged the baby and then just sort of went back to her speech in a way that was like watching a great shortstop throw out the runner at first—totally graceful, like she wasn't even trying. It was just immediately apparent—Wow, this person's really good at this.

Chakrabarti: We had a big canvassing event the day we launched her campaign, and from it we raised a bunch of money, around $30,000, which held over almost through the end of the year. There was this core group of between four and eight people showing up every week. But Alexandria was managing so much of the campaign herself, and it was so tough, while she was working a full-time job. She was managing a restaurant, and so she had kind of odd hours. She basically worked like 12-hour days, four days a week, and then got like three days off.

Lears: In January of 2018, she was getting ready to quit her job at the restaurant, and it was a tough time in the campaign. It was also a tough time for me with the film. There were these weird parallels between independent filmmaking and grassroots campaigning, where you'd have to be constantly trying to convince people to give you money and to believe that you can do something that they have no reason to necessarily believe that you can do. Right around the time I considered giving up the film project, she was considering giving up the campaign. We did this interview in her apartment, and she was feeling very demoralized. Within the next couple of months, I did the Kickstarter campaign and her online fundraising started to take off, but it's easy to forget that those kinds of things were so hard.

Exley: I was doing this fellowship at Harvard and working on all these plans that later became the meat of the Green New Deal. Alex heard that I was doing this, and she had friends in Boston, so she wanted to visit. We basically walked around for a couple of days and talked about economics and how we could rebuild and the role that the government would have. I tried to introduce her to professors and my fellow fellows, but none of them wanted to. I had told them all about this project I was working on to elect new members of Congress, and they all just thought it was ridiculous and silly. None of them wanted to waste any time talking to some kid who had no chance of winning—then, of course, after she won, they're all frantically emailing me because they want her to come speak in their classes.

Chakrabarti: It all felt like we were play-acting at a campaign and just doing it anyway, the best we could. And then right after the petition period, and she actually got on the ballot, things exploded.

Rojas: I moved to New York full time around March 2018. We were really sensitive about spending to begin with, let alone learning how to ask people for a lot of money. We were counting on just out-hustling Crowley in every possible way. That's why Alex wore out of her shoes and knocked on so many doors. Instead of making 5,000 calls, we made hundreds of thousands of calls. At the beginning, it was just out of people's houses, but we finally got an office in Queens. It was so loud every time the subway went by; it was so sweaty. Everybody was everywhere. A lot of us were young Latinas.

Taube: We had never won anything in DSA. We still had people at meetings saying, "The Democrats are like the graveyard, and I really don't think it's comfortable for us to endorse a Democrat." She's never identified as a socialist before this; she doesn't BDS. We sold people on the fact that this draws a line in the sand and shows that, like, DSA is willing to take a stand and willing to take on this fight against the county organization. Because nobody—nobody—endorsed her. And one thing that swung people on her within DSA was abolishing ICE. She was really one of the first people to say that. There were several votes, and we endorsed her on April 22. Originally her ties to DSA wasn't mentioned on their website, and we were like, "Hey, would you put some stuff on the website?" And then she did. And she was supportive of the organization all through the campaign, and yeah, she was a socialist candidate. The media was obsessed with her being a socialist.

Chakrabarti: There were big moments at the exact right time. One of those was Crowley not showing up to the debate, which prompted the New York *Times* to write that piece about him, and then they just kept coming one after another. The video went viral. And then the actual debate. The thing about Alexandria is that she's a really good student, but to this day I've never seen her actually write the points she's going to make and then hit those points. We prepped so much for it, but she was on fire. Crowley was expecting to go in there and just be a gracious, magnanimous leader of the party and school this young woman on how things actually work. And that just didn't happen.

Taube: Two weeks before the election, I had a canvas shift in Sunnyside. You could tell there was something happening. Door after door after door, people had heard of her, they were aware of her. They liked her.

Chakrabarti: We had done a poll three weeks out that showed Crowley up by around 30 points. But at the same time there was this energy on the ground. You think, *Well, polls are bullshit a lot of the time.*

Lears: People were coming up on the streets saying, "I voted for you." It wasn't a guarantee that things were gonna go her way. Alexandria had a slightly different attitude about all of it from the other candidates I was following. She was younger; she didn't have children. It isn't like she wasn't taking a huge risk—she was. But I think she was more prepared to lose.

Rojas: Before Election Day, I was so sick—a few days before I had a full-on 100-degree fever. I had stayed almost all night in the Queens office setting up different tables and packets for Election

Day. I slept for two hours, went back to Saikat's apartment, where I was sleeping on the floor, and was back at the office by six. I had to be on the dialer. When I saw the amount of people that were there from like six until the time the polls close, it was clear we could actually win this. But I had seen the poll so I was trying not to get my hopes up. I got to the Election Night party very early, and polls closed around nine, and I looked at the TV like, *Why is she up?* Why is it saying that she's at like 70 percent right now? Crowley should have had Queens down, because he's Queen's Democratic Party chair, and they started counting Queens first, so we were very confused.

Lears: I had already arranged to be in the car with Alexandria going over to the party. She wanted everyone to turn off their cell phones—at the moment the polls closed, the first results that were released had her a little bit ahead, and then she didn't get any more information until she got to the party. So we drove over and we found a place to park. I'm walking over to the location, and she can see that people are celebrating inside, and she starts running to get in and has to explain to the guard at the door who she is to get into her own party.

Rojas: I saw the TV, and then I looked to my left, and I saw her, we started freaking out, and everyone started screaming again. I just started sobbing, I couldn't talk. I just kept saying, *Why isn't it going down?*

Chakrabarti: We thought if she won, it would be like when Eric Cantor got beat—like, *Oh, we'll get a lot of press for a week*. We had to capitalize on this as much as possible. Corbin [Trent] booked the most insane day of media for her the next day—in retrospect, it's completely amazing that she knocked it out of the park, and it was a crazy thing to do late. It was a grueling day. We basically went home from that party at like two; I woke up at like 4:30 a.m. and picked her up at the Bronx and started doing media at six. Just walking around New York, there were cameras jumping out of bushes. It was overwhelming. And the whole time we were thinking the spotlight was going to go away.

12

Amazon:

Beating
Bezos

~~~

By

ANDREW RICE

In 2017, Amazon announced a contest
in which North American cities were
asked to compete to win something
called HQ2—HQ1 being Seattle, near
where the company was founded. The
prize would come with $5 billion in pri-
vate investment and 50,000 new jobs.
More than 200 cities submitted entries.
New York City, already booming and
home to thousands of other tech jobs, had

the idea of using the complex to anchor the redevelopment of a stretch of post-industrial waterfront in Queens just one subway stop across the East River from midtown. The plan had the backing of New York's political leadership: Mayor Bill de Blasio had Manhattan's skyscrapers lit orange, and then-Governor Andrew Cuomo joked that he would change his name to "Amazon Cuomo" if it would help. A group of 70 local elected officials, business leaders, and unions signed an open letter in support of the project.

In November 2018, a week after the midterm elections in which AOC was elected, the company announced it had two winners: Arlington, Virginia—just outside Washington, D.C.—and the Queens site. Each location was to receive, within ten years, at least 25,000 new jobs with an average salary of $150,000, many of which would go to residents of AOC's district, which begins just north of the Amazon tract and stretches up into the Bronx. In return, the government promised subsidies and tax incentives, mostly to be paid out of tax revenues generated by Amazon itself. The plan promised to spark a boom for restaurants and retail in the surrounding neighborhood of Long Island City, which was already bristling with new and under-construction apartment towers. Which meant it

would be a clear win for developers, too. For most politicians, it would be something to boast about, not undermine; a boon, not a boondoggle. The deal depended on the usual land-use approvals and tax incentives, but those seemed a foregone conclusion. Then @AOC tweeted.

"We've been getting calls and outreach from Queens residents all day about this," she began on November 12, 2018, linking to a news story about the announcement. "The community's response? Outrage."

This was an overstatement: Actually, polls showed the project was broadly popular, both in New York as a whole and in Queens in particular. But the deal offered the young congresswoman a chance to advance, in spectacularly confrontational fashion, her socialist critique of economic-development policy. To lure Amazon, the city and state government were offering billions of dollars in subsidies and tax incentives— giveaways that would line the pockets of an already-rich and well-connected conglomerate, AOC argued, that was expanding in New York anyway.

"Amazon is a billion-dollar company," @AOC continued. "The idea that it will receive hundreds of millions of dollars in tax breaks at a time when our subway is crumbling and our communities need

MORE investment, not less, is extremely concerning to residents here."

She went on, over a total of six tweets, to question Amazon's commitment to hiring local residents, its hostility toward unions, and the wave of gentrification that some housing activists feared it would bring. "Displacement is not community development," she wrote. "Investing in luxury condos is not the same thing as investing in people and families."

And that was it. Those were the 224 words that killed one of the largest economic-development projects in the city's recent history. "Very simply," said someone involved with the Amazon project, "AOC is the reason it didn't happen." In the process, she upset the old civic consensus about development—which treated social good as a by-product of economic growth and valued private investment above all else. For the young socialist and her movement, it was a catalyzing moment—one that demonstrated her power to shape the city while advancing a new, insurgent ideology of equity and opposition to corporate power.

How did a newly elected member of Congress who had no role in approving local land-use decisions scuttle the deal? Ocasio-Cortez's primary victory had been a national sensation, and a particular shock to the system in Queens, where Joe Crowley had run the local Democratic machine for two decades, promoting allies and doling out patronage. When she deposed the boss, party regulars started to fear the growing power of this impatient and uncooperative new left. The local city councilman and state senator, initially both supporters of the Amazon deal, switched sides and started to fiercely attack the company. The City Council Speaker, Corey Johnson, who was thinking of running for mayor, likewise came out in opposition to "vulture capitalism." Amazon has an imperious relationship with its home city, Seattle, and, historically, has expected similar deference elsewhere. Bezos quickly retreated, moving the entire HQ2 project to Arlington, Virginia. "Anything is possible," @AOC tweeted in celebration.

It symbolized exactly what the Establishment feared about the new generation of leaders on the left. Years later, New York's political class is still picking through the rubble and recriminations. "What made me so crazy is she didn't even try to figure out what the hell was going on," said Alicia Glen, the city's deputy mayor for economic development at the time. "She just went nuclear, and that is so irresponsible to your constituents." Proponents of the project said that the deal would have brought amenities like a public park, a new 600-seat school, and investments in transit to a stretch of industrial waterfront that happened to be adjacent to many thousands of new and planned apartment units in rapidly developing western Queens.

Ocasio-Cortez called that "dressed-up trickle-down economics." Like other critics of the deal, she seized on the size of the subsidy package, which would have maxed out at just under $3 billion. Those who supported the plan pointed out that the "billions" that were offered were conditional, tied to the tax revenues and number of new jobs Amazon managed to create, but that nuance was lost in the commotion AOC started. She characterized the deal as a gigantic corporate gift. "When you give a $3 billion tax break to the richest company in the world," she told the writer Anand Giridharadas, "that means you're giving up on our schools. You're giving up our infrastructure. You're giving up our community development." She questioned whether Amazon would benefit residents of the adjacent Queensbridge housing projects, which, she said, "went without heat and hot water in the dead of winter." She also claimed that an influx of new tech workers would turbocharge the ongoing gentrification of the neighborhood and that speculators were already jacking up rents by "two, three hundred dollars a month."

In fact, the Amazon deal had a lot of fans in the Queensbridge projects who were furious about AOC's opposition. "She doesn't know what poor, lower-income people need," said April Simpson, president of the housing project's tenants association. To win local support, Amazon and the government had floated ideas for a jointly funded employment center at Brooklyn Navy Yard, a $15 million jobs-and-technology-training program, and other inducements. (In 2021, Amazon would pledge $2 billion to a fund to create affordable housing in localities where it has headquarters, including Arlington, a Virginia neighborhood that happily accepted HQ2.) When the Amazon agreement died, those community investments did too. Rents kept on increasing even without Amazon, as the neighborhood filled with young AOC voters. Simpson can only recall seeing her congresswoman in the projects once: when thousands of Bernie Sanders supporters tramped through for a big endorsement rally at Queensbridge Park. "I know she's not for the people because she's never come over here," Simpson said. "But she has so much to say about Queensbridge."

After the deal collapsed, polls showed voters blamed Ocasio-Cortez, and she tried to deflect responsibility. "Everyone thinks I'm the one who kicked out Amazon," she told students at John Jay College in April 2019. "And it's like, *I wish!* I wish my five tweets defeated the richest man in the world. I would love to gas myself up and think that." But in the years since, emboldened activist groups have managed to scuttle other ambitious development projects, demonstrating that in a one-party system with low-turnout primaries, impassioned ideologues can exert enormous power. The city's real-estate industry and business community are frightened by the surge in anti-development sentiment. "That is a death knell for New York City," Glen said. Amazon, meanwhile, has continued about its business, further consolidating its grip on the retail sector during the pandemic. In late 2019, it announced plans to lease space for more than 1,500 workers in Hudson Yards, the new megadevelopment on the West Side of Manhattan (which itself has already received $6 billion in government subsidies). The next year, it bought the shuttered Lord & Taylor department store on Fifth Avenue, in which it housed another 2,000 employees.

These new jobs represent just a fraction of what Amazon promised at HQ2, and Amazon won't be making any public investments in return. And the expansion is coming to Manhattan—not Queens. Still, @AOC struck a triumphal pose, posting a photo of herself with her feet kicked up. "Me waiting on the haters to apologize after we were proven right on Amazon and saved the public billions," she wrote. "These jobs are for FREE." From her own perspective, the case against subsidized development seems to reflect an optimistic belief in the inherent vitality of the metropolis she represents. The city doesn't need to pander to big corporations, or sell itself at a bargain, because New York is . . . New York. In December 2020, an unrepentant AOC told a podcast interviewer, "There will always be another Amazon."

13

The Sit-in:

AOC vs. Nancy Pelosi, Day One

By

KATE ARONOFF

Τ
he moment that would transform Alexandria Ocasio-Cortez
into the most influential voice
of the climate movement almost didn't
happen. That it would focus on the Green
New Deal wasn't clear until 36 hours
beforehand. That AOC would show up
for it at all wasn't clear until she did.

For months, an upstart climate group
called the Sunrise Movement had been

planning an event intended to upend the debate over climate action: a sit-in at House Speaker Nancy Pelosi's office. Sunrise envisioned the protest as a soft launch for a sweeping range of climate solutions. The goal was to force Democrats to move beyond the timid half-measures they had long favored and confront global warming with the urgency it demanded.

AOC, for her part, was looking for a way to make her mark in Congress. "After she won, we had all these conversations about what we would do next," recalled Saikat Chakrabarti, her then–chief of staff. "She was still discovering her power in some ways." Zack Exley, who along with Chakrabarti had recruited AOC to run for Congress, had spoken to Sunrise two months earlier, but nothing had come of the conversation.

Just four days before the sit-in, the Sunrisers knew they needed to go bigger. Unless they could find someone prominent to support the demonstration, it wouldn't draw much notice on Capitol Hill. By that point, AOC already boasted more than a million followers on Twitter. And the protest would take place on her first day of orientation in Congress. But Sunrise's members knew they couldn't ask her to take on Pelosi by showing up in person. At best, they figured, all they could hope for was a tweet.

There in the office, the Sunrisers joined hands for an impromptu prayer circle. Then Evan Weber, the group's political director, made a call to Exley. "That was it," he recalled. "We'd had one conversation with Exley, then no conversations, and then a conversation the Friday before the sit-in that basically put everything into motion." Exley patched Sunrise through to Chakrabarti, who floated the tweet proposal to AOC. As he pitched the idea, he made a joke. "You could always join them," he said.

His boss didn't miss a beat. "Yeah," she said. "I'm gonna join them."

Chakrabarti was floored. AOC hadn't even been sworn in, and she was planning to protest her new boss at an event that was designed to end in arrests. Given Pelosi's iron-fisted enforcement of party discipline, the move could have effectively ended AOC's career before it even began.

But AOC understood how high the stakes were. The sit-in would take place at a moment when conservative Democrats were trying to oust Pelosi as Speaker. Given that AOC had just scored a big win against the party Establishment, she knew that barging into the Speaker's office with an army of activists might—understandably—be construed as part of the coup attempt. She would have to strike a perfect balance between supporting the cause and not stumbling onto the wrong side of a fight.

How she struck that balance foreshadowed the kind of lawmaker she would become. At one point, according to Weber, AOC seriously considered getting arrested along with the protesters. What changed her mind wasn't a fear of angering Pelosi—it was the realization that being hauled off in handcuffs would force her to miss an orientation session on how to cast floor votes. It was a quiet but telling decision. Her heart might be with the activists who had helped elect her, but her place was in Congress.

The next few days were frenetic. Over the weekend, 250 young Sunrisers arrived in Washington, D.C., to attend training sessions before the action, sleeping on pews in a church in the northwest part of the city. The group, joined by AOC's fledgling staff, scrambled to figure out what the congresswoman-elect would bring with her to the sit-in. It wasn't enough, she felt, to say that Democrats needed to do more on climate change. She wanted to come with a concrete proposal—something that spelled out what they *should* do.

That it would be called the Green New Deal wasn't a forgone conclusion. The T-shirts Sunrise had prepared for the sit-in didn't include the phrase; the group didn't want its policy push to be confused with the Green Party's platform. AOC also had reservations about the branding. The original New Deal, after all, excluded many women and people of color from its core programs. She and her staff had been working for months with New Consensus, a policy shop co-founded by Exley, to map out an ambitious plan to tackle the climate crisis and spur the U.S. economy. In her view, what stood in the way was politics. "The idea that the Democratic Party needs to be moderate is what's holding us back on this," she told me the week before her primary election.

Now, in the days before the sit-in, organizers and AOC's staff scrambled to rework the New Consensus plan into a formal resolution. But they didn't know what to call it, and no one had any ideas better than the Green New Deal. So when the name showed up on top of a Google Doc that appeared in Weber's in-box, it stuck.

The first iteration of the Green New Deal didn't call on Congress to pass a specific set of policy proposals. Rather, it urged the House to begin drafting climate legislation immediately, so Democrats would be ready to act swiftly if they succeeded at taking back the White House and Senate in 2020. The resolution spelled out a far-reaching set of goals the climate plan should meet, including going all-in on renewable energy and upgrading every home, office, and factory with state-of-the-art energy efficiency. It also called for guaranteeing jobs for all Americans, combating income inequality and racial injustice, and giving labor unions a voice in the transition to a green economy. It was, as Vox observed, a "full-spectrum vision of a sustainable social democracy—a level of progressive ambition that most U.S. citizens have likely never encountered."

Over the weekend, Chakrabarti attended the training sessions that Sunrise was holding in the church. Impressed, he recommended that AOC and her fellow Squad member Rashida Tlaib pay a visit the day before the sit-in. The two women tried to enter quietly, through the back of the church, so as not to interrupt the training. But Sunrise, smartly, had revamped the evening's agenda so their arrival would coincide with a pizza break. As soon as they were spotted, the young activists raced to greet them. It was a moment of generational transformation—two women of color elected to Congress, one of them still in her 20s, surrounded by hundreds of students and recent graduates who already viewed them as personal role models and avatars of change.

AOC seized the moment. Balancing in high heels on a folding table at the back of the chapel, she spoke to the young protesters. "We are busting down the doors," she declared.

"We cannot do it alone," she continued. "We need to show people that this is the fight for our fucking lives." By the time she finished, there wasn't a dry eye in the room.

After she spoke, Ocasio-Cortez walked through the crowd, posing for selfies and hugging tearful attendees as they told her how much it meant to them for her to be there. It was being in that church—seeing Sunrise's willingness to sacrifice potential donations and political support—that quashed any misgivings AOC had about jumping into the fray.

That didn't mean she was leaving anything to chance. Hours before the sit-in, she was still making last-minute tweaks to what she would say, honing a message that would neither start a battle with Pelosi nor play into the hands of those seeking to unseat her. By the time she made her appearance in Pelosi's office, the sit-in was already under way.

Framed by a semi-circle of activists seated on the floor, AOC made clear that the grassroots energy behind the sit-in was not just a climate call to arms—it was also a potential source of strength for Democrats. "Should Leader Pelosi become the next Speaker of the House," she declared, "we need to tell her that we've got her back in showing and pursuing the most aggressive energy agenda that this country has ever seen."

AOC's appearance unleashed a torrent of media coverage. In an instant, she had not only become the most important leader of America's climate movement but also made clear where her loyalties lay. "She made the decision in that moment—maybe for the first time—to be the conduit between social movements like ours and the halls of power," Weber said.

Following the sit-in, AOC and Senator Ed Markey spent a month working with Sunrise and New Consensus to draft a more detailed and comprehensive framework for climate action. Organized around a series of projects designed to cut carbon emissions to zero by 2050, the joint resolution called for clean air and water for all Americans, healthy and affordable food, safe housing, and green jobs. "It's not a bill," AOC explained at a press conference, wearing a bright-green suit amid her many male co-sponsors in dark ones. "It is a resolution. Our first step is to define the problem and the scope of the solution. Small, incremental policy solutions are not enough."

The resolution made the Green New Deal the center of gravity in the climate debate. The European Union embraced it, and officials from Spain to South Korea crafted their own versions of it. In November 2020, less than two years after AOC attended the sit-in at Pelosi's office, four insurgent candidates who ran on the Green New Deal were elected to Congress. And President Joe Biden created two new Cabinet-level posts charged with cutting carbon emissions to zero. "If she didn't actually care," Weber said, "none of this shit would have worked."

14

The Ikea Tutorial:

A PEOPLE'S ECONOMY

"Some things in society should not be for sale."

— JUNE 17, 2019 —

~~~~~

➡ AOC's Instagram Live feeds have a signature structure, moving deftly from the casual to the intimate to the didactic before crescendoing to a call to arms. This one, which was a sequel to an earlier feed in which she also assembled furniture, is typical. On June 17, 2019, she went live from her living room, where the plan was to talk to her audience about economic equity while **putting together a filing cabinet from Ikea.** She was wearing a T-shirt that read "Rematriate the Land," meaning return it to its natural state. In the end, she didn't get very far on the filing cabinet and had a glass of OJ.

1

She starts with the offhanded opening . . .

"Hey, everybody. Good to see ya. I'm back to making furniture, everyone. We're still trying to put together some semblance of a place to stay in D.C. So I have to make a file cabinet to hold my very important files from my house. I'm going to try to answer some questions while I do this multitask."

2

Before assuming the role of an (earthbound) lifestyle guru . . .

"I try not to be wasteful with furniture. The first rule is to get pieces that are all wood. If you're light with them, you can have them last a very, very long time."

3

Setting up the gentle rebuke . . .

"Don't be a person that just buys stuff and tosses it out. That's really not good for the environment. Always buy used furniture. Really lean on Craigslist . . . and flea markets and thrift stores and stuff like that."

4

Circling to the bigger picture . . .

"People are saying the economy's going great and we should all be thankful. And you're just kind of looking up and you're like, *Am I crazy?* You feel like you're really struggling to get by . . . I think that capitalism and the idea of capitalism gets confused by a lot of people. They're like, 'Oh, capitalism—that means businesses, right? That means a free market, right?' That's not what capitalism is. You can have free-market economies with democratic-socialist businesses. What are democratic-socialist businesses? A perfect example of that is a worker cooperative. If you ever go to Vermont, there'll be worker cooperatives that are employee owned. So it's really about democracy in the economy."

5

Which she underscores with a generational-bonding moment . . .

"I think we are experiencing generational shifts in attitudes across a wide variety of political issues. When you actually look at the shifts in political opening, they happen more along age than . . . a lot of other indicators. Younger generations have grown up in a vastly different [world than] older generations and baby boomers. We've never seen a capitalist society that has resulted in the true benefit of the many. But we have lived in a world where big business has owned and bought our government."

6

Before pivoting to the rallying cry . . .

"I wouldn't even call myself an ideologue as much as folks like to portray me as one . . . How can we alter our future? At a bare, bare minimum, where we can go is guarantee a living wage, guarantee health care to all people. Let's see—a minimum wage, Medicare for All . . . Until we are able to build enough political power [for] transformative changes in our policies . . . we need to organize."

7

Then back to the folksy . . .

"I thrift a lot of my clothes. The blue dress in my profile photo is . . . no joke, a designer dress that I got from a thrift store for like 35 bucks that normally retails for something like, honestly, maybe it's like a $500 wool dress. You use it, you wear it, and you love it. And you can wear it until there are holes in it."

8

. . . And out.

"All right. So I'm going to go finish making this furniture because I am not doing a good job. But I see you all; thank you all so much for joining. Bye."

15

The Squad:

A Sisterhood
That Shook
Washington

By

CLARE MALONE

L ike so many women in Instagram posts with nearly 210,000 likes, they are young-looking and striking: newly elected representatives Ayanna Pressley, Rashida Tlaib, Ilhan Omar, and Alexandria Ocasio-Cortez— the last two born in the 1980s—seated at a conference table and dressed in the high-necked attire of Washington,

D.C., bottles of water and thin microphones lined up neatly in front of them. Ocasio-Cortez—farthest from the camera, wearing a cream suit and satisfied smile—captioned the November 12, 2018, photo "Squad."

Tlaib's caption of a similar photo from that day reached for a more Gen X reference: "#DreamTeam in Congress." (Like Pressley, she was born in the 1970s.) But "Squad" stuck, soon becoming "the Squad." All four women were members of Justice Democrats, a group with ideological roots in Bernie Sanders's 2016 campaign that recruited progressive middle-class people to run for Congress. They had been thrown together by ideology to begin with, but the solidarity, friendship, and generational change read into that otherwise banal 2018 photo has come to define their political lives. At the time, a writer for *Glamour* giddily described her excitement for "these inspiring women," who were "already hatching plans to change the world together." Months after the post, the "Squad" phenom had grown so much as to merit an earnest Vox explainer on the term's hip-hop roots and its cultural appropriation (somehow it did so without mentioning Taylor Swift's *1989* album tour). There were those who found the term "embarrassing" and "mildly sexist and infantilizing" when

applied to these four history-making members of Congress: the youngest woman, the first Black woman from Massachusetts, the first Muslim women to serve in Congress. (It's worth noting that one Urban Dictionary definition of *squad* is: "A dumb word only used by white middle schoolers in suburban areas to describe their group of friends and try to sound ghetto.")

Ocasio-Cortez, Pressley, Tlaib, and Omar publicly embraced the term anyway. Together, they attracted the ire of the president of the United States, the Speaker of the House, and Fox News. They accumulated power—and generated jealousy—within their party. The Squad elicited no weak opinions.

• • •

The Squad as we know it almost wasn't. "You know, there was talk at one point right before [Pressley's] election about withdrawing the endorsement," Corbin Trent, a co-founder of Justice Democrats, said.

The ideological fissures of the 2016 Democratic primary were still fresh during the 2018 midterm season, and Pressley had endorsed Hillary Clinton, not Sanders. The Justice Democrats had sprung up during the 2018 midterms, providing endorsements and fundraising support for candidates in underdog primaries. The group kept in weekly touch with the women who would come to be known as the Squad, and it even ended up staffing Ocasio-Cortez's campaign once it became clear that its shoestring resources would be most effective if funneled into a single upstart's coffers.

While there were a raft of Justice Democrat candidates in 2018, Ocasio-Cortez, Pressley, Tlaib, and Omar emerged as the most visible and viable ones. But in contrast to Pressley, Omar and Tlaib were strong Sanders supporters and Ocasio-Cortez had worked for his campaign. The women's shared public image today belies differences like this. These differences aren't just political ones, either; the four Squad congresswomen depart from one another on belief, strategy, and personality. It's why Trent said "the Squad's not a thing." To him, it's more a mirage of the media's creation.

But the women are, in fact, close, in no small part because of that very media creation, a sort of self-fulfilling prophecy of friendship. At first, theirs was an amiable, helpmates-like connection. Ocasio-Cortez went out of her way to stump for the other women as she became a national sensation during the 2018 primaries. Later, she and Tlaib excitedly tweeted a video of their attendance at Pressley's final Boston City Council

meeting, eagerly performative fangirls for the cause. Once they got to Congress, their ties to Justice Democrats kept the group tactically aligned in a mini-caucus, one whose ethos was far cooler than, but not wholly dissimilar to, the anti-Establishment one of the right-wing Freedom Caucus. They immediately attracted media coverage incommensurate with your average House freshman. This ticked many people—including fellow Democrats—off.

The Squad photo that started it all was taken at an orientation specifically for incoming progressive members. Waleed Shahid, the communications director for Justice Democrats, said the event was meant to encourage the new members to "talk to each other, set up a group chat, all this basic stuff." The people with whom Saikat Chakrabarti, Ocasio-Cortez's then–chief of staff, spoke the most while in Washington were the other Squad members' chiefs of staff. "We had a running text thread going," he said, "to strategize together on vote recommendations for our bosses." They discussed a plan to "try to take over the Committee on Financial Services, turn that into a progressive committee," he recalled. Tlaib, Pressley, and Ocasio-Cortez got the committee assignment, along with other progressive newcomers such as Katie Porter of

California. (Porter, a white suburban mom from wealthy Orange County, California, is not a Squad member despite their shared political beliefs and an upset victory.)

The group's fame dovetailed with and helped accelerate the melding of pop culture and politics in Donald Trump's America. Ocasio-Cortez, Pressley, and Tlaib went viral for yet another photo in February 2019. In this one, they were shooting daggers at a testifying Michael Cohen. "The Destiny's Child of the Senate," Mashable inaccurately if adoringly captioned the photo. It was a level of fame that crossed over from D.C. celebrity to actual celebrity. The public—both those admiring of the foursome and those inclined to dislike them—seemed united in its intense curiosity. Americans have always felt entitled to the internal and personal lives of women in the spotlight, but the loudness and newness of the Squad in the congressional context—their skin color, their gender—fanned interest even more intensely. The women became the faces of creeping socialism—and a multiracial society—on Fox News. Tucker Carlson called Ocasio-Cortez a "moron," and Newt Gingrich told Sean Hannity that Omar showed "contempt for the country which she's been living in." During their first six months in office, Ocasio-Cortez was mentioned three times as much on Fox as she was on CNN and MSNBC, and Omar received similarly frenetic coverage from Fox. This inevitably drew the attention of cable-addicted Trump, who tweeted that the Squad was "endorsing Socialism, hate of Israel and the USA! Not good for the Democrats." Omar was assigned a Capitol Police special agent to track all her death threats.

If they had always been friendly collaborators, the Squad bonded deeply thanks to Congress's hostile breed of office politics, which spilled out into the open as time went on. The summer of 2019 was perhaps what lashed them together the most, after Nancy Pelosi dismissed "their public whatever and their Twitter world." Days later, Trump tweeted that the congresswomen should go back to their "crime infested" homes. It was a shot that seemed aimed, specifically, at Omar, who was born in Somalia and spent time in refugee camps before coming to America. The four quickly held a joint press conference, a circling-of-the-wagons move that's since become characteristic.

"They had all been turned into polarizing figures not by their own volition," Chakrabarti said. "I know for them, a large part of their friendship and bond was about supporting each other through that experience."

The Squad.

Wearing a liquid-drape cherry-red dress, Pressley took the podium first with a denunciation of Trump and an articulation of what united the foursome, the values their admirers saw the women as embodying: "Our squad is big. Our squad includes any person committed to building a more equitable and just world." When the first question came from the press, Ocasio-Cortez, Omar, and Tlaib all turned to Pressley, who strode to the microphone to answer. "She's very commanding, a mature mother hen," Trent said. (She's fifteen years older than AOC.) "You know, among them, she's sort of the senior role, if you will. She's sort of the leader."

In particular, "AOC looks very much up to Ayanna," he said. Both Ocasio-Cortez and Pressley are East Coasters with polished public personae who attended Boston University and worked for Kennedy congressional offices—Ocasio-Cortez interned in Ted's Senate office, while Pressley worked as an aide in Representative Joe II's. Their first meeting, in June 2018, was caught on video (of course), each in de rigueur "suffragette white" jackets, pumping up a small crowd of donors as they vibed off each other's stump speech, a little living-room display of political kismet. Afterward, Ocasio-Cortez gushed on Twitter about "BFF applications" being

in. So much of the Squad relationship is for public consumption, but even if they aren't friends in the constantly buzzing group-text kind of way, there's a sisterhood to it—the bond formed by very different people thrown together by circumstance.

Still, Ocasio-Cortez and Pressley seem like the kind of friends who could have happened without the wind of an out-of-control national phenomenon at their backs. Sarah Groh, Pressley's longtime chief of staff, knows Ocasio-Cortez from when they were both in college in the Boston area. Both Pressley and Ocasio-Cortez lost a parent to cancer, and they share the self-possessed, unbothered seriousness of the kind of woman who did Model U.N. and never skipped a college class. "You know how there are people who have Instagram relationships? This is not an Instagram relationship," Pressley said in 2019 of Ocasio-Cortez. "Our relationship is not static, it is not one-dimensional, it is dynamic, it is deep, it is meaningful, it is real, and it grows by the day." They also share the experience of sexual assault. In an Instagram Live retelling of her experience of the January 6 insurrection, Ocasio-Cortez recounted heading to Pressley's office in the aftermath of the attack and staying until four in the morning. Pressley fed her, listened to her story, and recognized it as traumatic. "I look back on that and she really helped my healing," Ocasio-Cortez said.

The two have seemingly learned to play the Washington insider's game better than Tlaib and Omar, who are both midwestern and have more of an underdog's fire about them. Tlaib has felt comfortable calling out Pelosi in uncomfortable ways—she admonished the Speaker to "uplift the women, especially the women of color, in your caucus"— while Omar ran afoul of the Democratic mainstream for her at best ignorant and at worst anti-Semitic comments about Israel. "I am, by nature, a starter of fires," Omar writes in her autobiography. Tlaib and Omar were both banned from Israel in 2019, which led to another Squad circling of the wagons—Ocasio-Cortez and Pressley pointed out it was remarkably terrible treatment for two prominent women of color. Still, in the eyes of the party Establishment, it only served to add another black mark to Tlaib's and Omar's résumé. Members were beginning to tire of the attention their dustups attracted. By contrast, when Ocasio-Cortez's staff began to cause trouble for her within the caucus with inflammatory tweets about Pelosi, they were pushed out. ("Staff are meant to be seen and not heard," a senior

Democratic aide told Vox at the time.) By March 2020, Politico was writing about "the 'new' AOC," who was more attuned to internal party politics. Pressley worked hard to blend in better too. "We don't land in the same place on every vote. We are each our own people," she said of the Squad. She had been worried from the outset that the excitement over the women's collective identity would distract from their day-to-day work. The Squad's rah-rah, you-go-girl, feel-good multiculturalism is memorable branding, but it threatens to flatten their remarkable individual selves. While there is never any public unpleasantness, it's clear that the group has disagreements, and they seem to occasionally chafe at the performative togetherness the label "Squad" has wrought. While they text regularly, it's not like they have standing brunch dates or consult with one another on all legislation. But they vocally endorsed one another during tough 2020 primary challenges for Tlaib and Omar, and all enthusiastically blurbed the latter's book, with Tlaib and Ocasio-Cortez calling Omar a "sister" and Pressley professing her to be a woman she loves "so fiercely." People close to the four are reluctant to talk about any behind-the-scenes disagreements on the record, a testament to both the power of their public friendship and the fear that gossip could trivialize it.

But more than a few were caught off guard, and headlines were generated, when Omar tweeted in late 2020 that it was "disturbing to see members be 1st to get [the] vaccine while most frontline workers, elderly and infirm in our districts, wait." The tweet seemed rather pointed, given that Ocasio-Cortez had posted an Instagram video of herself the day before receiving the shot. Ocasio-Cortez later tweeted out an explanation ("continuity of governance"), with no mention of Omar—whose father died in June of COVID-19 complications— though she did write "there's also a real risk in this age of misinfo of how it would be weaponized if leaders refused to take it en masse."

In the early days, the Squad shared a lot of "besties" social-media content of one another: a cartoon rendering of Omar and Ocasio-Cortez walking, an extremely cute video of Omar's young daughter visiting Congress and hanging with her mom and her mom's friends, and more pointed content at an "#In-DefenseofIlhan rally." Omar and Tlaib have always seemed more prone to posting casual or less highly produced promotional snaps of the group—there's a particularly winsome joie de vivre in Tlaib's account, lots of pictures of her family and door-to-door canvassing in an "I Have People in Detroit" beanie— while from the outset, Pressley was likelier to post a magazine shoot. There are more and more of those professional photos these days, like the August 2020 *Vanity Fair* Squad group portrait pegged to the summer of Black Lives Matter protests. They all posted it.

The Squad does not agree on every policy. Pressley voted against a financial boycott of Israel, hewing more to the traditional Democratic Party line, while Ocasio-Cortez supported it alongside Omar and Tlaib, who are both Muslim and were outspoken in their support for the Palestinian side. That position was painted by some as being anti-Semitic, a temperature-raising accusation, especially when made against the first two Muslim women in Congress. In the early days of the COVID-19 crisis, Ocasio-Cortez was the only Democratic member to vote against a relief package that she felt gave too much to big business. She thought she wouldn't be alone in her act of defiance, not having gotten a heads-up about minute changes of heart from certain colleagues who had told her they'd probably vote no, too. Ocasio-Cortez said she walked home from the vote in the rain, feeling lonely and discouraged. "I was just, like, heartbroken," she said.

The outsize individual celebrity of Ocasio-Cortez divides the group sometimes. Trent's analogy: "It's like going to the party with a drunk person," for the other, less famous three. "Yeah, they're fun, and they're your buddy, but sometimes they're a little embarrassing, and they're kind of gonna inhibit your ability to meet new people." While Ocasio-Cortez can chart her own course, he said, Pressley, Tlaib, and Omar risk staying in her shadow. Like actual sisters, the closeness can grate.

Odd metaphors aside, by 2020 the Squad had become a tool to grow the progressive caucus. In June 2020, 44-year-old middle-school principal Jamaal Bowman—a Justice Democrats recruit who was dubbed "this year's AOC"—beat a 16-term incumbent easily. Cori Bush's upset victory in Missouri indicated a bit of strategic maturity from the progressive campaign apparatus. Bush ran as a Justice Democrat candidate alongside the proto-Squad in 2018 and lost her race by 20 points. This time around, she had $150,000 of ad buys from Justice Democrats in the final week of her campaign.

Bowman and Bush have been marked as Squad intimates, at least publicly. While other progressives won in 2020, they were the most electrifying to the public, which now seems like the entrée necessary for membership in the friend group-cum-caucus. Bush seemed to meld with it most easily; it helps that she's a woman, adept at the blending of personal and political that the Squad does so well on social media. Bowman's Instagrams are more blah and professional; he'll probably never explain his makeup routine while expounding on progressive policy, as Ocasio-Cortez did for *Vogue*. After she won, Bush tweeted about the difficulty of shopping for a congressional wardrobe on a budget. Tlaib responded that she wore her old maternity shirts under blazers, and Ocasio-Cortez chimed in with advice about thrifting and renting clothes. "Thanks sis!" Bush replied, and Ocasio-Cortez proposed a shopping trip. It's clear the OG Squad is just fine with wielding their media power in order to propagate the caucus. Friendship for the cause. And now the GOP is trying to co-opt it: New York Republican freshman representative Nicole Malliotakis said she would be forming a conservative knockoff of the group. A "Freedom Squad," she called it.

However formalized the Squad becomes, the Justice Democrats aren't going away, while the Congressional Progressives seem more serious than ever about exerting influence during a Democratic administration; things are professionalizing rapidly. Whether the latest Squad initiates will ever have to weather the same kind of organic, unruly fame (and infamy) seems unlikely; Ocasio-Cortez, Pressley, Tlaib, and Omar hacked out a path through the Washington, D.C., weeds for them to follow in that way. It's more plausible that the same kind of intimate, sisterly bond will be difficult to replicate as the group, and its power, grows. But given that the level of vitriol in our political culture shows no sign of abating, sisterhood could mean survival. "There was a time where the volume of threats had gotten so high that I didn't even know if I was going to live to my next term," Ocasio-Cortez said in 2020. "Their sisterhood and their friendship, it's not some political alliance. It's a very deep, unconditional human bond."

16

The Border:

"The United States is running concentration camps on our southern border."

~~~

Text and story by MICHELLE RUIZ
Art by PIA GUERRA

ON THE MORNING OF THE VISIT, PROPUBLICA PUBLISHED AN EXPOSÉ: CUSTOMS AND BORDER PROTECTION AGENTS HAD THREATENED OCASIO-CORTEZ AND ESCOBAR IN A SECRET FACEBOOK GROUP. "FUCK THE HOES," ONE PATROL SUPERVISOR WROTE. "THERE SHOULD BE NO PHOTO OPS FOR THESE SCUM BUCKETS," ANOTHER COMMENTED. DOCTORED IMAGES DEPICTED OCASIO-CORTEZ PERFORMING SEX ACTS ON A MIGRANT AND ON TRUMP.

"I FELT LIKE I NEEDED TO PROTECT MYSELF FROM CBP OFFICERS."

"ONE OF THE FIRST THINGS WE WERE TOLD IS THAT WE WERE NOT ALLOWED TO SPEAK TO THE MIGRANTS."

OCASIO-CORTEZ FORCED HER WAY IN.

"SOME WOMEN HAD BEEN SEPARATED FROM CHILDREN, SOME HAD BEEN HELD FOR MORE THAN 50 DAYS. SEVERAL HAD NOT RECEIVED THEIR MEDICATIONS, INCLUDING ONE FOR EPILEPSY."

MY HAIR IS FALLING OUT!

I HAVEN'T TAKEN A SHOWER FOR 15 DAYS!

THIS IS ALL I WAS GIVEN TO WASH MY BODY!

17

The Zuckerberg
Grilling:

SLAYING THE TECH GIANTS

"So, you won't take down lies, or you will take down lies?"

▶▶ Within two months of taking office, AOC established herself as one of the all-time masters of the art of interrogating witnesses in congressional hearings. Unlike many of her colleagues, she refused to indulge in the tedious, self-righteous grandstanding that has become the hallmark of such proceedings. Instead, she subjected witnesses to incisive and aggressive questioning, forcing them to admit the very things that they were trying to avoid saying out loud.

In February 2019, in one of her very first hearings, AOC's deliberate, step-by-step probing of Michael Cohen, Donald Trump's personal attorney, yielded concrete evidence that helped spark a criminal investigation into the president's shady financial dealings. And in October 2019, her pointed cross-examination of Facebook founder Mark Zuckerberg exposed how little one of the world's richest and most powerful men seemed to know about his own business—and how willing he apparently was to turn a blind eye to the way his platform was poisoning democracy.

*Hearing of the House Financial
Services Committee.*

— OCTOBER 23, 2019 —

AOC: It's good to see you, Mr. Zuckerberg. I think you, of all people, can appreciate using a person's past behavior in order to determine, predict, or make decisions about future behavior. And in order for us to make decisions about Libra [a private cryptocurrency being proposed by Facebook], I think we need to kind of dig into your past behavior and Facebook's past behavior with respect to our democracy. Mr. Zuckerberg, what year and month did you personally first become aware of Cambridge Analytica [the British consulting firm that harvested the data of 87 million Facebook users in 2016 to assist Donald Trump's campaign]?

MZ: I'm not—I'm not sure of the exact time, but it was probably around the time when it became public. I think it was around March of 2018. I could be wrong, though.

AOC: Mm-hmm. When did Facebook COO Sheryl Sandberg become aware of Cambridge Analytica?

MZ: I don't know off the top of my head.

AOC: You don't know . . . When was the issue discussed with your board member Peter Thiel?

MZ: Congresswoman, I don't—I don't know that offhand.

AOC: You don't know. This was the largest data scandal with respect to your company, that had catastrophic impacts on the 2016 election. You don't know?

MZ: Well, Congresswoman, I'm sure we discussed it after it—after we were aware of what happened.

AOC: Okay. You announced recently that the official policy of Facebook now allows politicians to pay to spread disinformation in 2020 elections and in the future. So I just want to know how far I can push this in the next year. Under your policy, you know, using Census data, as well, could I pay to target predominantly Black Zip Codes and advertise them the incorrect election date?

MZ: No, Congresswoman, you couldn't. We have—even for these policies around the newsworthiness of content that politicians say and the general principle that I believe that in a democracy—

AOC: But you said you're not going to fact-check my ads.

MZ: But we have—if anyone, including a politician, is saying things that can cause—that is calling for violence or could risk imminent physical harm or voter or Census suppression, when we roll out the Census suppression policy, we will take that content down.

AOC: So, you will—there is some threshold where you

will fact-check political advertisements. Is that what you're telling me?

MZ: Well, Congresswoman, yes, for specific things like that, where there's imminent risk of harm. But also—

AOC: Could I run ads targeting Republicans in primaries, saying that they voted for the Green New Deal?

MZ: Sorry, I—can you repeat that?

AOC: Would I be able to run advertisements on Facebook targeting Republicans in primaries, saying that they voted for the Green New Deal? I mean, if you're not fact-checking political advertisements, I'm just trying to understand the bounds here, what's fair game.

MZ: Congresswoman, I don't know the answer to that off the top of my head. I think probably?

AOC: So you don't know if I'll be able to do that.

MZ: I think probably.

AOC: Do you see a potential problem here with a complete lack of fact-checking on political advertisements?

MZ: Well, Congresswoman, I think lying is bad. And I think if you were to run an ad that had a lie, that would be bad. That's different from it being—from—in our position, the right thing to do to

Instructions on How to Grill a High-Profile Witness

Responding to a question on Twitch in November 2020, as she joined gamers for a marathon session of Among Us, *AOC offered a mini-tutorial on how to grill a high-profile witness.*

THE PRESSURE

It's very stressful. The two most intense, high-stakes questionings I did in my first term were Michael Cohen and Mark Zuckerberg. Those two were so nerve-racking. In fact, when I was questioning Cohen, I had my Apple Watch on and it did that thing where it's like, "Hey, uh, are you having a heart attack right now?"

prevent your constituents or people in an election from seeing that you had lied.

AOC: So, you won't take down lies, or you will take down lies? I think this is just a pretty simple yes or no.

MZ: Congresswoman, in—

AOC: I'm not talking about spin. I'm talking about actual disinformation.

MZ: Yes . . . I believe that people should be able to see for themselves what politicians, that they may or may not vote for, are saying—

AOC: So you won't take them down.

MZ: —And judge their character for themselves.

AOC: So you won't take—you may flag that it's wrong, but you won't take it down.

MZ: Congresswoman, it depends on the context that it shows up—organic post, ads. The treatment is a little bit different.

AOC: One more question. In your ongoing dinner parties with far-right figures, some of whom advance the conspiracy theory that white supremacy is a hoax, did you discuss so-called social-media bias against conservatives? And do you believe there is a bias?

MZ: Congresswoman, sorry, I don't remember everything that was in the question.

THE PREP

I worked really hard to draft the questions in advance. But sometimes I write them while I'm there, or I edit them a lot while I'm sitting there in the hearing, depending on people's answers. The Mark Zuckerberg questioning, I wrote pretty much during that hearing, listening to him.

THE DYNAMIC

The thing that's so crazy about these hearings is that they may have this huge legal team, these lawyers and stuff behind them. But at the end of the day, it's one versus one. It's a little bit of a battle of wits.

THE TRICK

They're all coached in the same way. They're all coached to filibuster the questioning. Which is why you heard him say "Congresswoman, Congresswoman, Congresswoman" every time he answered a

AOC: That's all right, I'll move on. Can you explain why you've named the Daily Caller, a publication well documented with ties to white supremacists, as an official fact-checker for Facebook?

MZ: Congresswoman, sure. We actually don't appoint the independent fact-checkers. They go through an independent organization called the Independent Fact-Checking Network that has a rigorous standard for who they allow to serve as a fact-checker.

AOC: So, you would say that white-supremacist-tied publications meet a rigorous standard for fact-checking? Thank you.

question. Because he's trying to kill time . . . If you ask a witness a yes-or-no question, they will never answer yes or no, because that saves time. Which is why, after the hearing, people were saying, "Oh, she was so rude. She was interrupting him." But the thing is, once they start stammering, they're either not going to answer your question, or you have to press them. Or you got them.

18

The Climate Culture War:

What the Green New Deal Is and Isn't

By

DAVID WALLACE-WELLS

When Alexandria Ocasio-Cortez clasped her hands over her mouth at the Park Billiards Cafe & Sports Bar on Primary Night in June 2018, nobody had really heard of the Green New Deal, which would become not just her signature policy crusade but perhaps the central battlefield in America's culture war over climate.

It had been, two years before, the name of third-party spoiler Jill Stein's climate policy and, before that, had popped up in a book by Van Jones (one in which he also tried to coin the terms "green-collar jobs" and "green-collar economy"). When Nancy Pelosi wanted to disparage it, she flailed, sputtering, "The Green Dream, or whatever they call it." For a while, you could even hear confused climate people transposing the words: "New Green Deal." Across the Atlantic, they called their version the "European Green Deal," which dropped the FDR reference altogether and made the proposition sound like a bargain between the Brussels elite and the environmental left—which maybe it was.

But what was it here? There is not even a splinter green party to speak of in the United States, which means environmental concerns were always likely to appear, first, in costume when they assumed center stage. And which helps explain why, beyond its ambition, the most striking thing about the short list of talking points unveiled by AOC and Senator Ed Markey in February 2019, just a month after AOC was sworn in, is that the Green New Deal wasn't, and isn't, a real work of policy, or a piece of legislation, or even, really, a climate agenda. Its advocates often speak about it as a rolling program of policy

experiments, as the original New Deal was, guided not just by the goal of decarbonization but by principles of equity and justice—some experiments would fizzle, they admitted, and others, they hoped, would take root.

One day, the Green New Deal may well become that. In the meantime, as abstract as a vision board or a statement of values, it has already achieved something that long seemed nearly impossible: reversing the conventional rhetorical framing about climate change that had predominated since the very beginning of concern about warming and that had effectively prevented anything at all from ever being done about it. That framing held that warming was, yes, perhaps worrisome, but also that combating it was expensive—making the fight to take action a moral one, to be waged against the logic of dollars and cents. The Green New Deal was, and is, an alternate vision, of prosperity and justice delivered through climate action. And unlike Al Gore's shtick about light bulbs, which drew from the same rhetorical well, it didn't seem transparently inadequate to anyone looking at the science—or at the inevitable climate disruption, cascading into political failure and societal disarray, that the science forecast. Instead, the Green New Deal offered a climate revolution. Those who worried about it worried in the other direction—that it "went too far."

But by the time AOC—and Markey—stood for reelection, less than two years later, the revolution had already, improbably, been won. There had been some backlash on the right, and through the 2020 elections, you could catch references in conservative attack ads to that ill-advised, quickly retracted Green New Deal FAQ that spoke of cow farts and eliminating airplanes. But while AOC had somewhat stumbled into climate as her central calling card with that impromptu visit to the Sunrise sit-in in 2018, she paid no price in 2020 for having done so. You could see Ed Markey coasting to reelection on a wave of Green New Deal sentiment, buoyed past the finish line in his primary against Joe Kennedy by a savvy and combative ad produced by Sunrise—the most celebrated in the cycle, which included a billion-dollar presidential race. That race, too, concluded with a blitz of climate advertising from Joe Biden, who had been transformed, in the space of a single year, into someone who could plausibly claim the title of "first climate president"—and who promised, along the way, $2 trillion in climate spending, many multiples of what his former boss, Barack Obama, had achieved.

In all of this, the Green New Deal was both surfer and wave. Over the past few years, with climate disasters finally striking the global north and ever more intense ones battering the planet's baked equatorial band, those trying to raise the alarm have found themselves worrying that crescendos of catastrophe, far from awakening the world, might put it to sleep instead, as even those in the direct path of wildfires and hurricanes normalized not just the new intensity of change but also its accelerating rate. The worry is real: There was less horror, for instance, about the 2021 California wildfires than the 2018 ones, which were not nearly as damaging but did not unfold in the midst of a pandemic, and less outrage about the 2020 Amazon fires than the 2019 ones, which provoked an international outcry.

And yet it is just as important, I think, to note that we are witnessing, simultaneously, another kind of normalization, a *good* normalization—the normalization of climate alarm. Because even as we fail to make time to reckon explicitly with the present tense of the climate crisis, our intuitions about it, and the future it portends for us, climate alarm has grown much more central to the political and social discourse in America and elsewhere. Indeed, while the world's attention has been focused on the coronavirus, with little appetite for debate about the threat of warming, our collective, planetary response to the pandemic has brought along with it a sort of secret sidecar of unprecedented climate action. Even compromised by a Republican Senate, the last COVID relief package of 2020 smuggled in $35 billion in clean-energy spending—about half the size of Obama's biggest piece of climate spending, with presumably much more to come under a Biden administration and a Democratic Senate.

This shift has been spurred, in part, by the lessons about fighting warming that come from COVID-19, which teaches us that we are not invulnerable to the natural world, however modern and advanced we may feel; that it is better to respond quickly to emergent challenges, rather than wait until the terrifying future takes concrete shape before us; and that while adapting to that new future may seem easier than preventing it in the first place, it almost always pays off to invest in mitigation first, if only to reduce the amount of adaptation you have to do later. It also has to do with the "radicalization" of previously centrist Establishment forces, particularly in the field of economics and public policy. We now have the IMF publishing papers questioning neoliberalism, the Fed arguing that corporate power has been undermining the health of the economy for decades, and right-wing policy advisers suggesting we discard GDP as a measure of human well-being.

But on climate action in particular, much of the movement undoubtedly comes from how worried the world has become about the medium-term threat of dramatic warming. Even when we don't make time for news about locust plagues or fires in the Amazon, foreboding about the climate crisis has come to shape the country's political, social, and emotional relationship to its own future much more profoundly than ever before. Our politics and policy can't help but reflect those priorities, even when we aren't debating them directly. The Green New Deal didn't "win" by being voted into law; it won by changing the terms of debate. The question is no longer about the facts of climate science but about what action it requires of us— and how best to distribute the benefits of that action.

19

The Yoho Speech:

AOC ON

DECENCY

"Representative Yoho called me, and I quote, a 'fucking bitch.'"

In response, Ocasio-Cortez delivered a speech about sexism on the House floor.

*House Floor Speech Transcript
on Yoho Remarks.*

— JULY 23, 2020 —

66 About two days ago, I was walking up the steps of the Capitol when Representative Yoho suddenly turned a corner and he was accompanied by Representative Roger Williams, and accosted me on the steps right here in front of our nation's Capitol. I was minding my own business, walking up the steps and Representative Yoho put his finger in my face, he called me disgusting, he called me crazy, he called me out of my mind, and he called me dangerous. Then he took a few more steps and after I had recognized his comments as rude, he walked away and said I'm rude, you're calling me rude. I took a few steps ahead and I walked inside and cast my vote. Because my constituents send me here each and every day to fight for them and to make sure that they are able to keep a roof over their head, that they're able to feed their families and that they're able to carry their lives with dignity.

I walked back out and there were reporters in the front of the Capitol and in front of reporters Representative Yoho called me, and I quote, "a fucking bitch." These were the words that Representative Yoho levied against a congresswoman. The congresswoman that not only represents New York's 14th Congressional District, but every congresswoman and every woman in this country. Because all of us have had to deal with this in some form, some way, some shape, at some point in our lives. I want to be clear that Representative Yoho's comments were not deeply hurtful or piercing to me, because I have worked a working-class job. I have waited tables in restaurants. I have ridden the subway. I have walked the streets in New York City, and this kind of language is not new. I have encountered words uttered by Mr. Yoho and men uttering the same words as Mr. Yoho while I was being harassed in restaurants. I have tossed men out of bars that have used language like Mr. Yoho's and I have encountered this type of harassment riding the subway in New York City.

This is not new, and that is the problem. Mr. Yoho was not alone. He was walking shoulder to shoulder with Representative Roger Williams, and that's when we start to see that this issue is not about one incident. It is cultural. It is a culture of lack of impunity, of accepting of violence and violent language against women, and an entire structure of power that supports that. Because not only have I been spoken to disrespectfully, particularly by members of the Republican Party and elected officials in the Republican Party, not just here, but the President of the United States last year told me to go home to another country, with the implication that I don't even belong in America. The governor of Florida, Governor DeSantis, before I even was sworn in, called me a whatever that is. Dehumanizing language is not new, and what we are seeing is that incidents like these are happening in a pattern. This is a pattern of an attitude towards women and dehumanization of others.

So while I was not deeply hurt or offended by little comments that are made, when I was reflecting on this, I honestly thought that I was just going to pack it up and go home. It's just another day, right? But then yesterday, Representative Yoho decided to come to the floor of the House of Representatives and make excuses for his behavior, and that I could not let go. I could not allow my nieces, I could not allow the little girls that I go home to, I could not allow victims of verbal abuse and worse to see that, to see that excuse and to see our Congress accept it as legitimate and accept it as an apology and to accept silence as a form of acceptance. I could not allow that to stand which is why I am rising today to raise this point of personal privilege.

I do not need Representative Yoho to apologize to me. Clearly he does not want to. Clearly when given the opportunity he will not and I will not stay up late at night waiting for an apology from a man who has no remorse over calling women and using abusive language towards women, but what I do have issue with is using women, our wives and daughters, as shields and excuses for poor behavior. Mr. Yoho mentioned that he has a wife and two daughters. I am two years younger than Mr. Yoho's youngest daughter. I am someone's daughter too. My father, thankfully, is not alive to see how Mr. Yoho treated his daughter. My mother got to see Mr. Yoho's disrespect on the floor of this House towards me on television and I am here because I have to show my parents that I am their daughter and that they did not raise me to accept abuse from men.

Now what I am here to say is that this harm that Mr. Yoho levied, it tried to levy against me, was not just an incident directed at me, but when you do that to any woman, what Mr. Yoho did was give permission to other men to do that to his daughters. In using that language in front of the press, he gave permission to use that language against his wife, his daughters, women in his community, and I am here to stand up to say that is not acceptable. I do not care what your views are. It does not matter how much I disagree or how much it incenses me or how much I feel that people are dehumanizing others. I will not do that myself. I will not allow people to change and create hatred in our hearts.

And so what I believe is that having a daughter does not make a man decent. Having a wife does not make a decent man. Treating people with dignity and respect makes a decent man, and when a decent man messes up as we all are bound to do, he tries his best and does apologize. Not to save face, not to win a vote, he apologizes genuinely to repair and acknowledge the harm done so that we can all move on.

Lastly, what I want to express to Mr. Yoho is gratitude. I want to thank him for showing the world that you can be a powerful man and accost women. You can have daughters and accost women without remorse. You can be married and accost women. You can take photos and project an image to the world of being a family man and accost women without remorse and with a sense of impunity. It happens every day in this country. It happened here on the steps of our nation's Capitol. It happens when individuals who hold the highest office in this land admit, admit to hurting women and using this language against all of us. Once again, I thank my colleagues for joining us today. I will reserve the hour of my time and I will yield to my colleague, Representative Jayapal of Washington. Thank you.

20

The Night of
RBG's Death:

NOT GIVING UP

"Don't worry. We got you."

— SEPTEMBER 18, 2020 —

➤➤ On September 18, 2020, the Jewish New Year, Supreme Court Justice Ruth Bader Ginsburg died at the age of 87 with just enough time for Donald Trump to replace her.

AOC got on Instagram Live, and after acknowledging the grief and fighting back her own tears, didn't pretend that this could be stopped. Instead, she acknowledged the judicial harms to come and laid out practical steps for winning the next fight. She urged the long game. Ginsburg had preached the sort of incremental change that AOC often defined herself against. "Our ancestors have stared down the barrel of hopelessness before too," she said. "And they persisted." It was the right way to send off a foremother. —*IRIN CARMON*

314

1
She opens by creating a virtual mourner's circle . . .

"Hey everybody. Thank you for joining . . . It's a really incredibly sad day. Um, and sad evening if you haven't heard yet. Supreme Court Justice Ruth Bader Ginsburg just passed away this evening. One of the last statements that she gave to her granddaughter was that her final wish was that her vacancy on the Court that she would leave behind not be filled until a new president is able to fill it . . .

"I wanted to hop on because a lot of people were reaching out to me publicly and privately saying, 'What now? What do we do? I'm scared.'"

2
Sets up the stakes . . .

"For those of you who don't know, this vacancy on the Court is extremely, extremely significant. It's just earth, it's earth-shattering. It is not the time for cynicism. It is not the time to give up. It is not the time for us to say it's too late or it's too far gone, or I don't know what to do."

3
And the context . . .

"We're going to talk about it right now because it's that important, because the actual balance of our democracy rests in the actions that we choose to make between now and . . . Election Day and after. So now is the time to tune in to our everyday decisions . . . If you're a person that's saying, 'I don't know what to do right now,' don't worry. We've got you. Part of figuring out what to do is not just waiting for someone to tell you what to do, but it's actually looking into yourself and asking yourself, *What do I want to give? What am I willing to share?* . . . So let's talk about the ABC's. We want older people representing us in government. And we want younger people representing us in government. And one of the things that people ask me is why do we have a government that is . . . dominated by much, much older representatives and officials? . . . Well, it's because young people historically have not shown up . . . I, we're all tired, but that's how authoritarianism works. This is how authoritarianism works to wear you down until you give in. And right now, what we need to do is never give in."

4
And some practical steps . . .

"Our number one job right now is to not give in and is to not give up. So what can you do: vote, register to vote, organize, get involved in organizing and supporting organizers in your community . . .

"I need you to use your relationships. That's what we need you to do right now. Maybe you've got an uncle in Ohio. Maybe you've got family in Florida. Write down a list of five people. That for whatever reason you think that if you get through to them, whether it's getting them to switch their vote, making sure that they're registered . . . five names that you're going to check in on in the next week or the next two weeks."

5
. . . Ramping up to the rousing finish.

"These people do not care about democracy. They do not care about fairness. They do not care about equality. They do not care about justice. They care about money and making more money. They don't care who dies. They don't care whose rights get violated. So I need you to be ready because we need to be ready to organize. So our thing to do tonight is to identify what are you going to give? . . . Now is not the moment for hopelessness. We do not give up. And cynicism is not just unproductive. It's actively harmful for our democracy. Cynicism says it's over. Cynicism says we can't do it. Cynicism says don't bother trying. And if those are the sentiments coming out, then at this point, you are helping every person that is trying to marginalize the rights, the economic future, and the just prosperity of people . . . So listen, let this moment radicalize you. Look at your fear and turn it into fuel. Feel your fear. Feel the sweat. These are tools that we are going to have to use for the rest of our lives too because this is not over in November. I'm sorry, you're not going back to brunch."

21

The Teens:

~~~

"I hope to become my own version of AOC one day—they'll call me SHR."

SKYLAR, 18

"For the first time in my life I was able to see someone young, someone with student debt, someone still trying to balance their identity and their role in society— someone like me— ascend to power. I used to believe that utopias were just fantasies. It's time for a revolution and it's time to make it happen."

CARLOS, 18

"I saw the video of her talking about Representative Yoho and the names that he called her, and I was like, *This sounds like someone I want to know more about.* I wish I could be like her. She is the first political figure I really liked on my own."

TESS, 17

"I wish she would fight less with moderate Democrats, because it does lead to division within the party."

AMAYA, 17

"I love that people feel like they could know her as a friend."

CAROLYN, 19

"Many conservatives, including in my own family, try to tear AOC down for her past as a waitress. It makes my blood boil. But AOC pushes through that hate."

LILY, 16

"I'm a girl who spends lots of time in male-dominated fields because of my interest in STEM, so seeing AOC stand up to curses hurled at her has actually given me the self-confidence to speak my mind."

HUDA, 17

"There's an Amazon distribution center being built near my house, and I didn't think much of it until AOC spoke out against Amazon warehouse jobs."

OLIVIA, 17

"The video of her grilling Zuckerberg gives me life."

CAPRIANA, 19

♥

"Some of my friends, they're super-diehard AOC fans, but I started paying attention when she began advocating for the Green New Deal. She was super-persistent. As young girls we've been conditioned to be polite, but she contrasts the idea of what a girl should be while also getting her points across in an awesome way. I could never do that. I'm [too] hotheaded."

———

BRIGID, 17

♥

"I hope AOC can be president. I just worry that people are going to hurt her."

———

HANNAH, 18

♥

"I am a young progressive in a conservative town. Seeing another young Latina woman be so bold has taught me that being a feminist and progressive is something I can be proud of."

———

BREE, 17

♥

"People say when I give speeches I speak exactly like her. I want to run for Congress. I see myself in AOC, and I see a new system of the American government in her."

———

SCOTT, 18

LITTLE KIDS

~~~

"Is she from the movie Spy Kids*?"*

FRANCESCA, 7

———

"She's great because she's trying to change the world."

DAPHNE, 8

319

22

The Insurrection:

THE TERROR OF THE MOB

"I thought I was going to die."

— JANUARY 12, 2021 —

〜〜〜

➥ AOC took to Instagram Live to assuage the fears raised by the January 6 insurrection of the Capitol. It had a now-familiar rhetorical shape, moving from an intimate sermon to **a fire-and-brimstone speech**, as always without notes and in almost perfect spoken paragraphs:

1
She began with the direct address . . .

"Hi, everyone. Hey, everybody. How's it going? Thank you for joining. I figured I would take some time to answer, um, any and all questions that you may have after this violent and traumatizing week . . . I'll start by just lightly describing a little bit of what I went through on Wednesday, and what all of us went through. So Wednesday, as we know the president, frankly assisted by members of Congress, incited an attack on the United States Capitol. This is known as an act of insurrection. Frankly he is a traitor to our country, a traitor to the United States."

4
Put the event into an impassioned historical context . . .

"What was also traumatizing was how unsettling that day was because there was a sense that something was wrong and obviously with the violence, but there was a sense that something was wrong from the inside. What happens now? We know that Donald Trump cannot be president. He should not have been president the night of the attack. Because Republicans and the people around him are cowards . . . They care about white supremacy. They care about preserving the social order and the mythology of whiteness . . . They lust for power more than they care about democracy. With all of the rules rigged in their favor, the Electoral College is built on a compromise with slavers. The Senate is rigged in their favor. Gerrymandered districts are rigged [for] Republicans. They can't even win with the deck stacked in their favor. And so what they are willing to do is set a match and light our entire democracy on fire. It's nihilism, it's just destruction."

2
Shared her own experience, intimately and confessionally . . .

"Many congressional staffers were almost killed. Many children, children of members of Congress were there, children. As for myself, I had a pretty traumatizing event happen to me. And I do not know if I can even disclose the full details of that event due to security concerns, but I can tell you that I had a very close encounter where I thought I was going to die. You have all of those thoughts, where, you know, at the end of your life and all of these thoughts come rushing to you. That's what happened to a lot of us on Wednesday. I did not know if I was going to make it to the end of that day alive."

3
Connected to a broader, emotional point . . .

"I think it's an opportunity for a lot of us to talk about trauma as well. Whenever any person has an encounter where they think they're going to die and they go through that process, that is a traumatizing event."

5
. . . And then moved to the call to arms.

"We're going to have a lot of work to do because they created this mess . . . They created this violence for short, short-term gain, knowing the long-term loss. As long as they have a shred of personal gain to get in making the same mistake, same decisions, they will continue to make them. That's why they got to go. And that's why they need to experience consequences. Not because it's punishment but because consequences are the only way they will stop contributing to violence. That's what we gotta do. We gotta organize . . . Maybe we should just start voting on things based on whether we think it's right or not. And stop pretending that this is complicated because it's not, you're either with the people . . . or you're with that mob. Pretty clear-cut. Anyways, I'm going to answer some questions now that I went off on my rant."

2018: Behind the scenes of filming the documentary Knock Down the House.

Appendix

Note on Sources and Bibliography

Hundreds of interviews went into making this book. Sources on the record are noted in the text. In addition, many people spoke to us on the condition that they not be named, for fear of political or personal reprisal. These conversations guided our reporting and informed our perspective, especially when rendering a picture of Alexandria Ocasio-Cortez before she entered politics, during the phase of her life where the public record is not robust. Ocasio-Cortez did not participate in this book except in the fact-checking phase. We are grateful to all the people who spoke to us, often multiple times (and to multiple writers), to give us clarity and insight.

Ocasio-Cortez's prolific communication style gives a biographer a massive trove of material to mine. From her political beginnings, she has used social media constantly, like a public journal, to record her impressions, responses, and thoughts. Her Twitter feed and Instagram account have been invaluable to this effort, of course, as were the Ocasio-Cortez supporters and fans who preserved her early live-streams on YouTube. In addition, on a Facebook account called "Alex OC," now closed, she recorded the beginnings of her ascent, including the videos from the road trip to Standing Rock and documentation from her incipient primary campaign.

Especially at the beginning of her career, Ocasio-Cortez spoke intimately and at great length to certain interviewers. Four of these conversations are essential viewing for true AOC obsessives, and we found ourselves going back to them again and again: with *Ebro in the Morning* on Hot 97, July 12, 2018; with Ta-Nehisi Coates in person at Riverside Church on January 21, 2019; with students at John Jay College of Criminal Justice on April 24, 2019; and on *The Tightrope*, with Cornel West and Tricia Rose, on July 23, 2020.

Finally, we are indebted to all the other journalists who covered Ocasio-Cortez, especially those who saw and recorded the phenomenon early. These include the folks at the Intercept and the Young Turks, whose journalistic mission aligns with leftist politics, but also Charlotte Alter at *Time*, who first unearthed the "Alex OC" Facebook page, and whose 2019 magazine profile became the *The Ones We've Been Waiting For*, a book about the Ocasio-Cortez generation of politicians. *Knock Down the House*, the documentary directed by Rachel Lears, instantly became part of the Ocasio-Cortez canon. The Congressional beat reporters at the New York *Times* and the Washington *Post*, as well as at Politico and the Hill, kept constant measure of the battle lines inside the House. This bibliography credits all the journalists whose work informed ours. The interpretations are our own.

BOOKS AND FILM

Alter, Charlotte. *The Ones We've Been Waiting For: How a New Generation of Leaders Will Transform America* (New York: Penguin Books, 2020).

Blotnick, Robin, and Rachel Lears. *Knock Down the House*. Directed by Rachel Lears. Produced by Jubilee Films, Atlas Films, and Artemis Rising. Distributed by Netflix, released May 1, 2019.

Didion, Joan. "Insider Baseball." Republished in *Political Fictions* (New York: Alfred A. Knopf, 2001).

Freedlander, David. *The AOC Generation: How Millennials Are Seizing Power and Rewriting the Rules of American Politics* (Boston: Beacon Press, 2021).

Grim, Ryan. *We've Got People: From Jesse Jackson to AOC, the End of Big Money and the Rise of a Movement* (Washington D.C.: Strong Arm Press, 2019).

Hillstrom, Laurie Collier. *Alexandria Ocasio-Cortez: A Biography* (Santa Barbara, CA: ABC-CLIO, 2020).

Isserman, Maurice. *The Other American: The Life of Michael Harrington* (New York: PublicAffairs, 2000).

Kazin, Michael. *American Dreamers: How the Left Changed a Nation* (New York: Alfred A. Knopf, 2011).

Lopez, Lynda. *AOC: The Fearless Rise and Powerful Resonance of Alexandria Ocasio-Cortez* (New York: St. Martin's Press, 2020).

Ocasio-Cortez, Alexandria. *This Is What I Am* (New York: CreateSpace Independent Publishing Platform, 2019).

Omar, Ilhan. *This Is What America Looks Like: My Journey from Refugee to Congresswoman* (New York: Dey Street Books, 2021).

Page, Susan. *Madam Speaker: Nancy Pelosi and the Lessons of Power* (New York: Twelve Books, 2021).

Steinhauer, Jennifer. *The Firsts: The Inside Story of the Women Reshaping Congress* (Chapel Hill, NC: Algonquin Books, 2020).

Zarnow, Leandra Ruth. *Battling Bella: The Protest Politics of Bella Abzug* (Cambridge, MA: Harvard University Press, 2019).

Zelizer, Julian E. *Burning Down the House: Newt Gingrich, the Fall of a Speaker, and the Rise of the New Republican Party* (New York: Penguin Books, 2020).

FEATURE ARTICLES AND PROFILES

Aleksander, Irina. "How Alexandria Ocasio-Cortez and Other Progressives Are Defining the Midterms." *Vogue*, October 15, 2018.

Alter, Charlotte. "'Change Is Closer Than We Think': Inside Alexandria Ocasio-Cortez's Unlikely Rise." *Time*, March 21, 2019.

Barry, Dan, and Annie Correal. "The Epicenter." New York *Times*, December 3, 2020.

Beauchamp, Zack. "Bernie Sanders's Joe Rogan Experience." Vox, January 24, 2020.

Cadigan, Hilary. "Alexandria Ocasio-Cortez Learned Her Most Important Lessons from Restaurants." *Bon Appétit*, November 7, 2018.

Ceneta, Manuel Balce. "How Barbara Lee Became an Army of One." Politico, July 30, 2017.

Cerón, Ella. "AOC Loves a Press-On Nail." The Cut, January 14, 2019.

Chávez, Aída, and Ryan Grim. "A Primary Against the Machine: A Bronx Activist Looks to Dethrone Joseph Crowley, the King of Queens." The Intercept, May 22, 2018.

Cheslow, Jerry. "If You're Thinking of Living in: Parkchester." New York *Times*, May 10, 1992.

Dias, Elizabeth. "For Rashida Tlaib, Palestinian Heritage Infuses a Detroit Sense of Community." New York *Times*, August 14, 2018.

Dominus, Susan. "Hope and High Drama: A Year with Two New Democratic Congresswomen." *The New York Times Magazine*, November 18, 2019.

Edmondson, Catie. "How Alexandria Ocasio-Cortez Learned to Play by Washington's Rules." New York *Times*, September 18, 2019.

Freedlander, David. "One Year in Washington." *New York*, January 6, 2020.

Freedlander, David. "The 28-Year-Old Progressive Hoping to Unseat One of the Top Democrats in Congress." *New York*, June 25, 2018.

Golshan, Tara, and Ella Nilsen. "The Ongoing Feud Between House Democratic Leadership and Progressives, Explained." Vox, July 13, 2019.

Golshan, Tara, and Ella Nilsen. "Why Pelosi Calling Trump's Tweets Racist on the House Floor Turned into Chaos." Vox, July 16, 2019.

Gray, Briahna. "In Victory, Alexandria Ocasio-Cortez Showed That Authentic Progressive Values Can Redefine Political Reality." The Intercept, November 7, 2018.

Greenhouse, Linda. "Parkchester: Trouble in Paradise." *New York*, February 17, 1969.

Grim, Ryan, and Briahna Gray. "Alexandria Ocasio-Cortez Joins Environmental Activists in Protest at Democratic Leader Nancy Pelosi's Office." The Intercept, November 13, 2018.

Grunwald, Michael. "What AOC Gets That Bernie Didn't." Politico, April 16, 2020.

Hagen, Nick. "Elissa Slotkin Braces for a Democratic Civil War." Politico, November 13, 2020.

Haller, Vera. "Parkchester, the Bronx, Working as Planned." New York *Times*, October 26, 2016.

Helms, Andrew. "The Propagandists." The Ringer, October 10, 2018.

Jaffe, Greg, and Souad Mekhennet. "Ilhan Omar's American Story: It's

Complicated." Washington *Post*, July 6, 2019.

Lambiet, Jose. "'God Played Quite a Joke on Me with This Politics Stuff!' The Privacy-Loving Mother of Alexandria Ocasio-Cortez Whips Up Lasagna as She Tells How She Had to Flee New York Because of High Taxes and Gushes About Wedding Bells for Her Daughter." *Daily Mail*, March 4, 2019.

Leibovich, Mark. "For A.O.C., 'Existential Crises' as Her District Becomes the Coronavirus Epicenter." New York *Times*, May 4, 2020.

Macias, Miguel. "Portrait Of: Alexandria Ocasio-Cortez." Latino USA, October 26, 2018.

McIntosh, Don. "Talking Socialism: Catching Up with AOC." Democratic Left, Spring 2021.

Medina, Jennifer. "Jessica Cisneros on Challenging an Incumbent Democrat: 'There's a Lot He Has Never Had to Justify.'" New York *Times*, July 3, 2019.

Morris, Alex. "Alexandria Ocasio-Cortez Wants the Country to Think Big." *Rolling Stone*, February 27, 2019.

Nuzzi, Olivia. "Alexandria Ocasio-Cortez Is in the Building." *New York*, January 4, 2019.

Page, Susan. "Inside Nancy Pelosi's War with AOC and the Squad." Politico, April 15, 2021.

Read, Bridget. "36 Hours with Alexandria Ocasio-Cortez." *Vogue*, June 26, 2019.

Read, Bridget. "90 Minutes with Megan Hellerer." The Cut, October 28, 2019.

Relman, Eliza. "Alexandria Ocasio-Cortez's Partner Riley Roberts Stays Out of the Spotlight. He's onto Something." Insider, July 26, 2019.

Relman, Eliza. "Alexandria Ocasio-Cortez Triumphs over Her Wall Street–Backed Democratic Primary Opponent Michelle Caruso-Cabrera and All but Secures a 2nd Term." Insider, June 23, 2020.

Relman, Eliza. "The Story of How Democratic Rising Stars Alexandria Ocasio-Cortez and Ayanna Pressley First Met at a Manhattan House Party and Became 'BFFs.'" Insider, January 7, 2019.

Relman, Eliza. "The Truth About Alexandria Ocasio-Cortez: The Inside Story of How, in Just One Year, Sandy the Bartender Became a Lawmaker Who Triggers Both Parties." Insider, January 6, 2019.

Remnick, David. "Alexandria Ocasio-Cortez's Historic Win and the Future of the Democratic Party." *The New Yorker*, July 16, 2018.

Ruiz, Michelle. "Becoming AOC: Alexandria Ocasio-Cortez on How She Got Here and Where She's Headed." *Vanity Fair*, December 2020.

Sammon, Alexander. "How Progressives Built a Campaign Machine . . . Thanks to the DCCC." *The American Prospect*, September 15, 2020.

Tarleton, John, and Lydia McMullen-Laird. "Alexandria vs. Goliath." *Indypendent,* May 31, 2018.

Thompson, A. C. "Inside the Secret Border Patrol Facebook Group Where Agents Joke About Migrant Deaths and Post Sexist Memes." ProPublica, July 1, 2019.

Van Zuylen-Wood, Simon. "Pinkos Have More Fun." *New York,* March 3, 2019.

Wallace-Wells, Benjamin. "Bernie Sanders and Alexandria Ocasio-Cortez in Kansas." *The New Yorker,* July 23, 2018.

Yuan, Jada. "How a Middle-School Principal Used the Ocasio-Cortez Playbook Against a 16-Term Incumbent." Washington *Post,* July 16, 2020.

INTERVIEWS

"A Conversation with Alexandria Ocasio-Cortez." John Jay College of Criminal Justice. April 24, 2019.

"Alexandria Ocasio-Cortez on the Future of the Democratic Party." *The View,* ABC, June 29, 2018.

Baier, Bret. "Exclusive: AOC Blames Bernie's Lackluster Performance on Voter Suppression." *Special Report,* Fox News, March 12, 2020.

Bolduan, Kate. Interview with Alexandria Ocasio-Cortez. *At This Hour with Kate Bolduan,* CNN, July 15, 2019.

Coates,Ta-Nehisi. Alexandria Ocasio-Cortez in conversation with Ta-Nehisi Coates at Riverside Church. January 21, 2019.

Colbert, Stephen. "Alexandria Ocasio-Cortez: Trump Isn't Ready for a Girl from the Bronx." *The Late Show with Stephen Colbert,* CBS, June 29, 2018.

Colbert, Stephen. "Rep. Ocasio-Cortez Debunks Myths About a 70% Marginal Tax." *The Late Show with Stephen Colbert,* CBS, January 22, 2019.

Cooper, Anderson. "Alexandria Ocasio-Cortez: The Rookie Congresswoman Challenging the Democratic Establishment." *60 Minutes,* CBS, interview by Anderson Cooper, January 6, 2019.

Darden, Ebro. "Alexandria Ocasio-Cortez Makes History as First to Challenge NYC Congressional Seat in 14 Years." *Ebro in the Morning,* Hot97, June 25, 2018.

Darden, Ebro. "Alexandria Ocasio-Cortez on Being Underestimated, Her Humble Beginnings + Rep. Joe Crowley." *Ebro in the Morning,* Hot97, July 12, 2018.

Desus & Mero. "Rep. Alexandria Ocasio-Cortez." *Desus & Mero,* Showtime, February 5, 2019.

Desus & Mero. "AOC Goes Back to Bartending in the Bronx." Showtime, February 5, 2020.

Favreau, Jon. "Alexandria Ocasio-Cortez 2019 Full Interview." *Pod Save America,* August 15, 2019.

Gray, Briahna Joy. "Alexandria Ocasio-Cortez." SXSW, interviewed by Briahna Joy Gray. March 10, 2019.

Greenwald, Glenn. "Alexandria Ocasio-Cortez Talks to Glenn Greenwald About the Democratic Party and 2018 Midterms." The Intercept, June 12, 2018.

Hayes, Chris. "AOC on Coronavirus." *All In with Chris Hayes*, MSNBC, March 24, 2020.

Hayes, Chris. "Representative Ocasio-Cortez: It's Bad." *All In with Chris Hayes*, MSNBC, November 15, 2019.

Hoover, Margaret. "Alexandria Ocasio-Cortez." *Firing Line*, PBS, July 13, 2018.

Ioffe, Julia. "This Year's A.O.C., Jamaal Bowman, Says He's Ready to Fight." *GQ*, August 3, 2020.

Isikoff, Michael and Daniel Klaidman. "Ocasio-Cortez Says a Biden Presidential Run Doesn't 'Animate' Her." *Skullduggery*, Yahoo News, April 14, 2019.

Karl, Jonathan. "AOC Signals She'd Support Biden If He Was Dem Nominee: 'Absolutely' Must Beat Trump." *This Week*, ABC, June 16, 2019.

Katz, Evan Ross. Gabriel Ocasio-Cortez. *Shut Up Evan*, Apple Podcasts, March 2, 2021.

Kimmel, Jimmy. "Congressional Candidate Alexandria Ocasio-Cortez on Health Care, Education & Voting." *Jimmy Kimmel Live!*, ABC, October 18, 2018.

Lovett, Jon. "Alexandria Ocasio-Cortez 2018 Full Interview," *Pod Save America*, August 7, 2018.

Meyers, Seth. "Rep. Alexandria Ocasio-Cortez Responds to Fox News' Weird Obsession with Her." *Late Night with Seth Meyers*, NBC, March 22, 2019.

Michael, Michael Love. "Gabriel Ocasio-Cortez Is Building the Inclusive World He Wants to Live In," *Interview*, December 23, 2020.

Noah, Trevor. "Alexandria Ocasio-Cortez—Bringing Moral Courage to American Politics." *The Daily Show with Trevor Noah*, Comedy Central, July 26, 2018.

"Ocasio-Cortez Addresses 'Bernie Bros,'" *The View*, ABC, February 19, 2020.

Ocasio-Cortez, Alexandria. "Jabari Brisport and Alexandria Ocasio-Cortez Are Looking to Make All Kinds of Trouble," *Interview*, September 1, 2020.

Paiella, Gabriella. "The 28-Year-Old at the Center of One of This Year's Most Exciting Primaries." The Cut, June 25, 2018.

"Political Newcomer on Her Upset and the Road Ahead." *Morning Joe*, MSNBC, June 27, 2018.

Rapinoe, Megan. "Stimulus Package Q&A with AOC & Megan Rapinoe—IG Live," YouTube, March 29, 2020, https://www.youtube.com/watch?v=npIm-TXyjAc.

Remnick, David. "Alexandria Ocasio-Cortez on Breaking Up Homeland Security." *The New Yorker Radio Hour*, July 5, 2019.

Rogers, Matt, and Bowen Yang. "'You Owe It to the Bronx' (w/ Gabriel

Ocasio-Cortez)." Las Culturistas, September 2, 2020.

Scahill, Jeremy. "White Fear." *Intercepted*, May 30, 2018.

Schneps, Josh. "Who Is AOC? With US Congressmember Alexandria Ocasio-Cortez." *Schneps Connects*, December 20, 2020.

Stephanopoulos, George. "Trump in Office Is a 'Clear and Present Danger': Rep. Alexandria Ocasio-Cortez." *This Week*, ABC. January 10, 2021.

Tapper, Jake. "Ocasio-Cortez Says President Not Using His Defense Production Act Powers Will Cost Lives." *State of the Union*, CNN, March 22, 2020.

Tapper, Jake. "Ocasio-Cortez Slams Border Bill: US Should Not 'Be Throwing More Money to ICE,'" *The Lead*, CNN, June 27, 2019.

Tapper, Jake. "Rep. Ocasio-Cortez on What Biden's Win Means for Progressives." *State of the Union*, CNN, November 8, 2020.

West, Cornel, and Tricia Rose. "Alexandria Ocasio-Cortez Is Not Understood for Who She Is." *The Tight Rope*, July 23, 2020.

OPINION AND ANALYSIS

Berridge, Scott. "Millennials After the Great Recession." *Monthly Labor Review*, U.S. Bureau of Labor Statistics, September 2014.

Center for Information & Research on Civic Learning and Engagement (CIRCLE)."Election Week 2020: Young People Increase Turnout, Lead Biden to Victory." Jonathan M. Tisch College of Civic Life, Tufts University, November 25, 2020.

Cheney-Rice, Zak. "President Trump, Who Wanted Ivanka to Run World Bank, Blasts House Democrats as 'Inexperienced.'" Intelligencer, July 23, 2019.

Clyburn, James. "The Fake Fight Between Me and Cori Bush." Washington *Post*, December 6, 2020.

De Pinto, Jennifer. "The Big Question for Bernie Sanders: Can He Win Support from Minorities and Women?" CBS News, March 16, 2019.

Dowd, Maureen. "It's Nancy Pelosi's Parade." New York *Times*, July 6, 2019.

Editorial Board. "If You Want to Be Speaker, Mr. Crowley, Don't Take Voters for Granted." New York *Times*, June 19, 2018.

Fuller, Matt. "The Big Roadblock for Bernie Sanders's Agenda." HuffPost, February 13, 2020.

Gardner, Abby. "I'm Framing This Photo of Alexandria Ocasio-Cortez and the New Squad of Congresswomen Immediately." *Glamour*, November 13, 2018.

Gessen, Masha. "The Unimaginable Reality of American Concentration Camps." *The New Yorker*, June 21, 2019.

Hagle, Courtney. "Six Weeks of Fox's Alexandria Ocasio-Cortez

Obsession: 'Totalitarian,' 'Ignorant,' 'Scary,' and Waging a 'War on Cows.'" Media Matters for America, April 12, 2019.

Helmore, Edward. "How a Congressional Trip Highlighted Migrants' Detention Misery." *Guardian*, July 2, 2019.

Karbal, Ian. "Justice Democrats Secure Another Victory with Cori Bush, Unseating a Dynasty." Open Secrets, August 5, 2020.

Kessler, Glenn. "'Some People Did Something': Rep. Omar's Remarks in Context." Washington *Post*, April 11, 2019.

Krogstad, Jens Manuel, Mark Hugo Lopez, Gustavo López, Jeffrey S. Passel, and Eileen Patten. "Looking Forward to 2016: The Changing Latino Electorate." Pew Research Center, January 19, 2016.

Krugman, Paul. "More on a Job Guarantee (Wonkish)." New York *Times*, July 5, 2018.

Langer, Gary. "Wrapping Up a Wild Ride: A 2016 Exit Poll Review." ABC News, May 10, 2020.

Montare, Ariadne S. "Standing Rock: A Case Study in Civil Disobedience." American Bar Association, May 2018.

O'Rourke, Beto. "Beto O'Rourke: AOC Is a 'Phenomenal Leader.'" Politico, July 15, 2019.

O'Rourke, Ciara, "No, Alexandria Ocasio-Cortez Probably Didn't Say That." PolitiFact, March 27, 2019.

Ocasio-Cortez, Alexandria. "Alexandria Ocasio-Cortez on Her Catholic Faith and the Urgency of Criminal Justice Reform." *America: The Jesuit Review*, June 27, 2018.

Ocasio-Cortez, Alexandria. "The Effects of Antioxidants on Lifespan Using the *C. elegans* Model." Yorktown Science Research, 2007.

Pew Research Center. "In Clinton's March to Nomination, Many Democrats Changed Their Minds." July 25, 2016.

Reston, Maeve, and Gabe Ramirez. "Hillary Clinton Splits Younger, Older Democratic Women." CNN Politics, June 10, 2016.

Saad, Lydia. "Black Americans Want Police to Retain Local Presence." Gallup, August 5, 2020.

Sullivan, Margaret. "Alexandria Ocasio-Cortez's Victory Points to a Media Failure That Keeps Repeating." Washington *Post*, June 28, 2018.

Thiessen, Marc A. "Opinion: Alexandria Ocasio-Cortez Is an Economic Illiterate—and That's a Danger to America." Washington *Post*, February 21, 2019.

Thompson, Alex, and Holly Otterbein. "The 'New' AOC Divides the Left." Politico, March 30, 2020.

Traister, Rebecca. "The Imagined Threat of a Woman Who Governs Like a Man." The Cut, December 19, 2018.

Traister, Rebecca. "The New Face of Power Is Taking Shape." The Cut, November 7, 2018.

Warren, Elizabeth. "Alexandria Ocasio-Cortez." *Time*, April 17, 2019.

NEWS CLIPS

Acevedo, Nicole. "AOC Says Puerto Rico Self-Determination Bill 'Does Not Oppose Statehood.'" NBC News, June 17, 2021.

"Alexandria Ocasio-Cortez Draws Huge Crowd at SXSW." *Kris 6 News*, March 9, 2019.

"Alexandria Ocasio-Cortez Joins Climate Change Activists in Protest at Nancy Pelosi's Office." YouTube, uploaded by *Time*, November 13, 2018.

"Alexandria Ocasio-Cortez, Other Lawmakers Visit Border Facility, Blast Conditions." YouTube, uploaded by NBC New York, July 2, 2019.

Arnold, Amanda. "AOC Will Stand with Sexual-Assault Survivors at the State of the Union." The Cut, February 4, 2019.

Bade, Rachael, and Heather Caygle. "Exasperated Democrats Try to Rein In Ocasio-Cortez." Politico, January 11, 2019.

Bade, Rachael and Mike DeBonis. "'Outright Disrespectful': Four House Women Struggle as Pelosi Isolates Them." Washington *Post*, June 10, 2019.

Baragona, Justin. "Rashida Tlaib Fires Back at Pelosi: 'Very Disappointing' That She's Trying to 'Diminish Our Voices.'" Daily Beast, July 7, 2019.

Barrón-López, Laura. "Ocasio-Cortez Stockpiling Campaign Cash after First Year in Congress." Politico, January 13, 2020.

Barrón-López, Laura. "Ocasio-Cortez Weighs a New Primary Target: Hakeem Jeffries." Politico, December 18, 2018.

Beauchamp, Zack. "The Ilhan Omar Anti-Semitism Controversy, Explained." Vox, March 6, 2019.

Beekman, Daniel. "Diverse Group of Startups Thriving at City-Sponsored Sunshine Bronx Business Incubator in Hunts Point." New York *Daily News*, July 17, 2012.

Bendery, Jennifer. "GOP Congressman Insults Alexandria Ocasio-Cortez, Then Fundraises Off of It." HuffPost, July 26, 2018.

Bloch, Matthew, Larry Buchanan, Josh Katz, and Kevin Quealy. "An Extremely Detailed Map of the 2016 Election." New York *Times*, July 25, 2018.

Borunda, Daniel. "Migrant Children Detention Concerns Continue on First Anniversary of Tornillo Protests." *El Paso Times*, June 24, 2019.

Branigin, Anne. "'This Is About the Preservation of Our Humanity': Democrats Speak Out About Vile Conditions, Racist Rhetoric at Border Facilities." The Root, July 2, 2019.

Breuninger, Kevin. "Nancy Pelosi Responds to Shock Election Upset in New York: 'It's Not About Me

Setting Somebody Up.'" NBC, June 27, 2018.

Brice-Saddler, Michael. "He Easily Found Hundreds of Death Threats Against Rep. Ilhan. He Wants Twitter to Stop Them." Washington *Post*, April 16, 2019.

BU Today Staff. "The Story Behind Ocasio-Cortez's Dancing Video— from Those Who Made It." *Bostonia*, January 4, 2019.

Budryk, Zack. "Biden Knocks Trump on Tweets About 'Smart as Hell' Ocasio-Cortez." The Hill, July 16, 2019.

Budryk, Zack. "Pressley Defends Breaking with 'Squad' on BDS Vote." The Hill, July 24, 2019.

Caygle, Heather, and Sarah Ferris. "'Do Not Tweet': Pelosi Scolds Progressives in Closed-Door Meeting." Politico, July 10, 2019.

Caygle, Heather, and Sarah Ferris. "How House Democratic Factions Ended Their Twitter Feud." Politico, July 18, 2019.

Caygle, Heather, and Sarah Ferris. "Pelosi Works to Placate Splintered Dems." Politico, July 9, 2019.

Caygle, Heather, Sarah Ferris, and John Bresnahan. "Progressive Caucus Eyes Shakeup to Boost Power Next Congress." Politico, October 26, 2020.

Caygle, Heather, Sarah Ferris, and John Bresnahan. "'Too Hot to Handle': Pelosi Predicts GOP Won't Trigger Another Shutdown." Politico, February 7, 2019.

Christopher, Tommy. "Joe Rogan's Bernie Endorsement Draws Outrage as Clip Surfaces Comparing Black Neighborhood to 'Planet of the Apes.'" Mediaite, January 24, 2020.

Conway, Kellyanne. "Kellyanne Conway Speaks Out on Census Showdown, Border Crisis." YouTube, uploaded by Fox News, July 9, 2019.

Cortellessa, Eric. "Obama Gave a House Candidate His Blessing— After Reading His Letter to a Rabbi." *Times of Israel*, August 4, 2020.

Da Silva, Chantal. "Alexandria Ocasio-Cortez Explains Why She Voted Against Coronavirus Relief Package." *Newsweek*, April 24, 2020.

DeBonis, Mike, Paul Kane, and Rachael Bade. "Pelosi Defends Handling of 4 House Women as Democrats Fume About Ocasio-Cortez's Top Aide." Washington *Post*, July 11, 2019.

DeCosta-Klipa, Nik. "Ayanna Pressley Says 'the Squad' Is 'Not a Monolith.'" Boston.com, August 15, 2019.

DeCosta-Klipa, Nik. "3 Members of the 'Squad' Are Reportedly Making 2020 Endorsements. Ayanna Pressley Is Holding Off." Boston .com, October 16, 2019.

Dessem, Matthew. "Alexandria Ocasio-Cortez Spent Her Weekend Dunking on Aaron Sorkin and Helping Raise Money for Trans Kids." Slate, January 21, 2019.

Díaz, Carmen Graciela. "Alexandria Ocasio Quiere Ser la Defensora de los Trabajadores." *El Nuevo Día*, July 7, 2018.

Dickerson, Caitlin. "'There Is a Stench': Soiled Clothes and No Baths for Migrant Children at a Texas Center." New York *Times*, June 21, 2019.

Dwyer, Devin. "Alexandria Ocasio-Cortez's Twitter Lesson for House Democrats." ABC News, January 17, 2019.

Edelman, Susan. "Relatives of Queens Pol Liz Crowley Allegedly Shown 'Favoritism' in School Jobs." New York *Post*, February 22, 2020.

Edmondson, Catie. "Ocasio-Cortez Builds Progressive Campaign Arm to Challenge Democrats." New York *Times*, February 21, 2020.

Ember, Sydney. "Bernie Sanders Had Heart Attack, His Doctors Say as He Leaves Hospital." New York *Times*, October 4, 2019.

Emma, Caitlin, and Sarah Ferris. "Trump Seeks $4.5 Billion in Emergency Border Aid." Politico, May 1, 2019.

Fearnow, Benjamin. "Alexandria Ocasio-Cortez, Boyfriend Offer White People Tips on Combating Racism: Chip Away 'Without Judgment.'" *Newsweek*, February 8, 2020.

Ferré-Sadurní, Luis, Andy Newman, and Vivian Wang. "Alexandria Ocasio-Cortez Emerges as a Political Star." New York *Times*, June 27, 2018.

Ferris, Sarah. "'History has proven her right': 'Barbara Lee's Anti-War Push Succeeds on Iran." Politico, January 10, 2020.

Ferry, Shannan. "Brooklyn Zip Code Has City's Highest Coronavirus Death Rate." *Spectrum News*, NY1, May 18, 2020.

Foran, Clare and Gregory Krieg. "AOC's PAC Throws Weight Behind 7 Progressive Women Candidates with Endorsements." CNN Politics, February 21, 2020.

Fuller, Matt. "The Rift in the House Democratic Caucus." HuffPost, November 13, 2020.

Gajanan, Mahita. "Alexandria Ocasio-Cortez's First House Speech Broke a C-Span Record. Here's What She Said." *Time*, January 18, 2019.

Gamboa, Suzanne. "Over Half of Eligible Latinos Voted in 2020—a Historic First." NBC, May 11, 2021.

Gibson, Brittany. "The Politician as Organizer." *The American Prospect*, October 15, 2020.

Giridharadas, Anand. "The New York Hustle of Amazon's Second Headquarters." *The New Yorker*, November 17, 2018.

Goldmacher, Shane, and Jonathan Martin. "Alexandria Ocasio-Cortez Defeats Joseph Crowley in Major Democratic House Upset." New York *Times*, June 26, 2018.

Goldmacher, Shane. "An Upset in the Making: Why Joe Crowley Never Saw Defeat Coming." New York *Times*, June 27, 2018.

Halbfinger, David M. "Helmsleys' Parkchester Condos Are Sold." New York *Times*, July 3, 1998.

Hawkings, David. "Joseph Crowley, 56 Years Young and Ready to Succeed the Old Guard." *Roll Call*, April 11, 2018.

Heintz, Paul. "AOC, Sanders Dine at Burlington's Penny Cluse Café." *Seven Days*, September 29, 2019.

Herndon, Astead W. "Alexandria Ocasio-Cortez on Biden's Win, House Losses, and What's Next for the Left." New York *Times*, November 7, 2020.

Hersher, Rebecca. "Key Moments in the Dakota Access Pipeline Fight." NPR, February 22, 2017.

Hoonhout, Tobias. "'It Was Like Pulling Teeth': AOC Backed Away from Sanders Campaign after Joe Rogan Endorsement." National Review, March 13, 2020.

Igoe, Katherine J. "Who Is Alexandria Ocasio-Cortez's Boyfriend Riley Roberts?" *Marie Claire*, September 14, 2020.

"Ilhan Omar Attack Ad Goes After $1.1M in Campaign Funds Paid to Her Husband's Firm." WCCO Minneapolis, July 22, 2020.

Jilani, Zaid, and Ryan Grim. "Data Suggest That Gentrifying Neighborhoods Powered Alexandria Ocasio-Cortez's Victory." The Intercept, July 1, 2018.

John, Arit. "A Brief History of Squads." New York *Times*, July 18, 2019.

Karoub, Jeff. "Commission: 'Systemic Racism' at Root of Flint Water Crisis." Associated Press, February 17, 2017.

King, Georgia Frances. "Alexandria Ocasio-Cortez Won a Prestigious Science-Fair Prize for Research Involving Free Radicals." Quartz, December 1, 2018.

Kormann, Carolyn. "Shock and Elation at Alexandria Ocasio-Cortez's Victory Party." *The New Yorker*, June 27, 2018.

Krieg, Gregory. "Bernie Sanders Distances Himself from Ocasio-Cortez's Comments, Says Medicare for All is 'Already a Compromise.'" CNN Politics, February 19, 2020.

Kurtzleben, Danielle. "Rep. Alexandria Ocasio-Cortez Releases Green New Deal Outline." NPR, February 7, 2019.

Lake, Eli. "Congress Set to Vote on Jerusalem." New York *Sun*, May 31, 2017.

Lees, Jaime. "Alexandria Ocasio-Cortez and Cori Bush Are Punk AF." *Riverfront Times*, July 23, 2018.

Leonhardt, Megan. "Alexandria Ocasio-Cortez, the Youngest Woman Ever Elected to Congress, Is Down to Less Than $7,000 in Savings." CNBC, November 16, 2018.

Levine, Jon. "AOC, Boyfriend Talk About 'Combating Racism as a White Person' in Instagram Stories." New York *Post*, November 8, 2020.

Marans, Daniel. "Alexandria Ocasio-Cortez Refused to Campaign More for Bernie Sanders." HuffPost, March 13, 2020.

McCammond, Alexi. "AOC Challenges Puerto Rico Governor over Statehood." Axios, March 5, 2021.

McCarthy, Tom. "Ocasio-Cortez Condemns College Republicans' Email Calling Her a Domestic Terrorist." *Guardian*, April 10, 2019.

McKinley, Jesse. "Jamaal Bowman Proves Ocasio-Cortez Was No Fluke." New York *Times*, July 17, 2020.

Medina, Jennifer. "A Vexing Question for Democrats: What Drives Latino Men to Republicans?" New York *Times*, March 5, 2021.

Mellins, Sam. "Many New York Judges Spend Their Way Toward Seats on the Bench. And It's Perfectly Legal." The City, December 9, 2020.

Nicolaou, Elena. "Alexandria Ocasio-Cortez and Her Boyfriend Riley Roberts Met in 'True Nerdy Fashion.'" Oprah Daily, November 4, 2020.

North, Anna. "How 4 Congresswomen Came to Be Called 'the Squad.'" Vox, July 17, 2019

Palmer, Anna, and Jake Sherman. "The Power of Incumbency." Politico, May 4, 2020.

Parés Arroyo, Marga. "A Alexandria Ocasio-Cortez 'le Encanta Venir a Puerto Rico.'" *El Nuevo Día*, November 8, 2018.

Paz, Isabella Grullón. "Read Bernie Sanders's Full Speech on Ending His Campaign." New York *Times*, April 8, 2020.

Raju, Manu. "AOC Warns She May Force House Members to Return for Stimulus Vote, Potentially Delaying Final Passage." CNN Politics, March 25, 2020.

Ramirez, Fernando. "Candidate for Congress Visits Texas Tent City, Wants to Abolish ICE." *Houston Chronicle*, June 27, 2018.

Rapier, Robert. "Highlights of Joe Biden's Energy Plan." *Forbes*, September 6, 2020.

"Rep. Alexandria Ocasio-Cortez (D-NY) Responds to Rep. Ted Yoho (R-FL)." C-Span, July 23, 2020.

Resnick, Gideon. "There Will Now Likely Be Two Democratic Socialists of America Members in Congress." Daily Beast, August 8, 2018.

Roberts, Chris. "How 'Free Speech' Works: Baseball Team Loses Sponsors over AOC Video." *Observer*, June 5, 2019.

Ryan, Lisa. "AOC and Elizabeth Warren Are Not Happy With the Way *Game of Thrones* Ended." The Cut, May 21, 2019.

Schwartz, Ian. "Rep. Rashida Tlaib to Border Center Protesters: 'We Are Putting America First,' 'I Will Outlove Your Hate.'" Real Clear Politics, July 1, 2019.

Schwartz, Ian. "Tucker Carlson: 'Screechy Moron' Alexandria Ocasio-Cortez Not Demanding China to Adopt 'Green New Deal.'" Real Clear Politics, February 13, 2019.

Sherfinski, David. "Ilhan Omar: Biden Team's Weak Signals Hurt $15 Minimum Wage Effort." Washington *Times*, March 9, 2021.

Sommerfeldt, Chris and Janon Fisher. "Ocasio-Cortez Rips Her Ex-Chief of Staff for 'Divisive' Tweet About Fellow Dems, but Insists He Left Her Office on Good Terms." New York *Daily News*, August 8, 2019.

Somnez, Felicia. "Ocasio-Cortez Rallies Protesters at Pelosi's Office, Expresses Admiration for Leader." Washington *Post*, November 13, 2018.

Sprunt, Barbara. "Here's What's in the American Rescue Plan." NPR, March 11, 2021.

Stein, Jeff. "What Ocasio-Cortez Wants for America After Beating Joe Crowley." *Washington Post*, June 27, 2018.

Stolberg, Sheryl Gay. "In Texas, a Lone House Democrat Has an 'A' Rating from the N.R.A. Can He Survive?" New York *Times*, September 9, 2019.

Sung, Morgan. "Astrology Twitter Is Fighting over Whether Alexandria Ocasio-Cortez Lied About Her Birth Time." Mashable, March 26, 2019.

Thebault, Reis. "Ocasio-Cortez's Chief of Staff Accuses Moderate Democrats of Enabling a 'Racist System.'" Washington *Post*, June 28, 2019.

Thompson, Alex. "Ocasio-Cortez Backs Campaign to Primary Fellow Democrats." Politico, November 17, 2018.

Villarreal, Daniel. "The Full Transcript of Alexandria Ocasio-Cortez's 60-Second Speech at the DNC." *Newsweek*, August 18, 2020.

Walsh, Joan. "Behind the Scenes of the House Democrats' Twitter War." *The Nation*, July 22, 2019.

Wang, Amy B. "Rep. Rashida Tlaib Profanely Promised to Impeach Trump. She's Not Sorry." Washington *Post*, January 4, 2019.

Weigel, David. "Alexandria Ocasio-Cortez: The Democrat Who Challenged Her Party's Establishment—and Won." Washington *Post*, June 27, 2018.

Wise, Justin. "Roseanne Barr Calls Ocasio-Cortez 'Farrakhan Loving,' 'Bug-Eyed Bitch.'" The Hill, February 21, 2019.

Wong, Scott. "Jeffries Defends Democratic Caucus Tweet Slamming Ocasio-Cortez Chief of Staff." The Hill, July 16, 2019.

Wong, Scott. "Ocasio-Cortez: GOP Attacks Are 'Incitement of Violence' Against Women of Color." The Hill, April 11, 2019.

Wong, Scott. "Some Dems Float Idea of Primary Challenge for Ocasio-Cortez." The Hill, January 29, 2019.

Wong, Scott. "The Five Lawmakers Who Voted Against $484B in Coronavirus Relief." The Hill, April 23, 2020.

MISC.

"Alexandria Ocasio-Cortez at Netroots Nation 2018." Netroots Nation, keynote address. YouTube, uploaded by Thomas Brown, August 4, 2018.

"Alexandria Ocasio-Cortez Calls Out Trump in Five-Minute Corruption Game." Congressional Hearing, uploaded by CNN, February 8, 2019.

"Before Alexandria Was Known as AOC, There Was a Movement That Recruited Her to Run." Justice Democrats, YouTube, January 16, 2019.

"Bernie Sanders, Alexandria Ocasio-Cortez & James Thompson Rally Wichita Kansas!" YouTube, uploaded by RedditforBernie, July 20, 2018.

"Category: Coffee & Conversation." *Dean of Students Coffee Conversation Category*, Boston University Dean of Students, www .bu.edu/dos/category/coffee -conversation/.

Congressional District 14, NY, censusreporter.org.

"Congresswoman Alexandria Ocasio-Cortez on Self-Love, Fighting the Power, and Her Signature Red Lip." *Vogue Beauty Secrets* video, August 21, 2020.

"Democratic Primary Debate: Crowley vs. Ocasio-Cortez, Part 1." *Inside City Hall*, NY1, June 15, 2018.

"Green New Deal." C-Span, May 13, 2019.

"House and Senate Democrats on Green New Deal." C-Span, February 7, 2019.

"House Debate on Coronavirus Economic Relief Bill." C-Span, March 27, 2020.

"Open Phones." C-Span, October 20, 2019.

Sanders, Bernie. "Bernie's Back Rally with AOC in New York." YouTube, October 19, 2019.

"'This Is the Beginning': Alexandria Ocasio-Cortez's Victory Speech." *Guardian* video, June 28, 2018.

September 13, 2021:
Ocasio-Cortez
captures the spotlight
at the Met Gala.

Contributors

Lisa Miller is on staff at *New York* Magazine, where she focuses on subjects including mental health, education, crime, and the lived experience of American women. Previously, she worked at *Newsweek*, *The Wall Street Journal*, and *The New Yorker*, and her work has appeared in the New York *Times* and the Washington *Post*. She is a three-time winner of the New York Newswomen's Club prize for feature writing, and a three-time winner of the Wilbur Award for her work on American religious beliefs and practices. Her 2013 article "Orders of Grief," about Newtown, Connecticut, a year after the mass shooting there, was a finalist for the National Magazine Award, and in 2016, she was on the team that produced the ASME-winning video "Guns and Empathy." Miller is the author of *Heaven* and is at work on *Morningside Park*, a book about the 2019 murder of the Barnard student Tessa Majors. She graduated from Oberlin College and lives in Brooklyn.

Rebecca Traister is a writer-at-large for *New York* Magazine and the author of three books, including the New York *Times* best sellers *All the Single Ladies* and *Good and Mad: The Revolutionary Power of Women's Anger.*

Michelle Ruiz is a *Vogue* contributing editor and a contributor to *Vanity Fair*, for which she authored the December 2020 cover profile of Representative Alexandria Ocasio-Cortez. A former senior editor at ABC News and *Cosmopolitan*, she has been published in the New York *Times*, *The Wall Street Journal*, and the Cut, among other outlets.

Andrew Rice has been a *New York* Magazine staff writer since 2012, covering a wide variety of subjects including real estate, affordable housing, climate change, and local and national politics. He is currently at work on a book about the year 2000 in Florida.

David Freedlander is the author of *The AOC Generation: How Millennials Are Seizing Power and Rewriting the Rules of American Politics*. He is a contributor to *New York* Magazine and to Politico and writes about politics, New York City, arts, and ideas for a variety of outlets, including *Vanity Fair, Air Mail*, the Daily Beast, *Art News*, and others. He lives deep in the heart of AOC Country in Jackson Heights, Queens.

Clare Malone is a freelance writer and reporter based in New York City. Her work has appeared in *New York* Magazine, the New York *Times*, *Harper's*, and FiveThirtyEight, where she covered politics as a senior writer. She is a former editorial staffer at *The New Yorker* and *The American Prospect*.

Molly Fischer is a writer at the Cut and *New York* Magazine. Previously, she hosted the podcast *The Cut on Tuesdays*. Her writing has also appeared in *n+1, Harper's, Bookforum*, and *The New York Times Book Review*. She lives in Brooklyn.

Josh Gondelman is a writer and comedian who incubated in Boston before moving to New York, where he lives with his wife, Maris, and their pug, Bizzy. He currently works as a writer and co-executive producer for *Desus & Mero* on Showtime, which is a lot of fun. Previously, he wrote for *Last Week Tonight with John Oliver* (also fun, if you're wondering). Gondelman has an essay collection called *Nice Try: Stories of Best Intentions and Mixed Results* and hosts a podcast called *Make My Day*. You can decide on your own whether those things are fun as well.

Timothy Shenk is a co-editor of *Dissent* and an assistant professor of history at George Washington University. He is writing an intellectual biography of American democracy for Farrar, Straus and Giroux.

Kate Aronoff is a staff writer at *The New Republic* covering climate and energy issues as well as the author of *Overheated: How Capitalism Broke the Planet—And How We Fight Back*. She is the co-author of *A Planet to Win: Why We Need a Green New Deal* and the co-editor of *We Own the Future: Democratic Socialism, American Style*.

Andrea González-Ramírez is a writer at the Cut and *New York* Magazine. She is originally from Vega Alta, Puerto Rico, and the founder of the Latinas in Journalism Mentorship Program. Her work has appeared in GEN by Medium, Refinery29, PRX's *Latino USA*, *El Diario Nueva York*, *Centro Voices*, and *Diálogo*, among other outlets. González-Ramírez is one of the authors of *AOC: The Fearless Rise and Powerful Resonance of Alexandria Ocasio-Cortez* and a 2019–20 Ida B. Wells Fellow at Type Investigations. She holds a master's of journalism with a concentration in international reporting from the Craig Newmark Graduate School of Journalism at CUNY and a degree in journalism and sociology from the University of Puerto Rico.

David Wallace-Wells is an editor-at-large at *New York* Magazine and the author of the New York *Times* best seller *The Uninhabitable Earth*.

Bridget Read is a senior writer at the Cut and *New York* Magazine. Before that, she was a culture writer at *Vogue*.

Eric Levitz is a senior writer at *New York* Magazine's Intelligencer.

Amelia Schonbek is a journalist whose work often focuses on how people experience and recover from trauma. Her reporting has been supported by Type Investigations, the Solutions Journalism Network, and the Center on Media, Crime, and Justice at John Jay College in New York. When not at work, she likes to sing, swim, and be outside.

Pia Guerra is the Joe Shuster and Eisner Award–winning penciller and co-creator of *Y: The Last Man*. Following the 2016 election, she got into editorial cartooning, and her work has appeared regularly at theNib.com and occasionally in the Washington *Post*. She also partners with her husband, the writer Ian Boothby, to draw cartoons for *The New Yorker*. Dan Rather tweeted about one of her cartoons, which she thinks is pretty darn neat.

Brock Colyar is a writer at *New York* Magazine. They live in Brooklyn.

Particular Thanks

This book is a special project of *New York* Magazine. The editors of it are grateful to Vox Media president Pam Wasserstein, the magazine's Editor-in-Chief David Haskell, and Managing Editor Ann Clarke for blessing the project and freeing up the resources to go forward. That includes especially the gift of Lisa Miller, the book's principal writer and conscience, without whom it would not in any way have been possible. Along the way, the book grew in its ambition and reach: Without singling out too many names you can also see on the next page, it is worth saying that the book might have fallen apart without Kaitlin Jessing-Butz's exceptional corralling and managing talents. Because the book's architecture is unconventional, it had to be imagined from scratch. Hitomi Sato was the gifted principal designer, working with the *New York* Magazine design and photo team. And the book is indebted, obviously, to all of its exceptional contributors, both within and beyond the magazine's staff. Finally, thanks to Edward Hart for his fact-checking guidance and Brock Colyar and Florence O'Connor for their research help, particularly in its first stages.

At Avid Reader Press, the book was lucky enough to be placed in the talented hands of Julianna Hauber. Jofie Ferrari-Adler did what great publishers do—supported and cajoled, in tandem. David Kuhn was the agent who believed in the book from the outset and negotiated in every sense the collaboration between *New York* and Avid Reader Press. Thanks to all.

Image Credits

Index

Ocasio-Cortez, Alexandria (AOC)
(*cont.*)